池本幹雄

When I renovated my home, I got to install a "catwalk," as I'd long yearned to. The surface is transparent tempered glass, so the view from below is outstanding.

I can behold paw pads clearly too, and have made many discoveries, like "Oh, that's how your back legs are in that pose?!"

I feel overwhelming joy simply from being able to look up at Lord Kitty from below. Cats really are loftier than people, eh.

I'm just stupidly in love with cats...

Or rather, I'm just stupid.

—Mikio Ikemoto, 2021

BORUTO
=NARUTO NEXT GENERATIONS=

VOLUME 15

SHONEN JUMP EDITION

Creator/Supervisor MASASHI KISHIMOTO
Art by MIKIO IKEMOTO

Translation: Mari Morimoto
Touch-Up Art & Lettering: Snir Aharon
Design: Alice Lewis
Editor: Alexis Kirsch

Printed in the U.S.A.

Published by VIZ Media, LLC
P.O. Box 77010
San Francisco, CA 94107

10 9 8 7 6 5 4 3 2 1
First printing, October 2022

PARENTAL ADVISORY
BORUTO is rated T for Teen and is
recommended for ages 13 and up.
This volume contains fantasy violence.

viz.com

BORUTO

-NARUTO NEXT GENERATIONS-

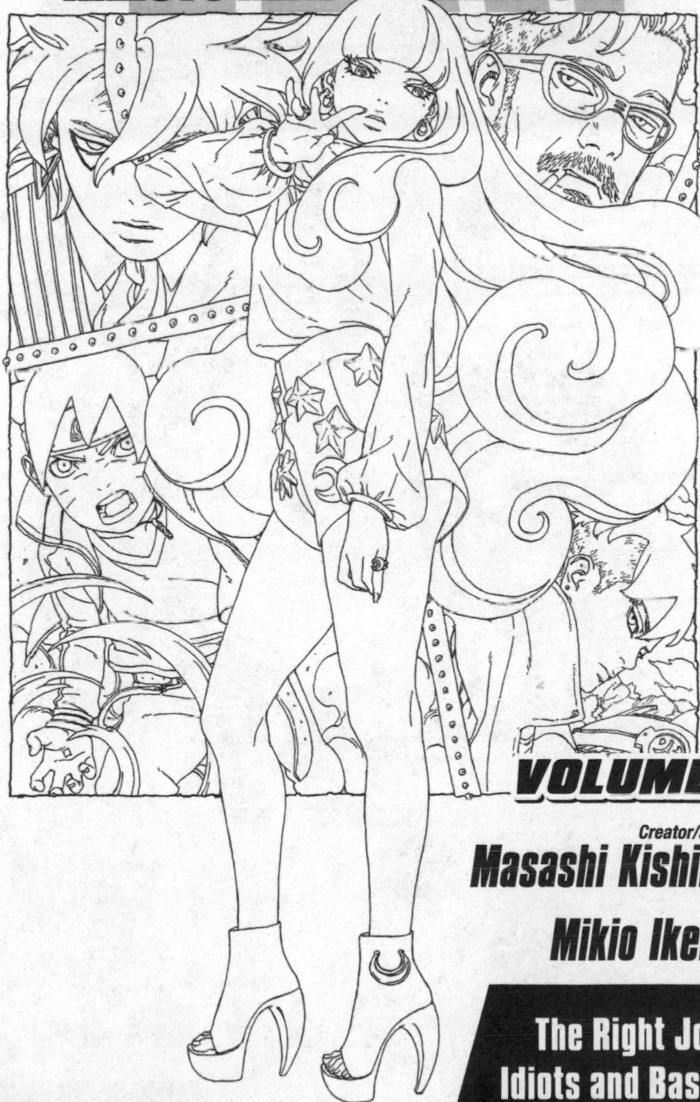

VOLUME 15

Creator/Supervisor
Masashi Kishimoto
Art by
Mikio Ikemoto

The Right Job for Idiots and Bastards

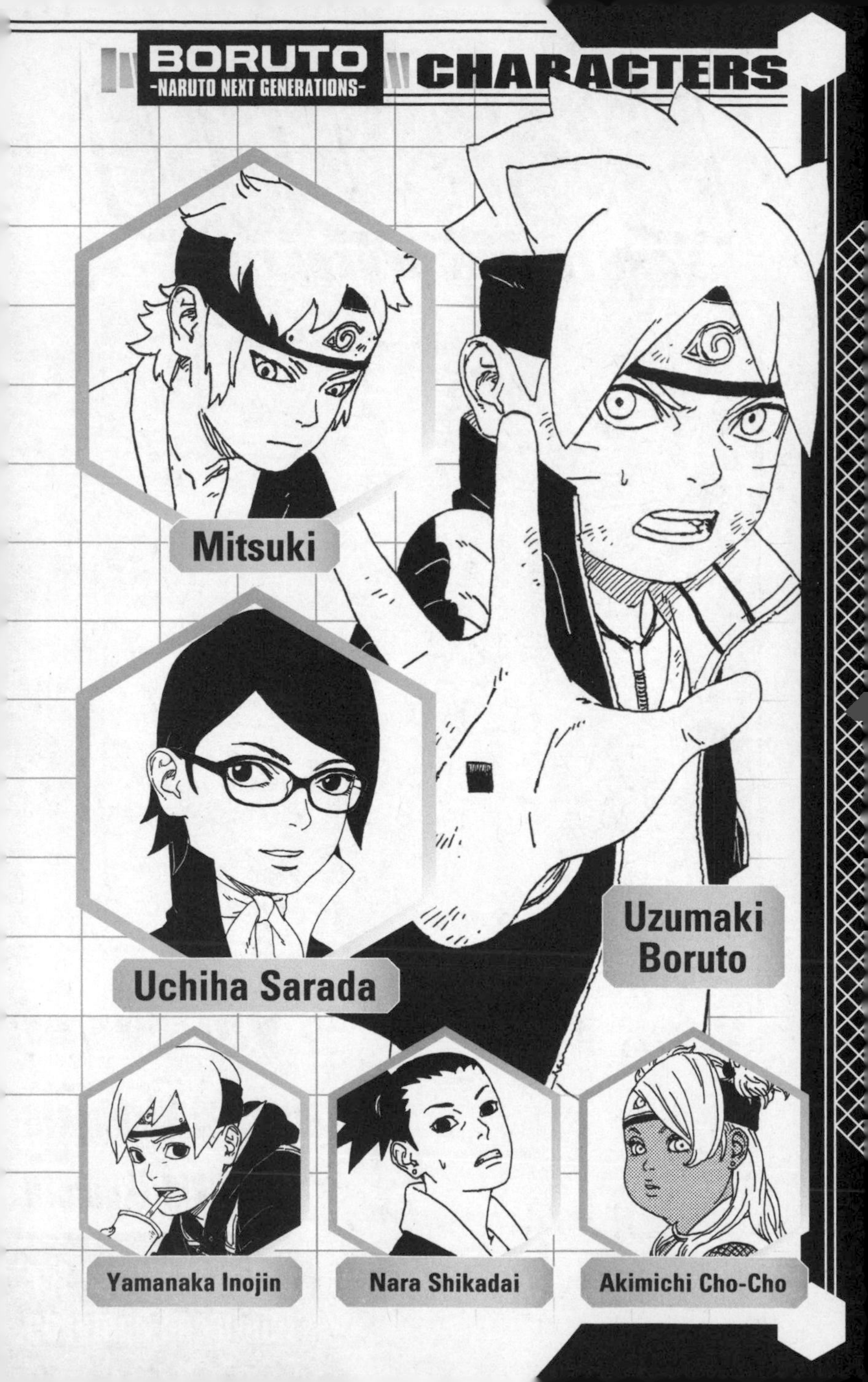
BORUTO
-NARUTO NEXT GENERATIONS-
CHARACTERS
Mitsuki
Uzumaki Boruto
Uchiha Sarada
Yamanaka Inojin
Nara Shikadai
Akimichi Cho-Cho

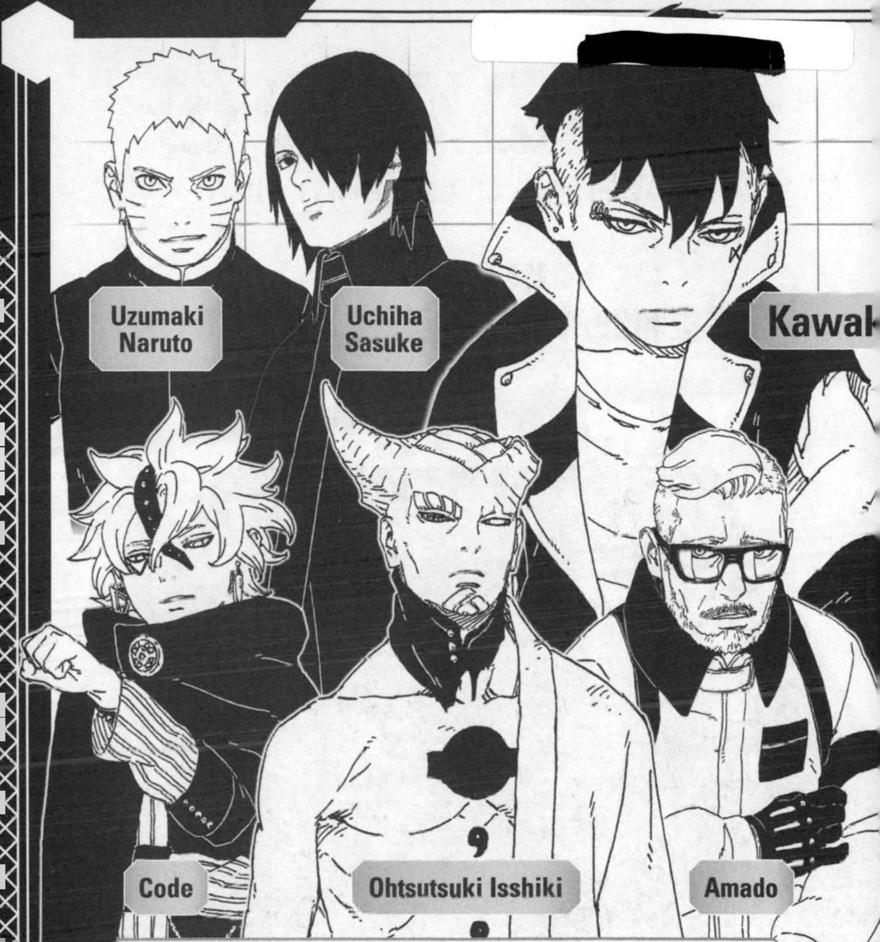
[redacted]
Uzumaki Naruto
Uchiha Sasuke
Kawak
Code
Ohtsutsuki Isshiki
Amado

STORY

The Great Ninja War that shook the world and shed much blood is now history. Naruto has become the Seventh Hokage, and the people of Konohagakure Village are enjoying peace. Yet Naruto's son Uzumaki Boruto has a glum life, perhaps due to his father's too-great influence.

But Ohtsutsuki Clan members attack, and leave a mysterious mark, the Karma, on Seventh Hokage Naruto's son Boruto...

Afterwards, Boruto happens upon a young man named Kawaki who bears the same Karma as himself. And it is he who is proven to be what Kara has been calling the Vessel.

In order to place Kawaki under his protection, Naruto moves him into his own home. Boruto and Kawaki keep butting heads, but Kawaki starts acclimating to the Village and begins to respect Naruto.

Later, Kara members Amado and Kashin Koji break off from Kara, and Amado defects to Konoha Village. With his life running out, Isshiki tries to resurrect in Kawaki's body, but the valiant efforts of Naruto and the others lead to his end. As he dies, Isshiki commands Kara's last officer, Code, to take up the Ohtsutsuki Will. Code vows to punish Boruto and the others.

BORUTO

-NARUTO NEXT GENERATIONS-

VOLUME 15
THE RIGHT JOB FOR IDIOTS AND BASTARDS

CONTENTS

Number 56: **Code** ·· 7

Number 57: **Eida** ·· 49

Number 58: **The Right Job for Idiots and Bastards** ······ 90

Number 59: **Knight** ·· 133

Number 56: Code

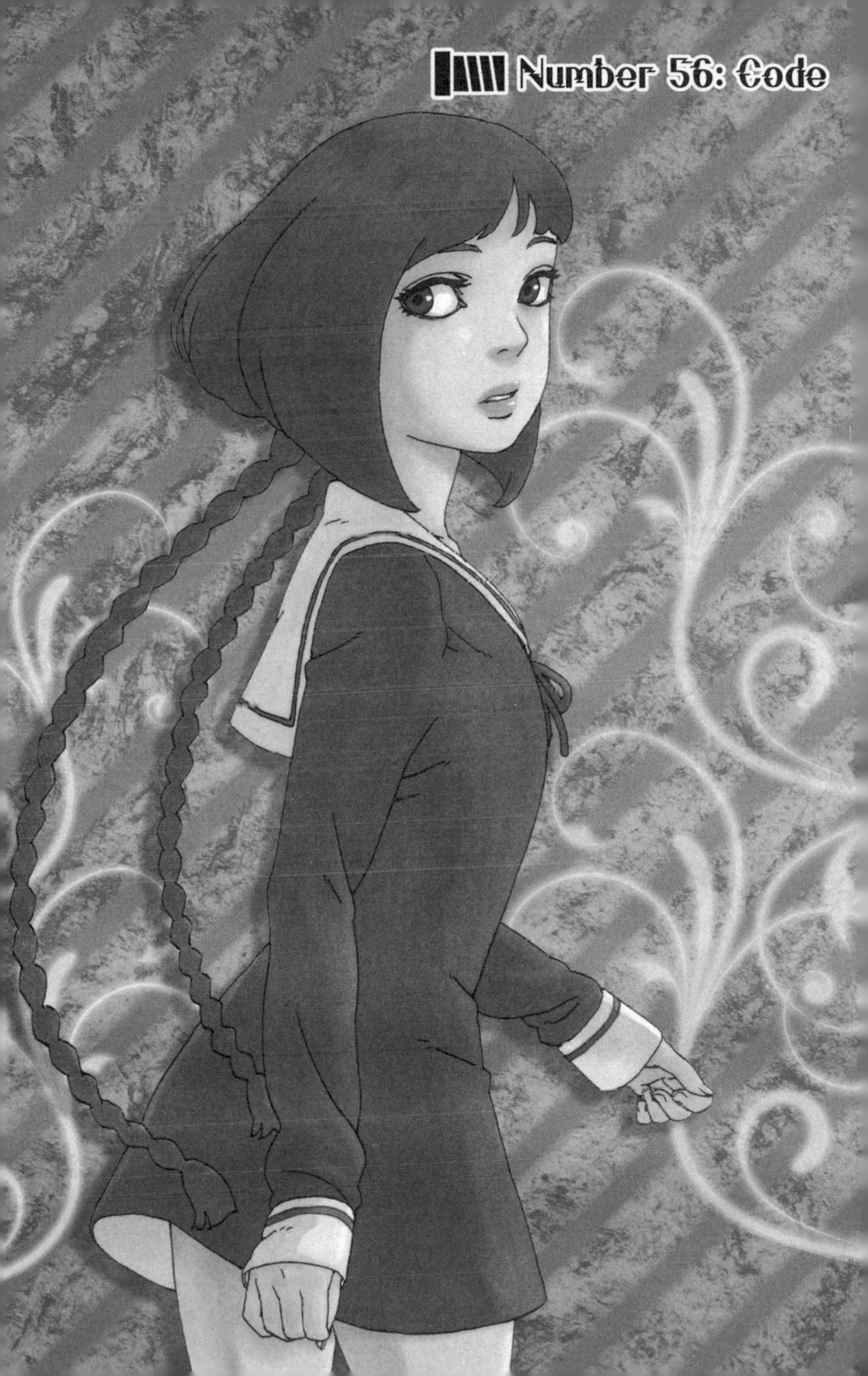

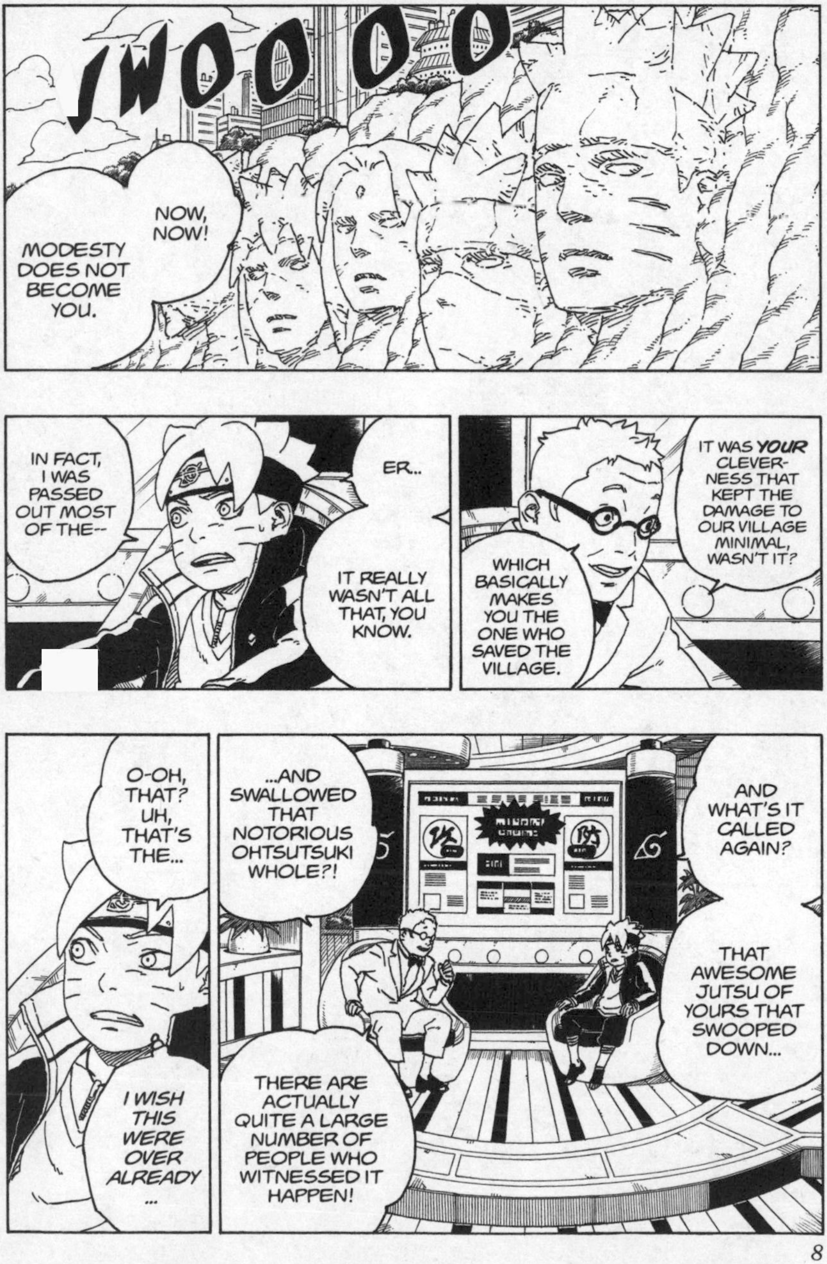
WOOOO
NOW, NOW!
MODESTY DOES NOT BECOME YOU.
IT WAS *YOUR* CLEVERNESS THAT KEPT THE DAMAGE TO OUR VILLAGE MINIMAL, WASN'T IT?
WHICH BASICALLY MAKES YOU THE ONE WHO SAVED THE VILLAGE.
ER...
IT REALLY WASN'T ALL THAT, YOU KNOW.
IN FACT, I WAS PASSED OUT MOST OF THE--
AND WHAT'S IT CALLED AGAIN?
THAT AWESOME JUTSU OF YOURS THAT SWOOPED DOWN...
...AND SWALLOWED THAT NOTORIOUS OHTSUTSUKI WHOLE?!
THERE ARE ACTUALLY QUITE A LARGE NUMBER OF PEOPLE WHO WITNESSED IT HAPPEN!
O-OH, THAT? UH, THAT'S THE...
I WISH THIS WERE OVER ALREADY...

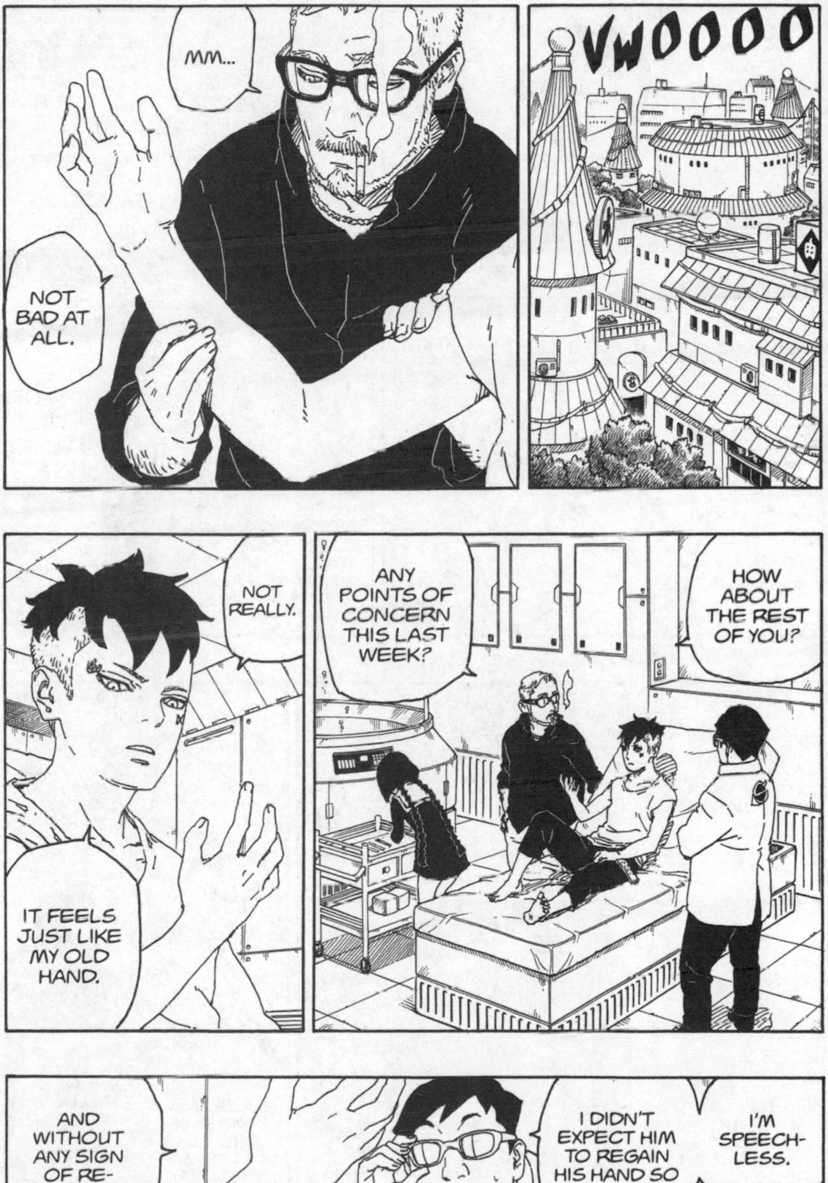
VWOOOO
MM...
NOT BAD AT ALL.
HOW ABOUT THE REST OF YOU?
ANY POINTS OF CONCERN THIS LAST WEEK?
NOT REALLY.
IT FEELS JUST LIKE MY OLD HAND.
I'M SPEECH-LESS.
I DIDN'T EXPECT HIM TO REGAIN HIS HAND SO QUICKLY.
AND WITHOUT ANY SIGN OF RE-JECTION...

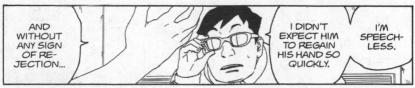

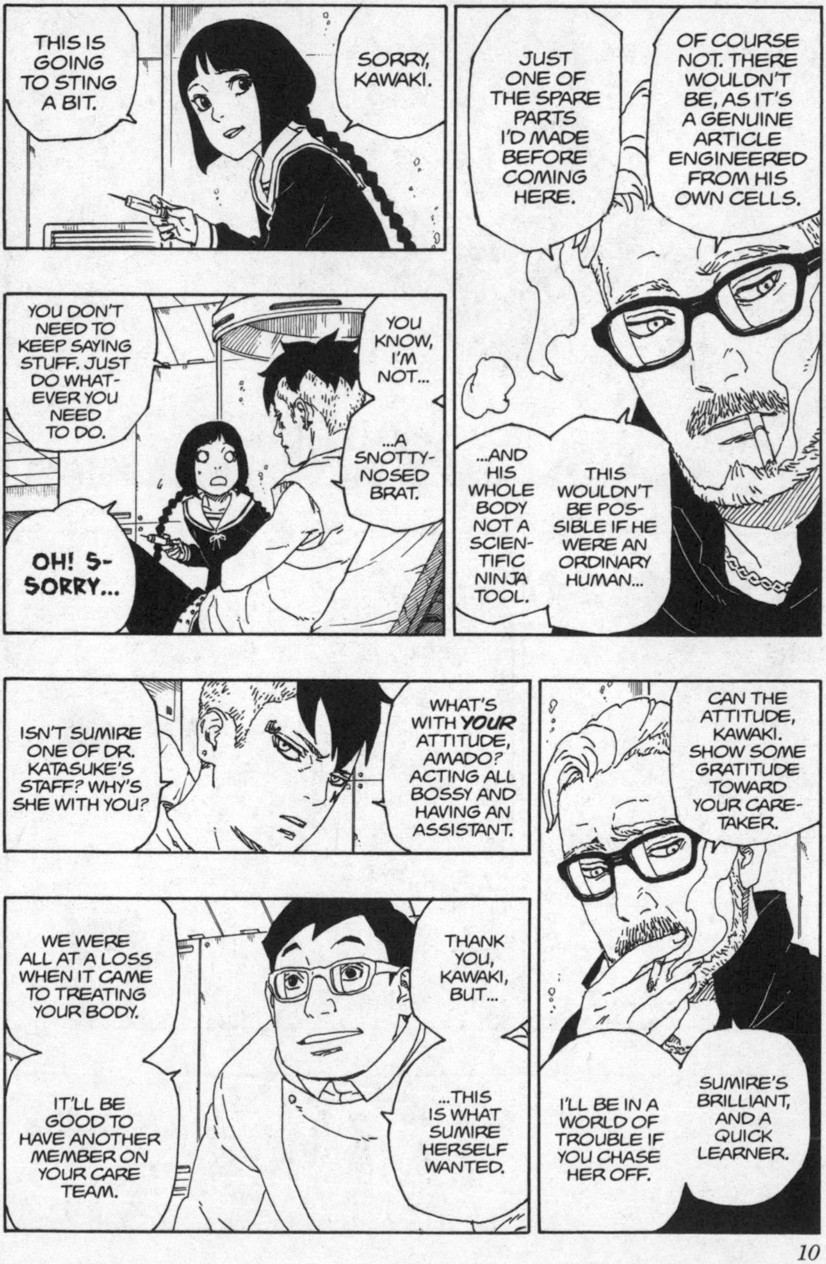
OF COURSE NOT. THERE WOULDN'T BE, AS IT'S A GENUINE ARTICLE ENGINEERED FROM HIS OWN CELLS.
JUST ONE OF THE SPARE PARTS I'D MADE BEFORE COMING HERE.
THIS WOULDN'T BE POSSIBLE IF HE WERE AN ORDINARY HUMAN...
...AND HIS WHOLE BODY NOT A SCIENTIFIC NINJA TOOL.
SORRY, KAWAKI.
THIS IS GOING TO STING A BIT.
YOU KNOW, I'M NOT...
...A SNOTTY-NOSED BRAT.
YOU DON'T NEED TO KEEP SAYING STUFF. JUST DO WHATEVER YOU NEED TO DO.
OH! S-SORRY...
CAN THE ATTITUDE, KAWAKI. SHOW SOME GRATITUDE TOWARD YOUR CARETAKER.
SUMIRE'S BRILLIANT, AND A QUICK LEARNER.
I'LL BE IN A WORLD OF TROUBLE IF YOU CHASE HER OFF.
WHAT'S WITH *YOUR* ATTITUDE, AMADO? ACTING ALL BOSSY AND HAVING AN ASSISTANT.
ISN'T SUMIRE ONE OF DR. KATASUKE'S STAFF? WHY'S SHE WITH YOU?
THANK YOU, KAWAKI, BUT...
...THIS IS WHAT SUMIRE HERSELF WANTED.
WE WERE ALL AT A LOSS WHEN IT CAME TO TREATING YOUR BODY.
IT'LL BE GOOD TO HAVE ANOTHER MEMBER ON YOUR CARE TEAM.

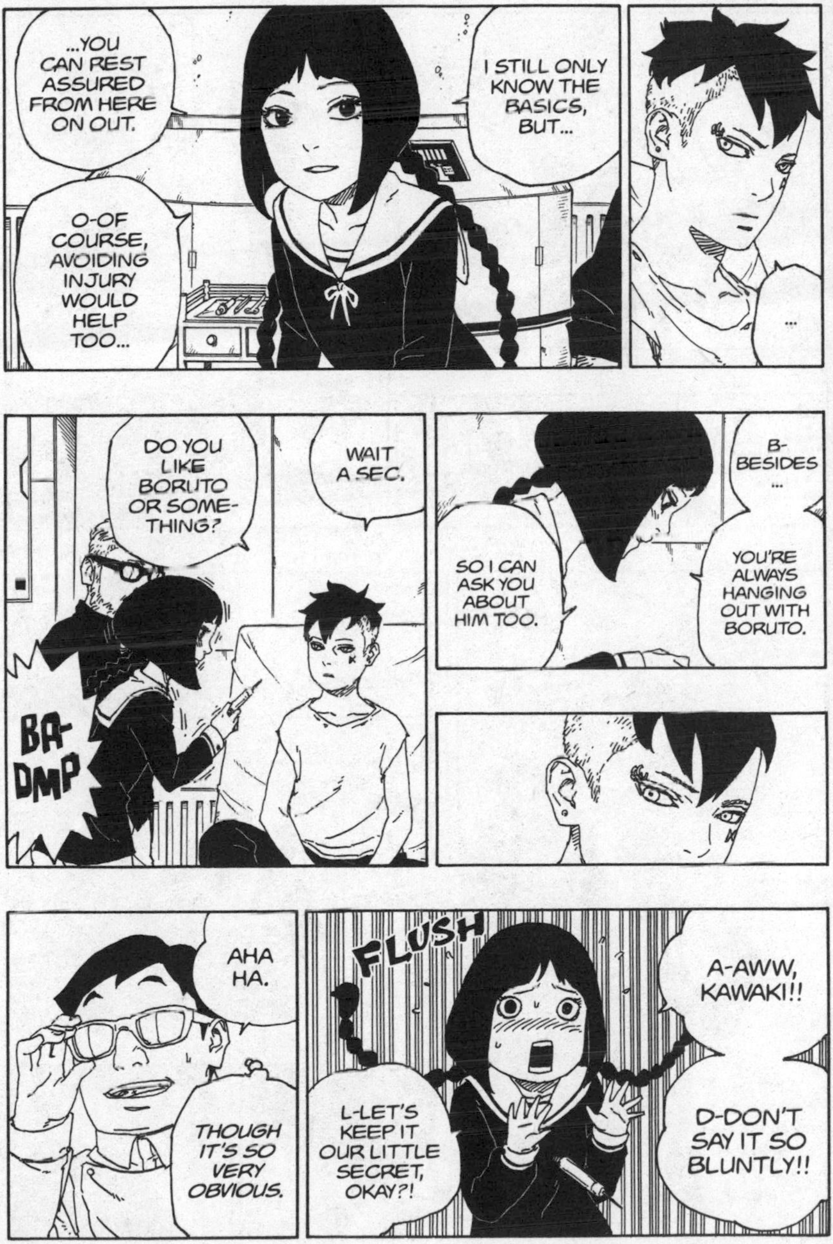
...
I STILL ONLY KNOW THE BASICS, BUT...
...YOU CAN REST ASSURED FROM HERE ON OUT.
O-OF COURSE, AVOIDING INJURY WOULD HELP TOO...
B-BESIDES...
YOU'RE ALWAYS HANGING OUT WITH BORUTO.
SO I CAN ASK YOU ABOUT HIM TOO.
WAIT A SEC.
DO YOU LIKE BORUTO OR SOME-THING?
BA-DMP
A-AWW, KAWAKI!!
FLUSH
D-DON'T SAY IT SO BLUNTLY!!
L-LET'S KEEP IT OUR LITTLE SECRET, OKAY?!
AHA HA.
THOUGH IT'S SO VERY OBVIOUS.

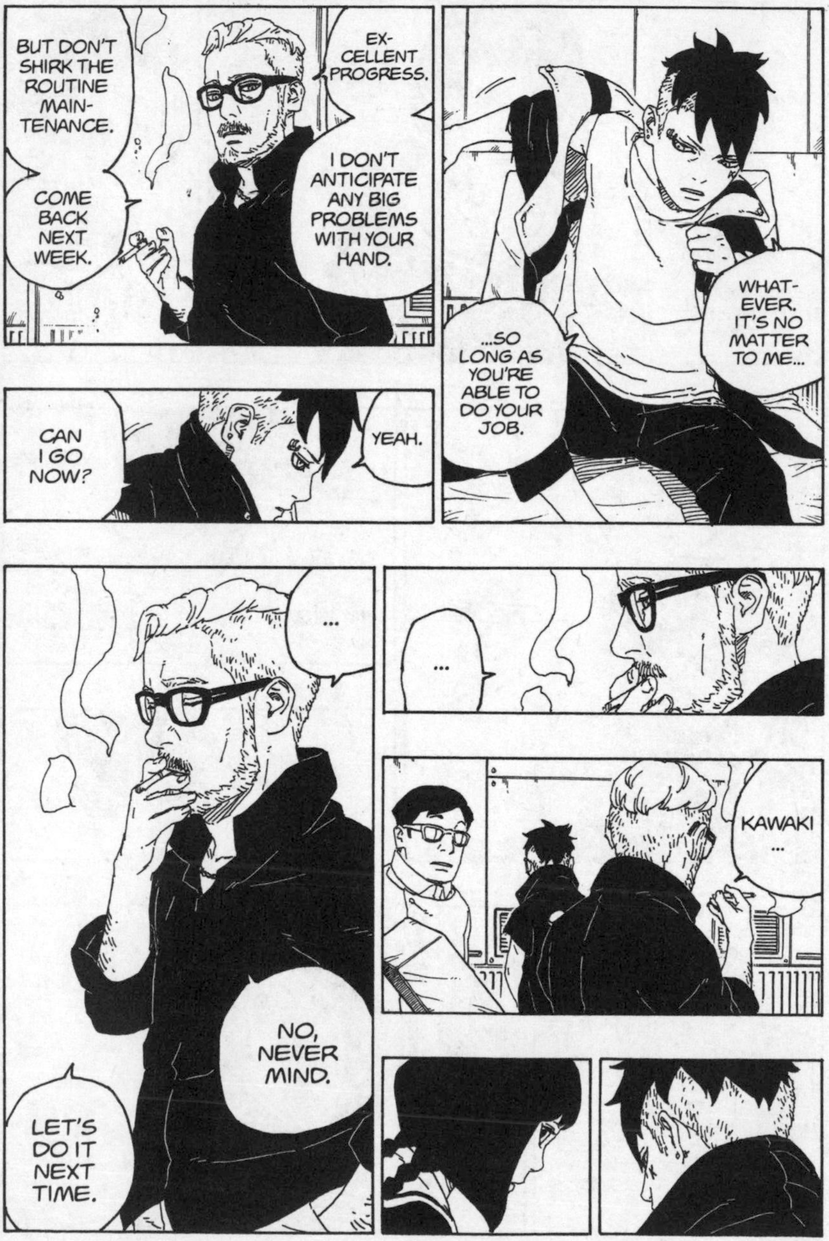
WHAT-EVER. IT'S NO MATTER TO ME...
...SO LONG AS YOU'RE ABLE TO DO YOUR JOB.
EX-CELLENT PROGRESS.
I DON'T ANTICIPATE ANY BIG PROBLEMS WITH YOUR HAND.
BUT DON'T SHIRK THE ROUTINE MAIN-TENANCE.
COME BACK NEXT WEEK.
YEAH.
CAN I GO NOW?
...
KAWAKI ...
...
NO, NEVER MIND.
LET'S DO IT NEXT TIME.

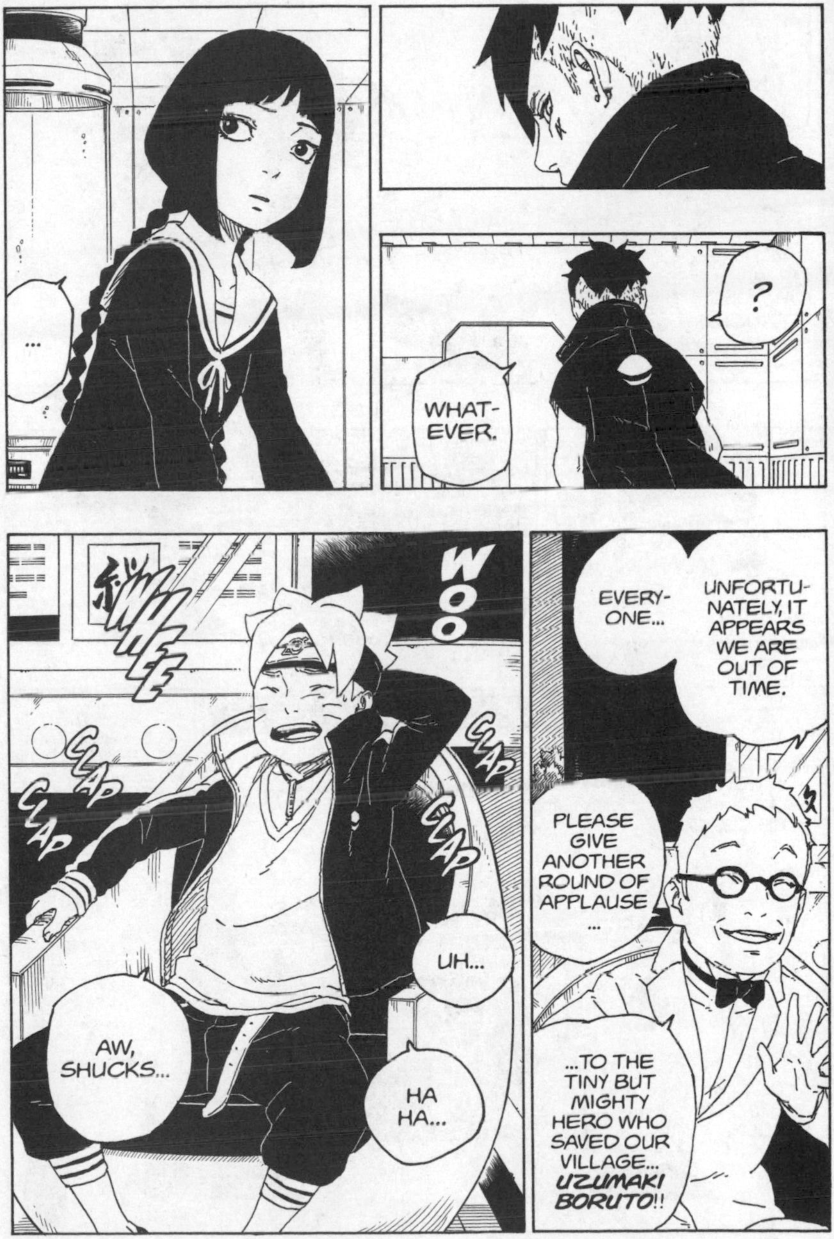
?
WHATEVER.
...
EVERYONE...
UNFORTUNATELY, IT APPEARS WE ARE OUT OF TIME.
PLEASE GIVE ANOTHER ROUND OF APPLAUSE...
...TO THE TINY BUT MIGHTY HERO WHO SAVED OUR VILLAGE... **UZUMAKI BORUTO**!!
WOO
WHEE
CLAP
CLAP
CLAP
CLAP
UH...
HA HA...
AW, SHUCKS...

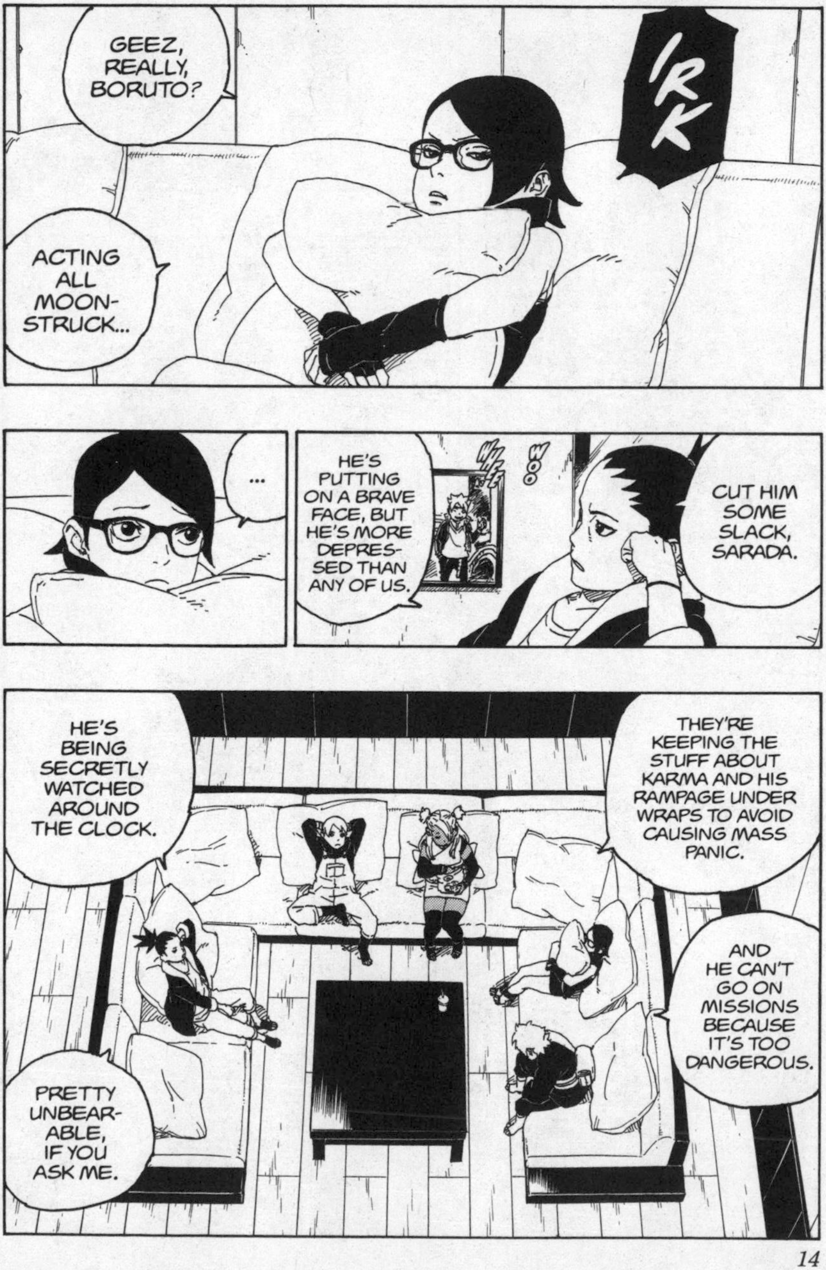
IRK
GEEZ, REALLY, BORUTO?
ACTING ALL MOON-STRUCK...
CUT HIM SOME SLACK, SARADA.
WOO
HE'S PUTTING ON A BRAVE FACE, BUT HE'S MORE DEPRES-SED THAN ANY OF US.
...
THEY'RE KEEPING THE STUFF ABOUT KARMA AND HIS RAMPAGE UNDER WRAPS TO AVOID CAUSING MASS PANIC.
AND HE CAN'T GO ON MISSIONS BECAUSE IT'S TOO DANGEROUS.
HE'S BEING SECRETLY WATCHED AROUND THE CLOCK.
PRETTY UNBEAR-ABLE, IF YOU ASK ME.

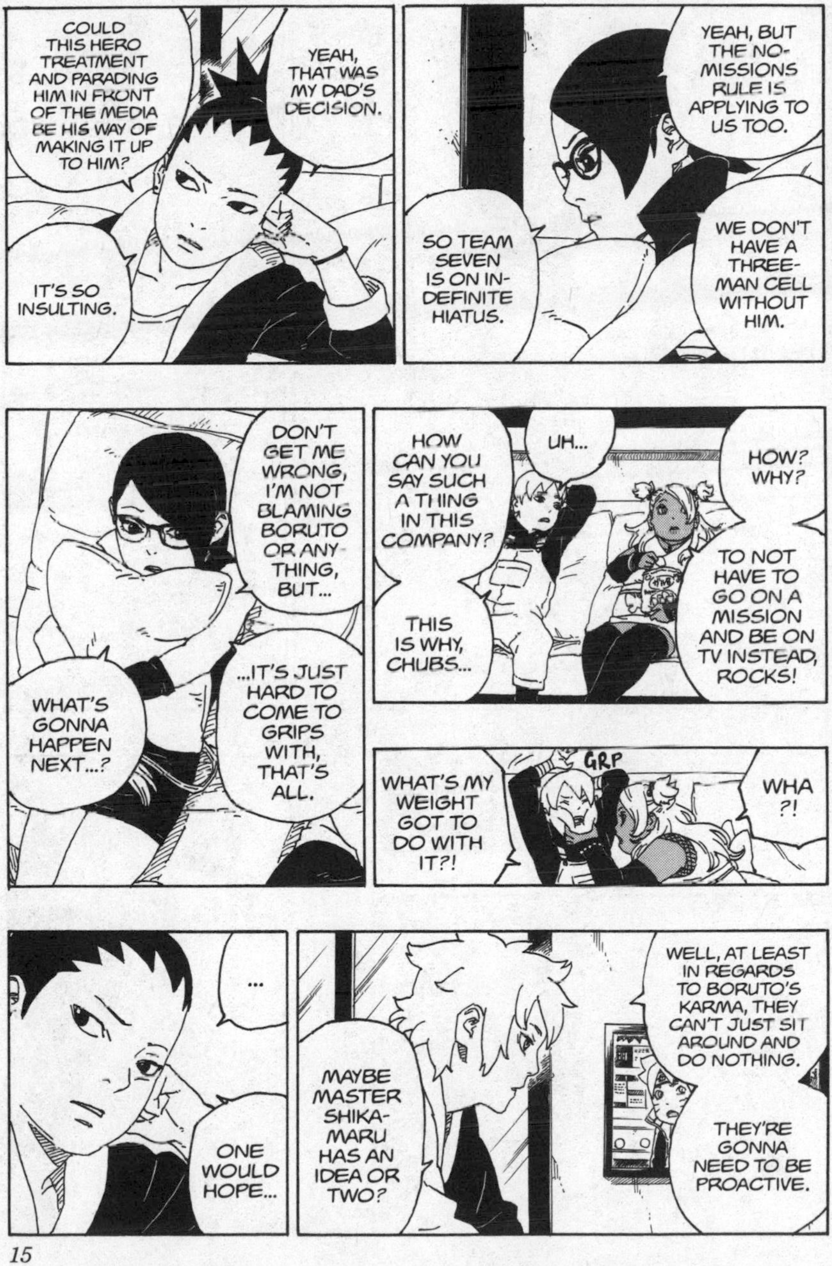
YEAH, BUT THE NO-MISSIONS RULE IS APPLYING TO US TOO.
WE DON'T HAVE A THREE-MAN CELL WITHOUT HIM.
SO TEAM SEVEN IS ON INDEFINITE HIATUS.
COULD THIS HERO TREATMENT AND PARADING HIM IN FRONT OF THE MEDIA BE HIS WAY OF MAKING IT UP TO HIM?
YEAH, THAT WAS MY DAD'S DECISION.
IT'S SO INSULTING.
HOW? WHY?
UH...
HOW CAN YOU SAY SUCH A THING IN THIS COMPANY?
TO NOT HAVE TO GO ON A MISSION AND BE ON TV INSTEAD, ROCKS!
THIS IS WHY, CHUBS...
WHA?!
GRP
WHAT'S MY WEIGHT GOT TO DO WITH IT?!
DON'T GET ME WRONG, I'M NOT BLAMING BORUTO OR ANYTHING, BUT...
...IT'S JUST HARD TO COME TO GRIPS WITH, THAT'S ALL.
WHAT'S GONNA HAPPEN NEXT...?
WELL, AT LEAST IN REGARDS TO BORUTO'S KARMA, THEY CAN'T JUST SIT AROUND AND DO NOTHING.
THEY'RE GONNA NEED TO BE PROACTIVE.
MAYBE MASTER SHIKAMARU HAS AN IDEA OR TWO?
...
ONE WOULD HOPE...

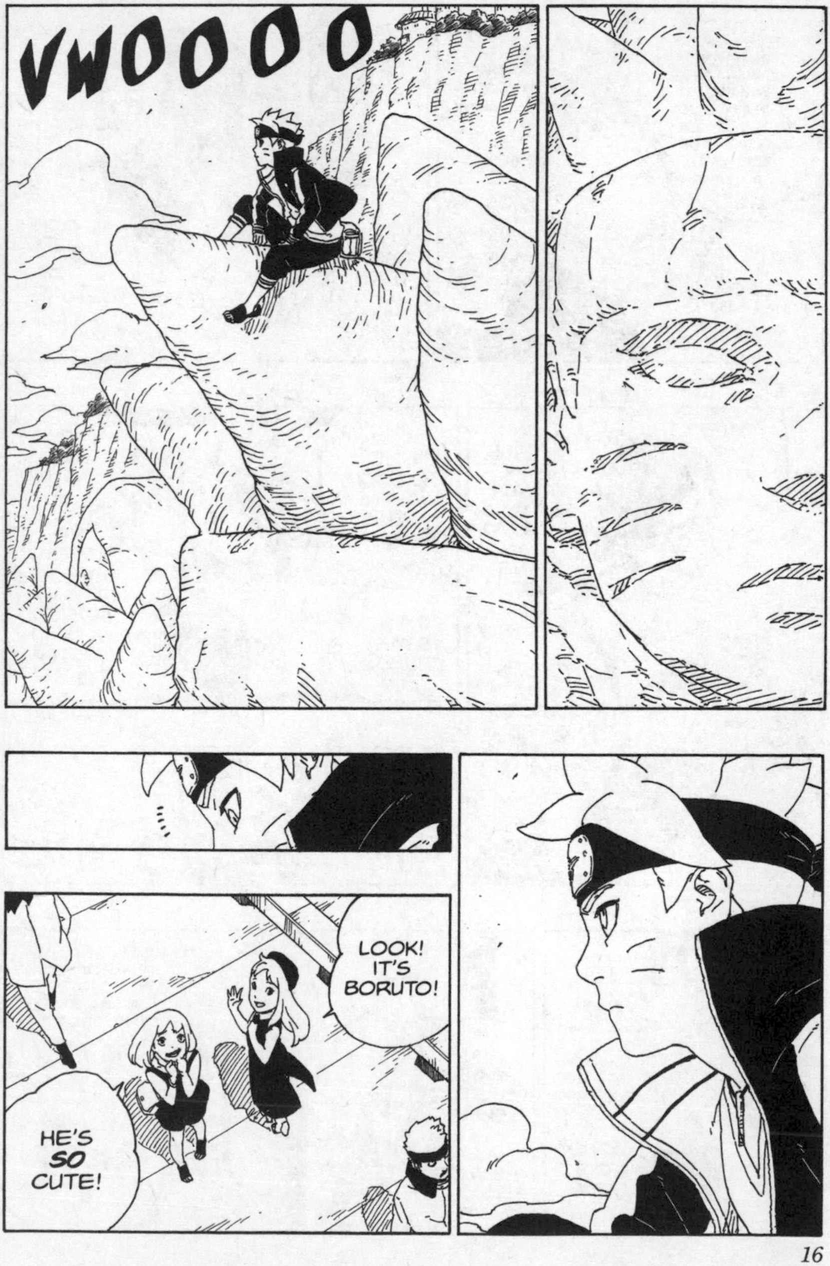
VWOOOO
LOOK! IT'S BORUTO!
HE'S *SO* CUTE!

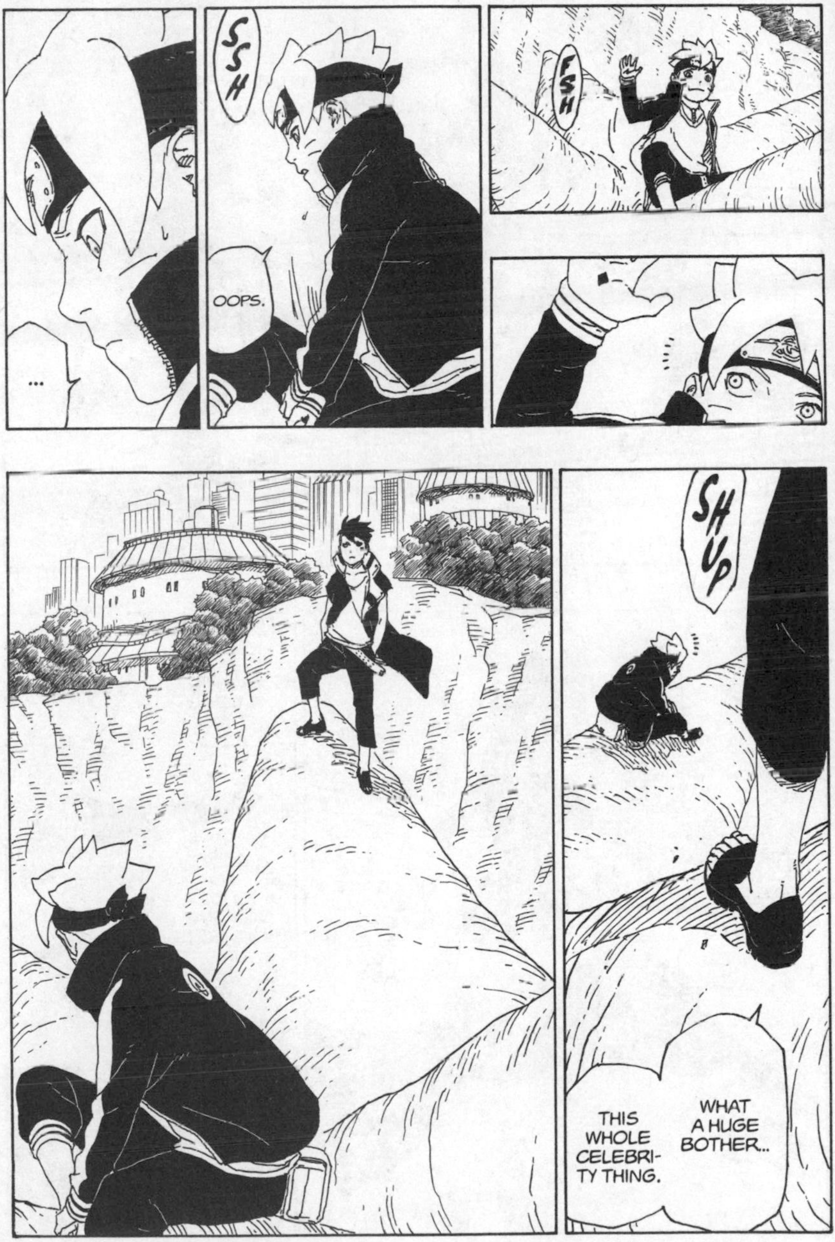
FSH
SSH
OOPS.
...
SHUP
WHAT A HUGE BOTHER...
THIS WHOLE CELEBRITY THING.

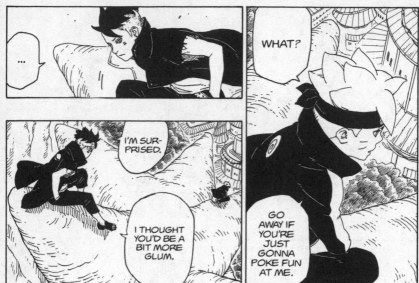

WHAT?
GO AWAY IF YOU'RE JUST GONNA POKE FUN AT ME.
...
I'M SUR-PRISED.
I THOUGHT YOU'D BE A BIT MORE GLUM.
ABOUT KARMA?
NAH. I WAS OVER IT A LONG TIME AGO.
IT'S JUST ...
I DON'T KNOW HOW TO ACT OR WHAT I SHOULD BE TRYING TO DO ABOUT IT.
BASED ON WHAT WE'VE LEARNED SO FAR...
...BOTH OF OUR BODIES ARE ABOUT 80 PERCENT OHTSUTSUKI-FIED ALREADY.
AND FOR YOU IN PARTICU-LAR...
THE OHTSUTSUKI DATA IS STILL CONTINUING TO EXTRACT ITSELF FROM YOUR KARMA.

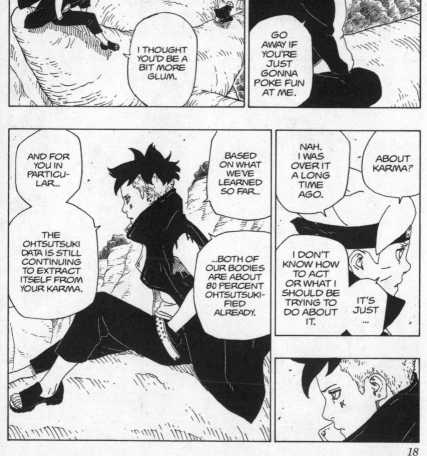

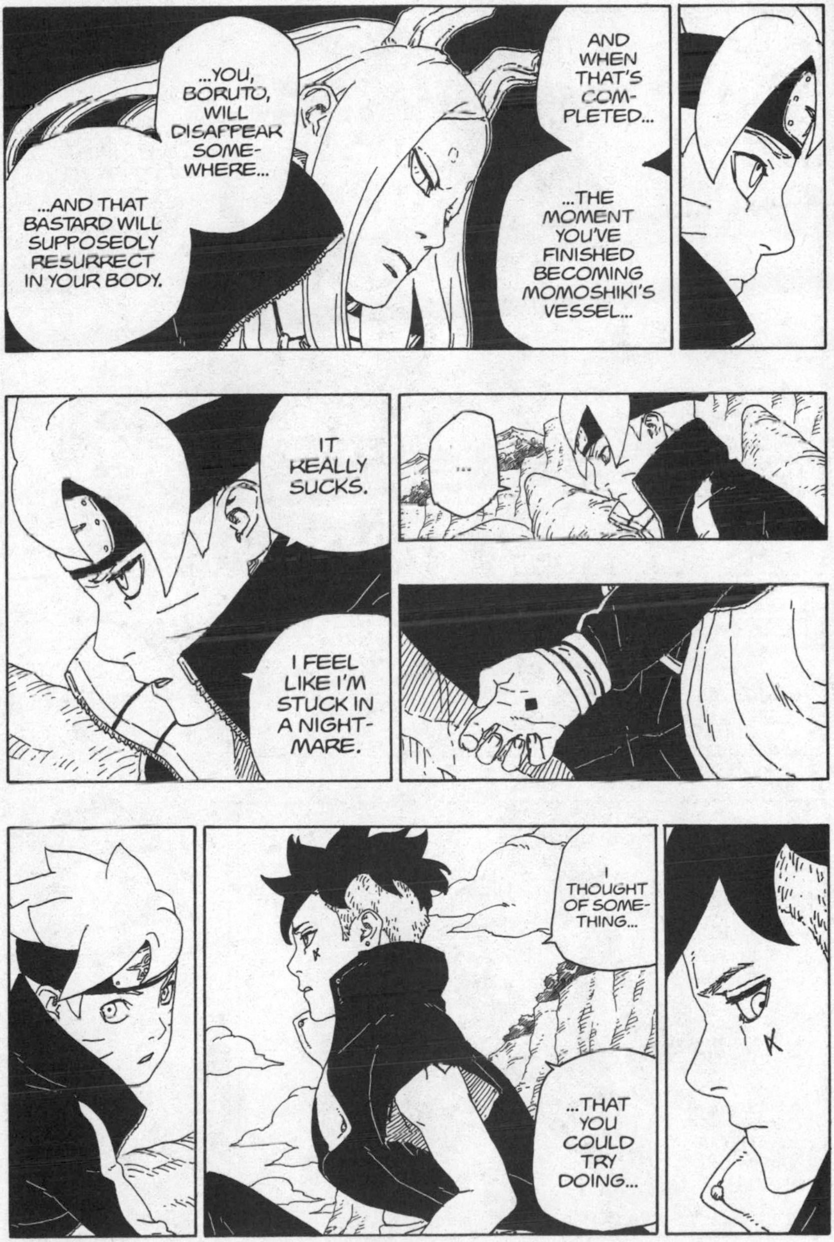
AND WHEN THAT'S COM-PLETED...
...THE MOMENT YOU'VE FINISHED BECOMING MOMOSHIKI'S VESSEL...
...YOU, BORUTO, WILL DISAPPEAR SOME-WHERE...
...AND THAT BASTARD WILL SUPPOSEDLY RESURRECT IN YOUR BODY.
...
IT REALLY SUCKS.
I FEEL LIKE I'M STUCK IN A NIGHT-MARE.
I THOUGHT OF SOME-THING...
...THAT YOU COULD TRY DOING...

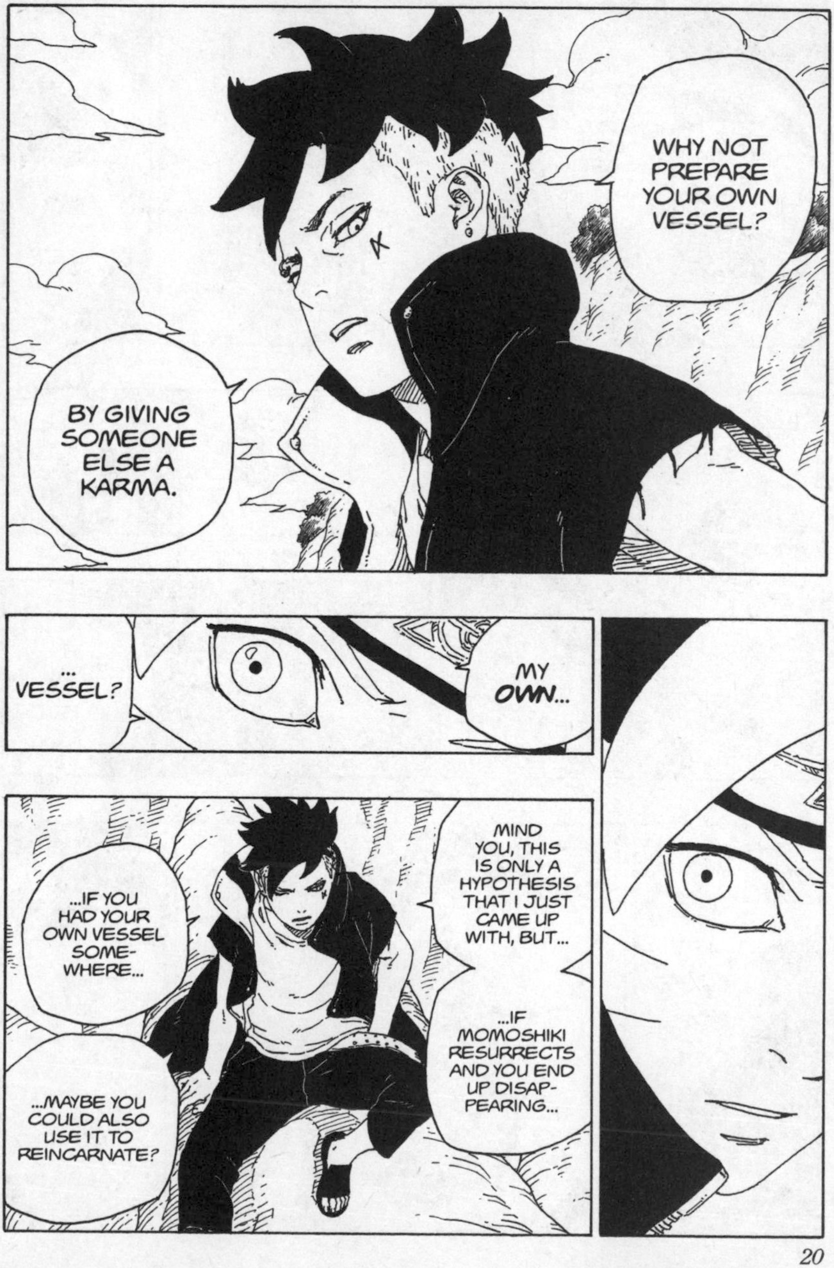
WHY NOT PREPARE YOUR OWN VESSEL?
BY GIVING SOMEONE ELSE A KARMA.
MY OWN...
... VESSEL?
MIND YOU, THIS IS ONLY A HYPOTHESIS THAT I JUST CAME UP WITH, BUT...
...IF YOU HAD YOUR OWN VESSEL SOME-WHERE...
...IF MOMOSHIKI RESURRECTS AND YOU END UP DISAP-PEARING...
...MAYBE YOU COULD ALSO USE IT TO REINCARNATE?

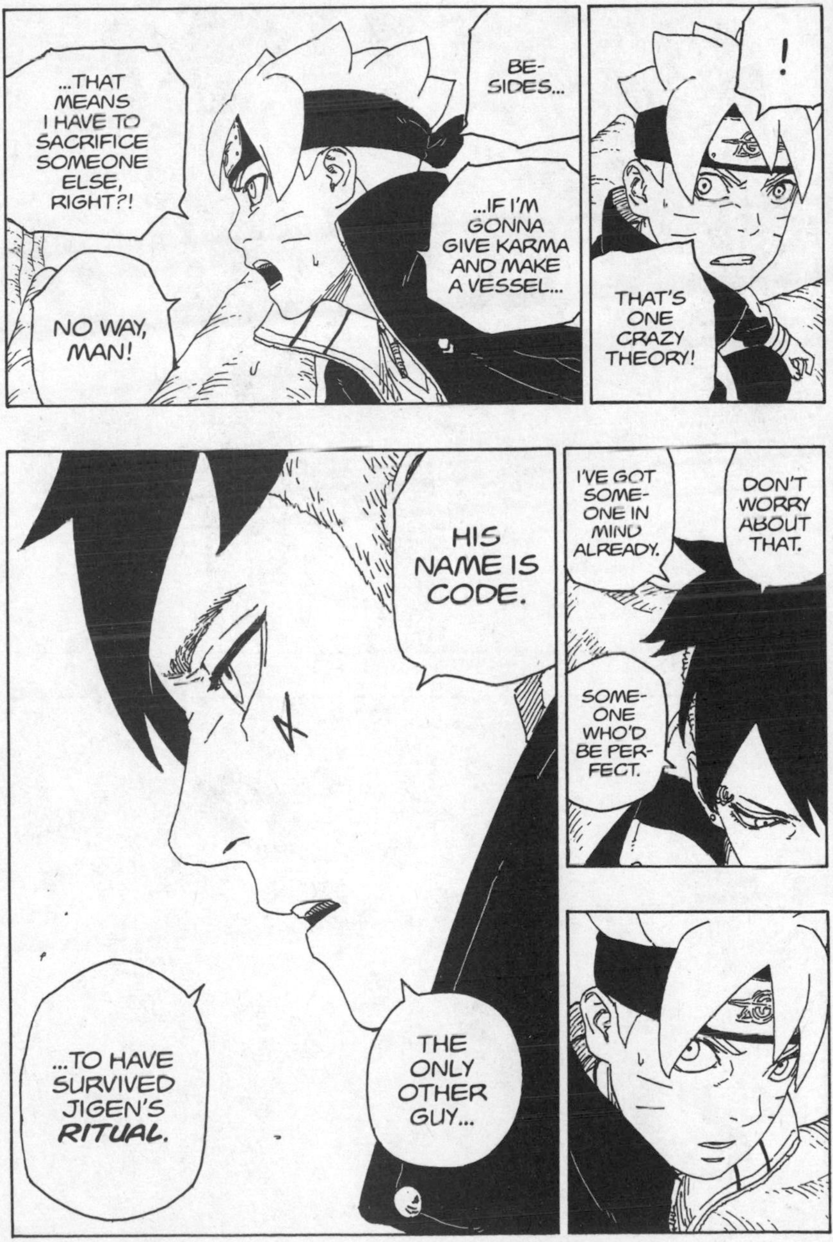
!
THAT'S ONE CRAZY THEORY!
BE-SIDES...
...IF I'M GONNA GIVE KARMA AND MAKE A VESSEL...
...THAT MEANS I HAVE TO SACRIFICE SOMEONE ELSE, RIGHT?!
NO WAY, MAN!
DON'T WORRY ABOUT THAT.
I'VE GOT SOME-ONE IN MIND ALREADY.
SOME-ONE WHO'D BE PER-FECT.
HIS NAME IS CODE.
THE ONLY OTHER GUY...
...TO HAVE SURVIVED JIGEN'S *RITUAL.*

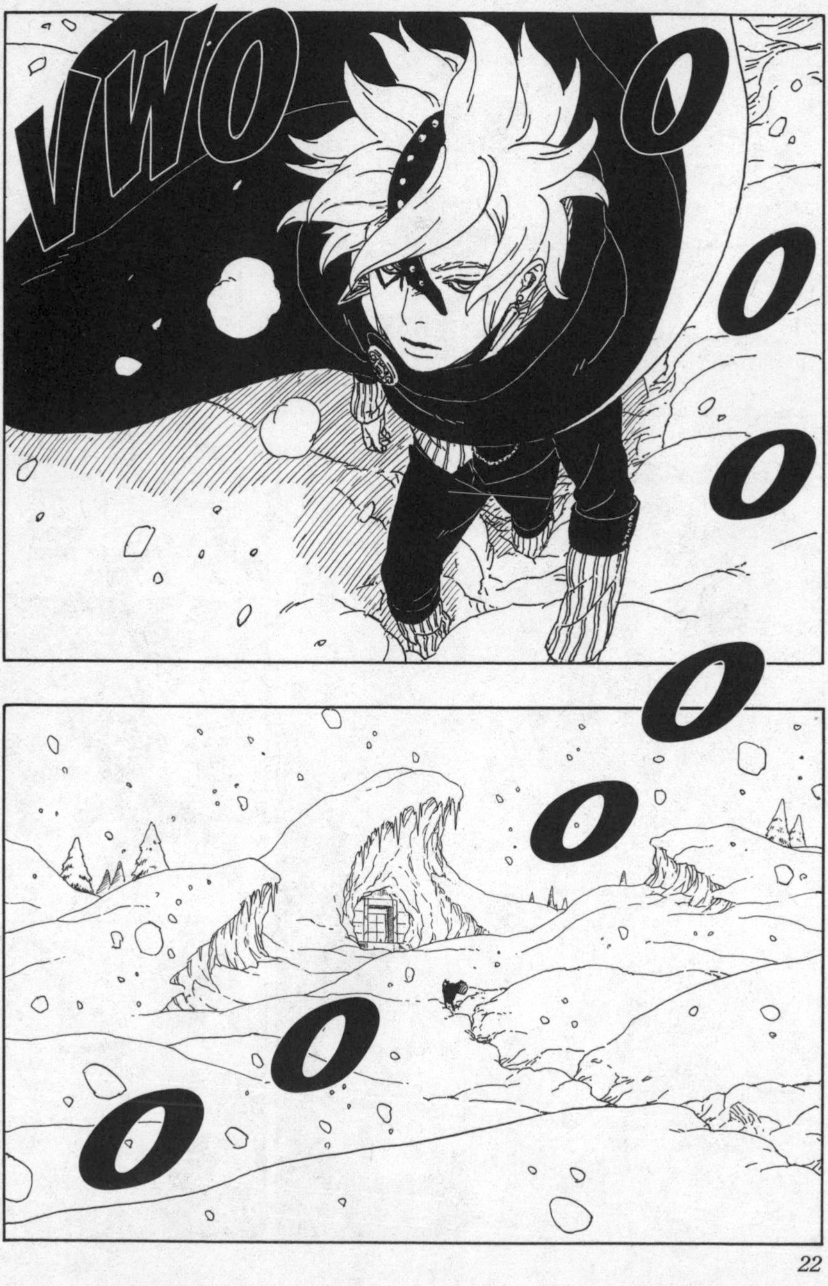
VWOOOOOOOO

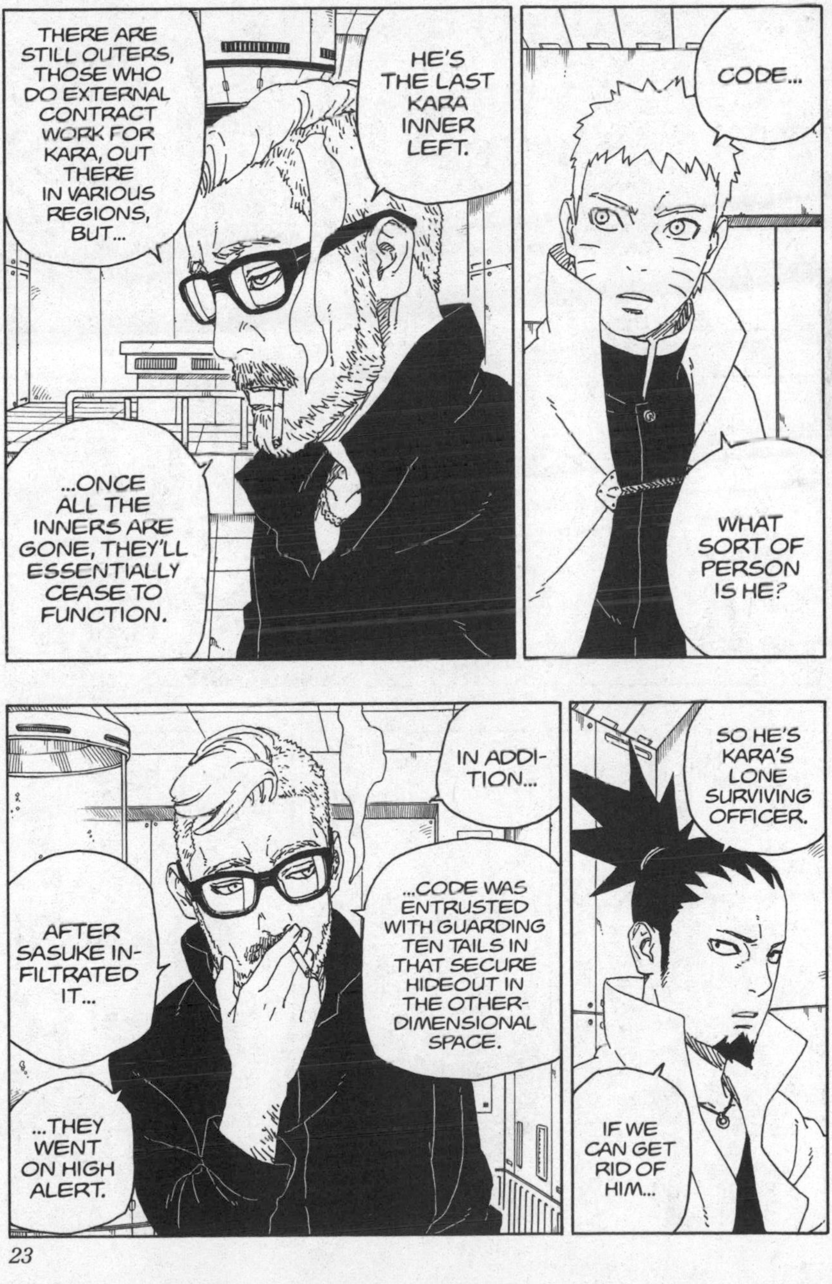
CODE...
WHAT SORT OF PERSON IS HE?
HE'S THE LAST KARA INNER LEFT.
THERE ARE STILL OUTERS, THOSE WHO DO EXTERNAL CONTRACT WORK FOR KARA, OUT THERE IN VARIOUS REGIONS, BUT...
...ONCE ALL THE INNERS ARE GONE, THEY'LL ESSENTIALLY CEASE TO FUNCTION.
SO HE'S KARA'S LONE SURVIVING OFFICER.
IF WE CAN GET RID OF HIM...
IN ADDITION...
...CODE WAS ENTRUSTED WITH GUARDING TEN TAILS IN THAT SECURE HIDEOUT IN THE OTHER-DIMENSIONAL SPACE.
AFTER SASUKE INFILTRATED IT...
...THEY WENT ON HIGH ALERT.

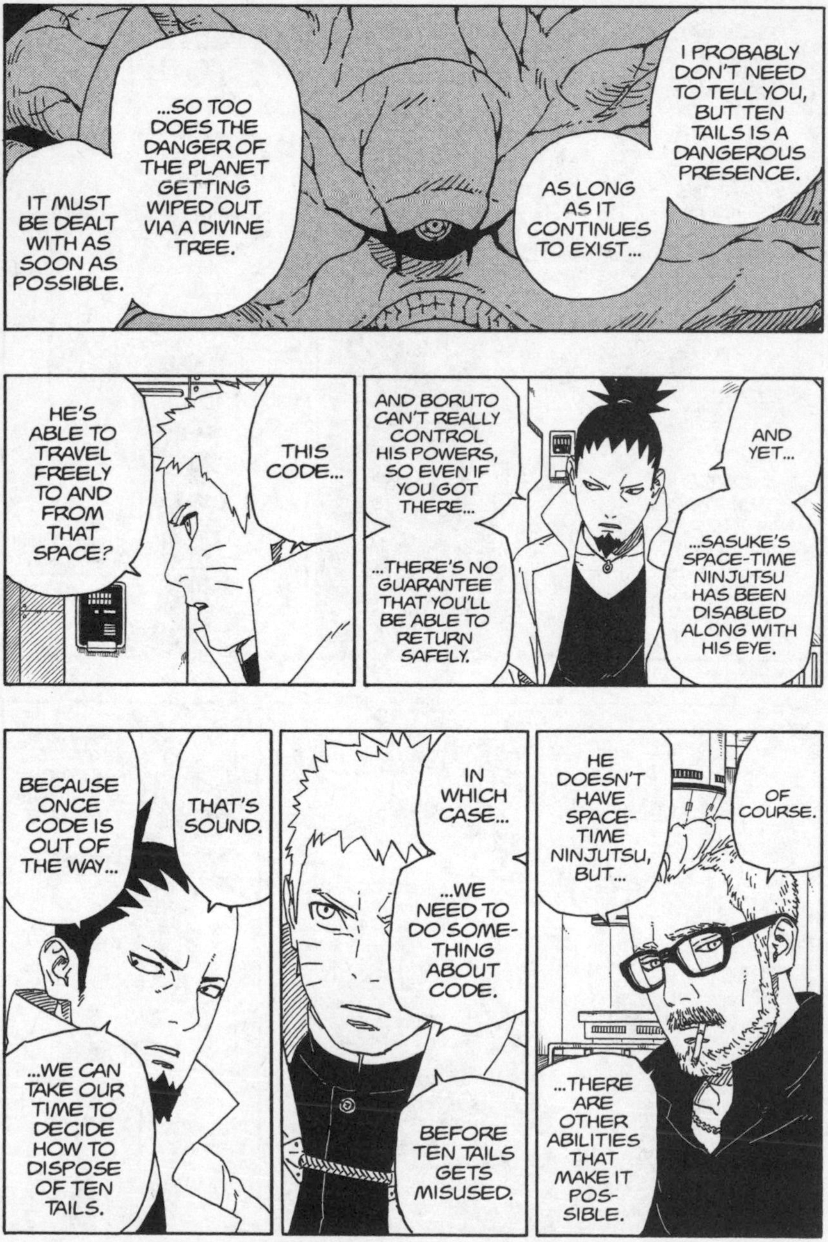
I PROBABLY DON'T NEED TO TELL YOU, BUT TEN TAILS IS A DANGEROUS PRESENCE.
AS LONG AS IT CONTINUES TO EXIST...
...SO TOO DOES THE DANGER OF THE PLANET GETTING WIPED OUT VIA A DIVINE TREE.
IT MUST BE DEALT WITH AS SOON AS POSSIBLE.
AND YET...
...SASUKE'S SPACE-TIME NINJUTSU HAS BEEN DISABLED ALONG WITH HIS EYE.
AND BORUTO CAN'T REALLY CONTROL HIS POWERS, SO EVEN IF YOU GOT THERE...
...THERE'S NO GUARANTEE THAT YOU'LL BE ABLE TO RETURN SAFELY.
THIS CODE...
HE'S ABLE TO TRAVEL FREELY TO AND FROM THAT SPACE?
OF COURSE.
HE DOESN'T HAVE SPACE-TIME NINJUTSU, BUT...
...THERE ARE OTHER ABILITIES THAT MAKE IT POSSIBLE.
IN WHICH CASE...
...WE NEED TO DO SOMETHING ABOUT CODE.
BEFORE TEN TAILS GETS MISUSED.
THAT'S SOUND.
BECAUSE ONCE CODE IS OUT OF THE WAY...
...WE CAN TAKE OUR TIME TO DECIDE HOW TO DISPOSE OF TEN TAILS.

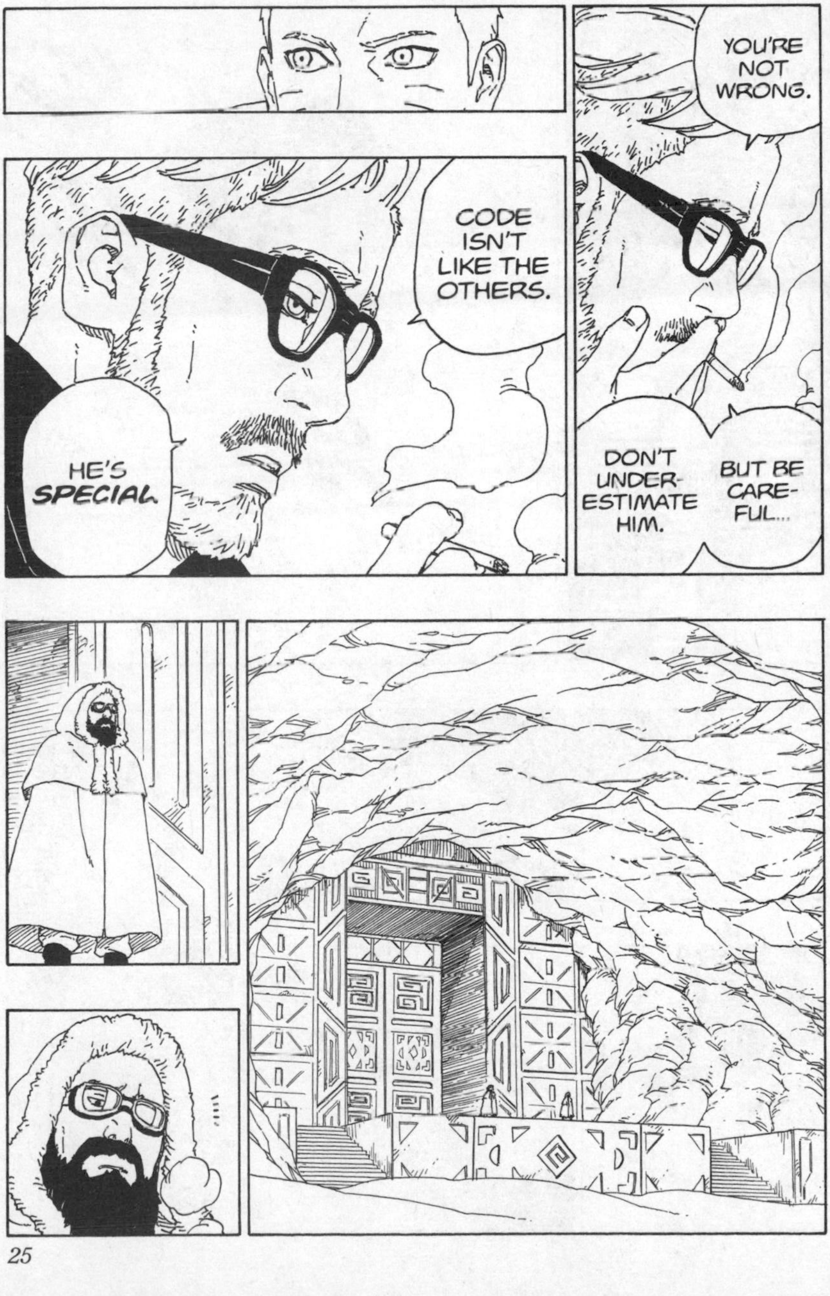
YOU'RE NOT WRONG.
BUT BE CARE-FUL...
DON'T UNDER-ESTIMATE HIM.
CODE ISN'T LIKE THE OTHERS.
HE'S *SPECIAL*.

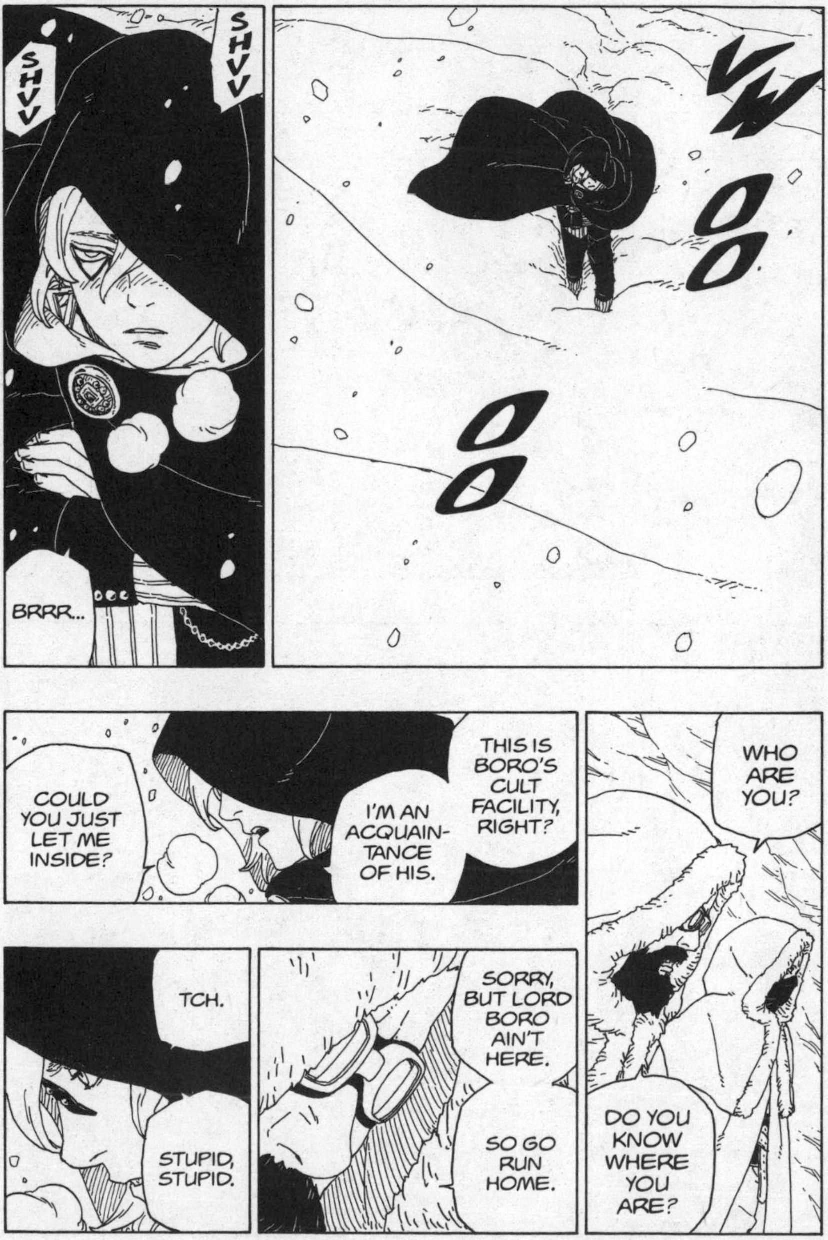
VWOOOO
SHVV
SHVV
BRRR...
WHO ARE YOU?
DO YOU KNOW WHERE YOU ARE?
THIS IS BORO'S CULT FACILITY, RIGHT?
I'M AN ACQUAIN-TANCE OF HIS.
COULD YOU JUST LET ME INSIDE?
SORRY, BUT LORD BORO AIN'T HERE.
SO GO RUN HOME.
TCH.
STUPID, STUPID.

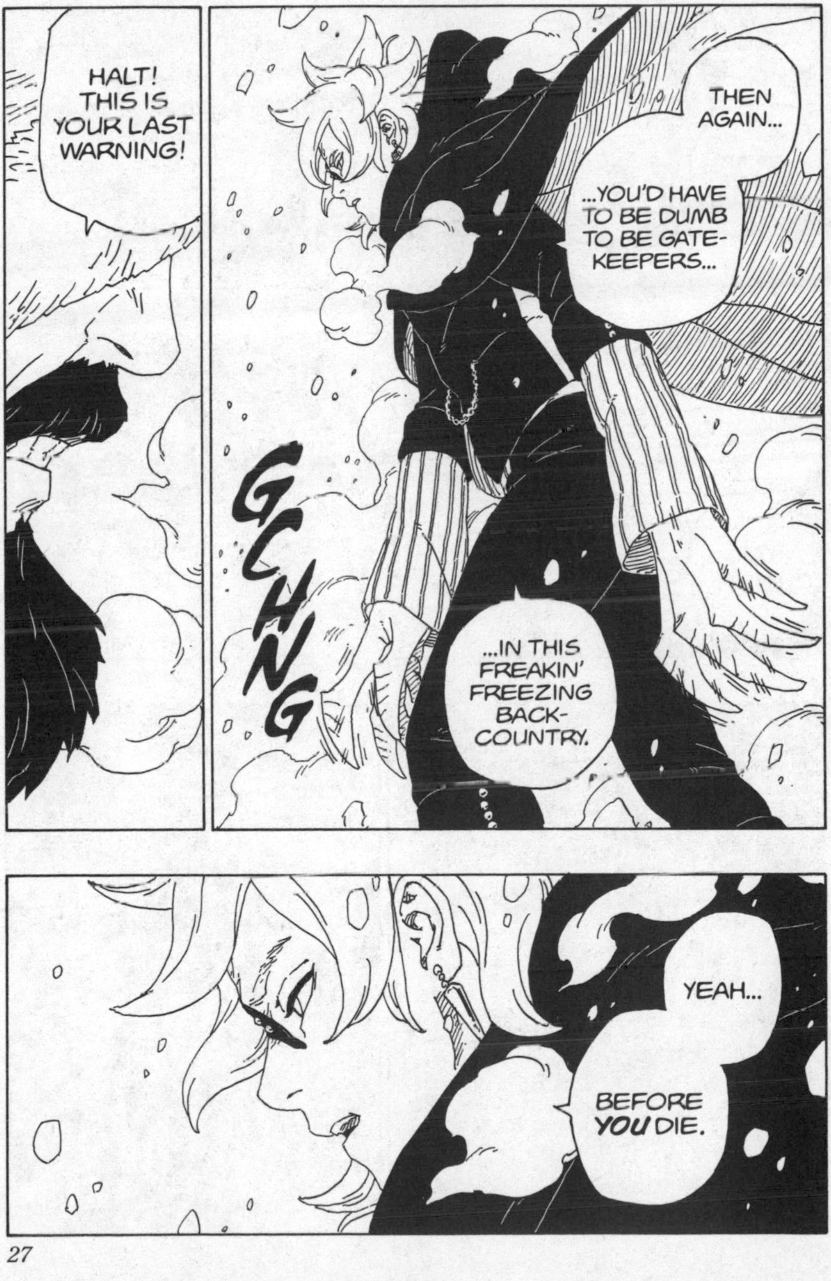
THEN AGAIN...
...YOU'D HAVE TO BE DUMB TO BE GATE-KEEPERS...
GCHNG
...IN THIS FREAKIN' FREEZING BACK-COUNTRY.
HALT! THIS IS YOUR LAST WARNING!
YEAH...
BEFORE *YOU* DIE.

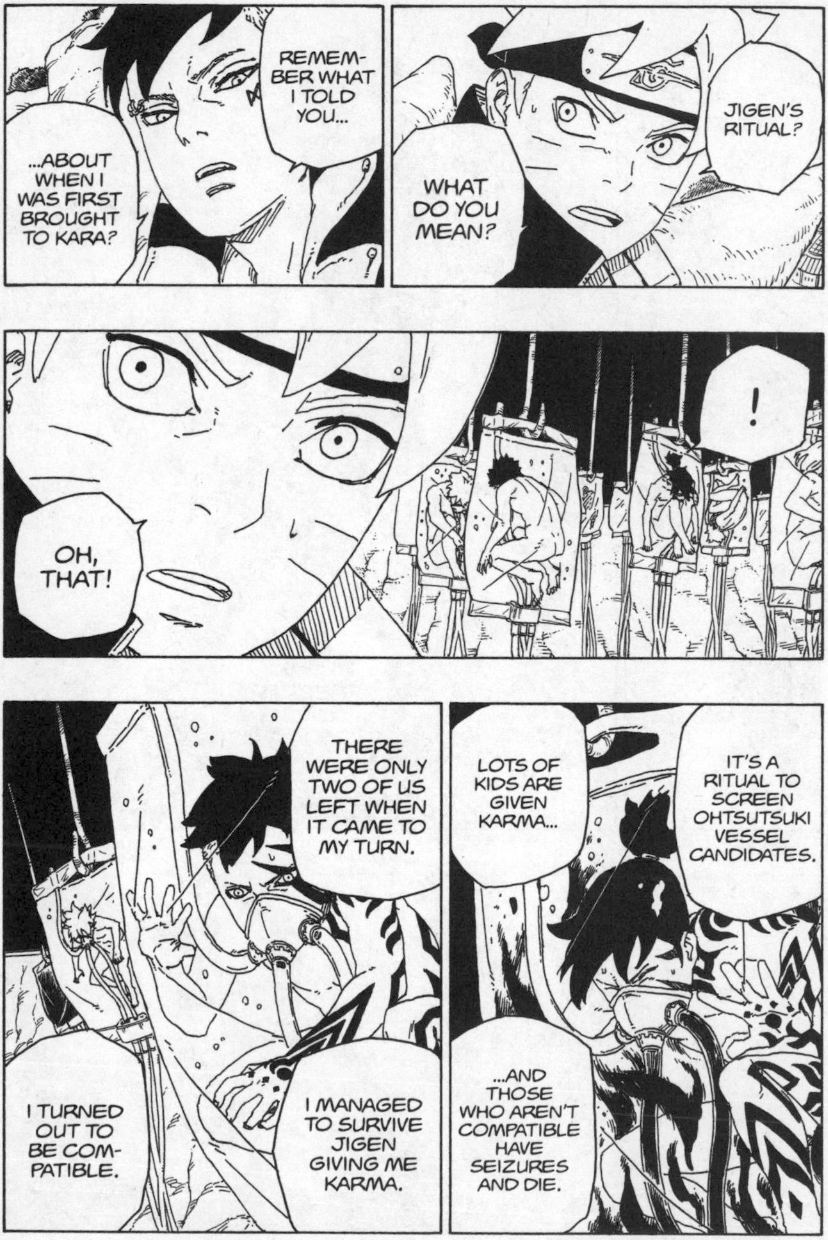
JIGEN'S RITUAL?
WHAT DO YOU MEAN?
REMEMBER WHAT I TOLD YOU...
...ABOUT WHEN I WAS FIRST BROUGHT TO KARA?
!
OH, THAT!
IT'S A RITUAL TO SCREEN OHTSUTSUKI VESSEL CANDIDATES.
LOTS OF KIDS ARE GIVEN KARMA...
...AND THOSE WHO AREN'T COMPATIBLE HAVE SEIZURES AND DIE.
THERE WERE ONLY TWO OF US LEFT WHEN IT CAME TO MY TURN.
I MANAGED TO SURVIVE JIGEN GIVING ME KARMA.
I TURNED OUT TO BE COMPATIBLE.

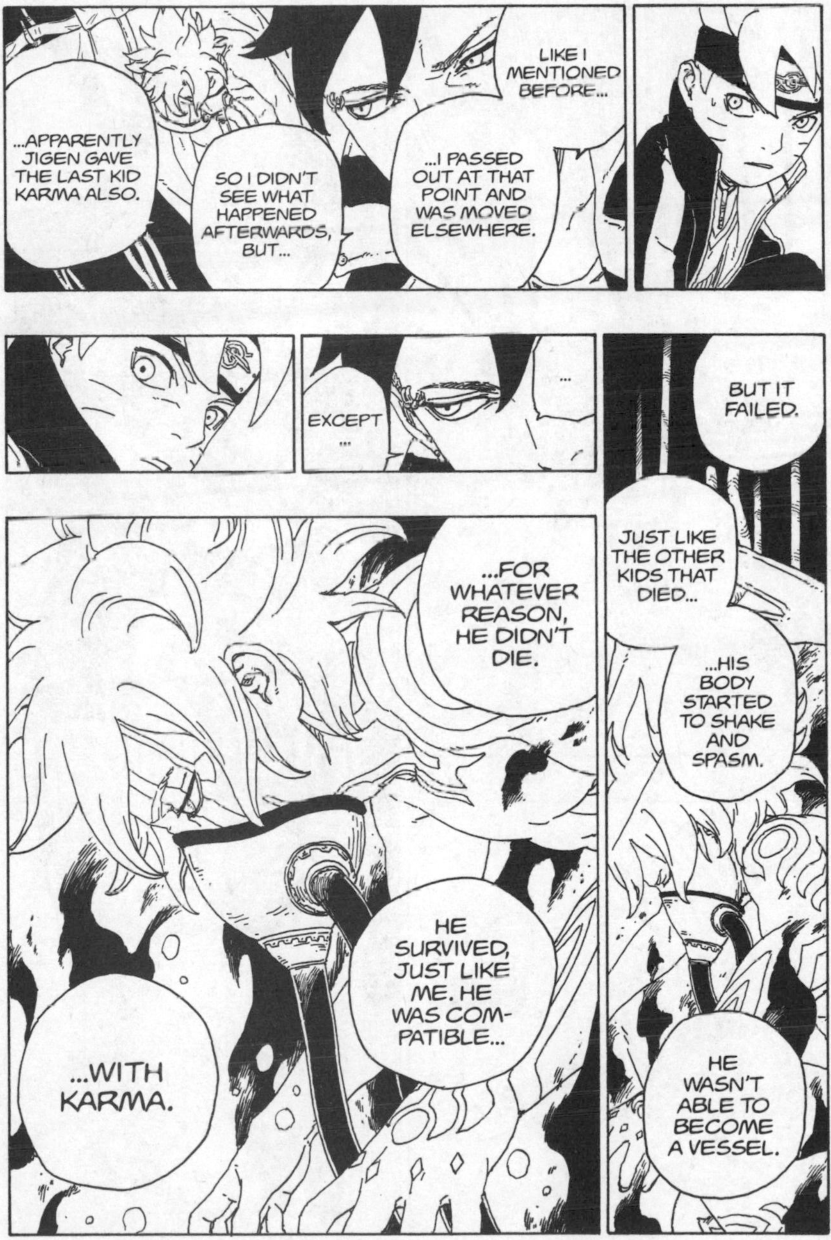
LIKE I MENTIONED BEFORE...
...I PASSED OUT AT THAT POINT AND WAS MOVED ELSEWHERE.
SO I DIDN'T SEE WHAT HAPPENED AFTERWARDS, BUT...
...APPARENTLY JIGEN GAVE THE LAST KID KARMA ALSO.
BUT IT FAILED.
JUST LIKE THE OTHER KIDS THAT DIED...
...HIS BODY STARTED TO SHAKE AND SPASM.
HE WASN'T ABLE TO BECOME A VESSEL.
...
EXCEPT ...
...FOR WHATEVER REASON, HE DIDN'T DIE.
HE SURVIVED, JUST LIKE ME. HE WAS COMPATIBLE...
...WITH KARMA.

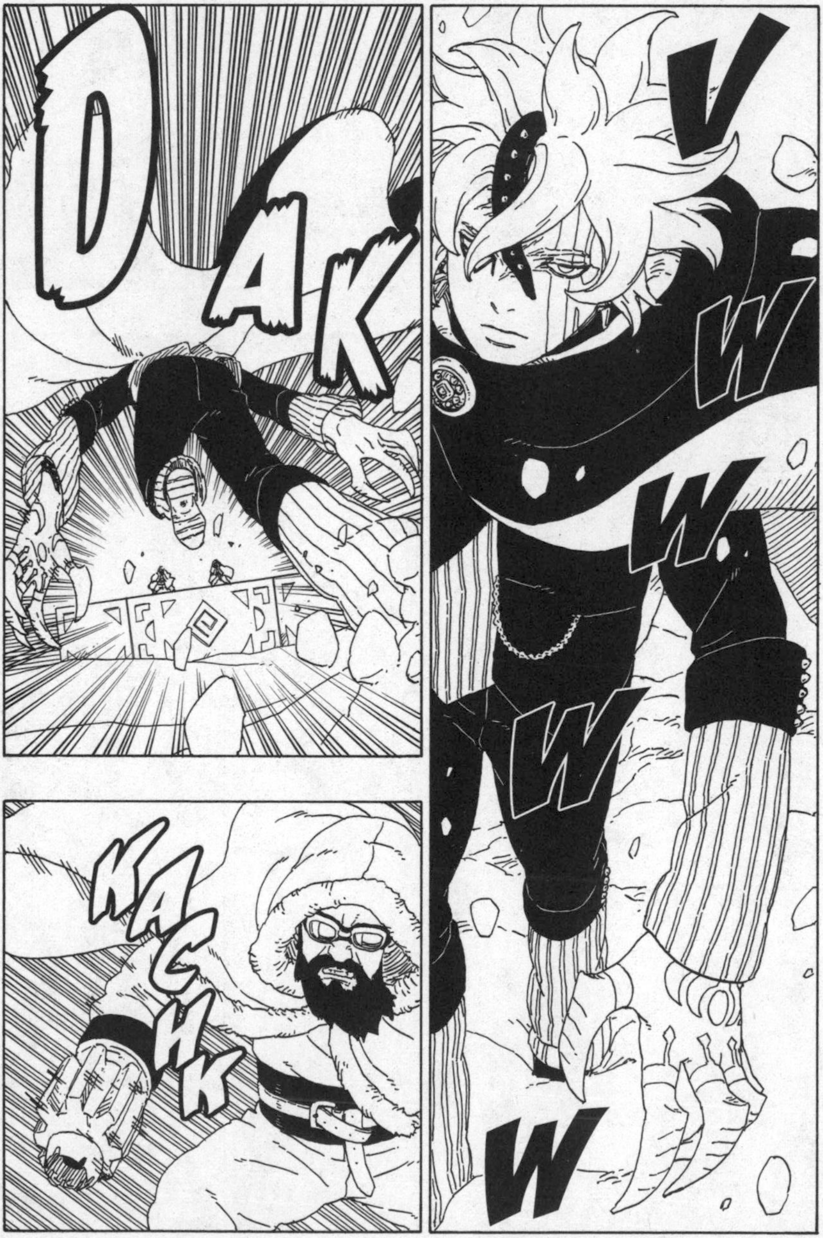
VWWWW
DAK
KACHK

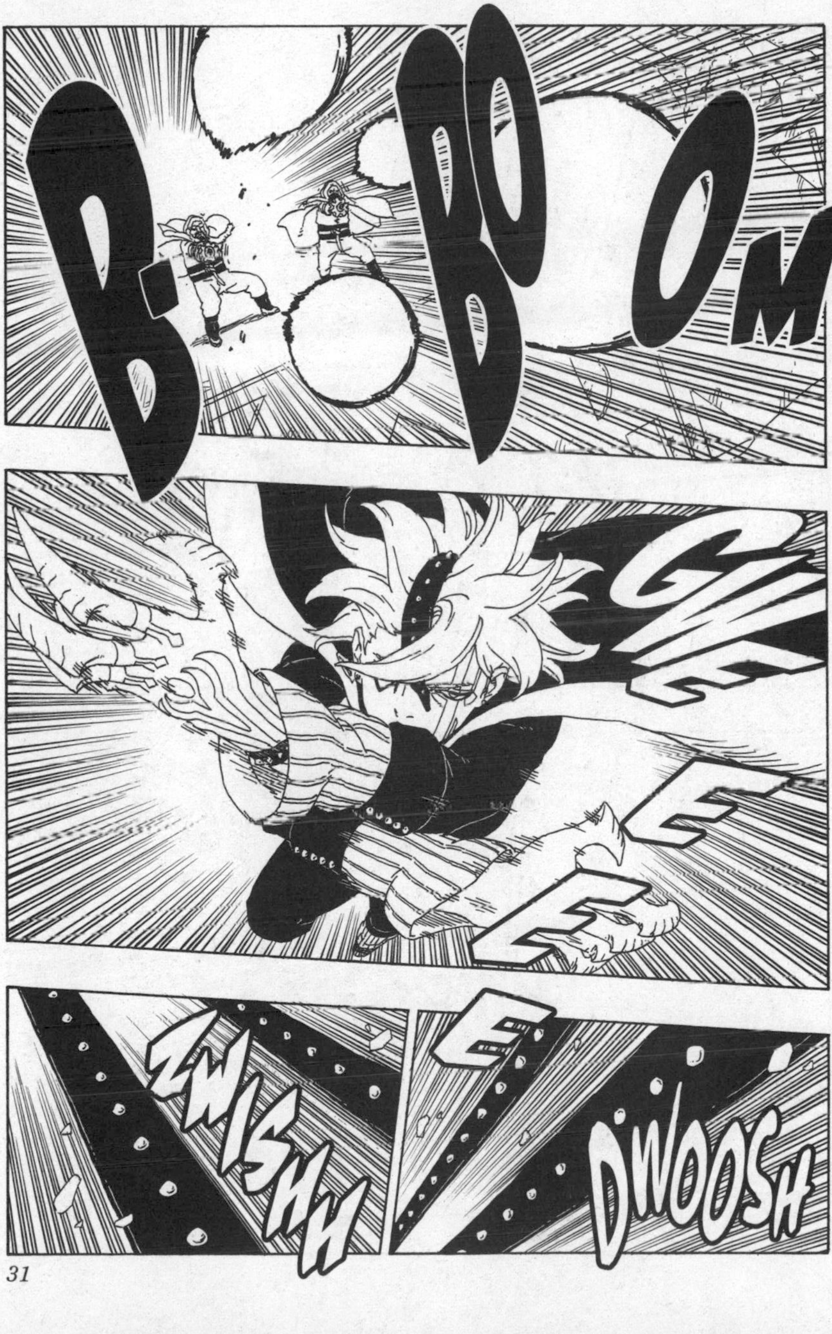
B-BOOM
GWEEE
E
DWOOSH
ZWISHH

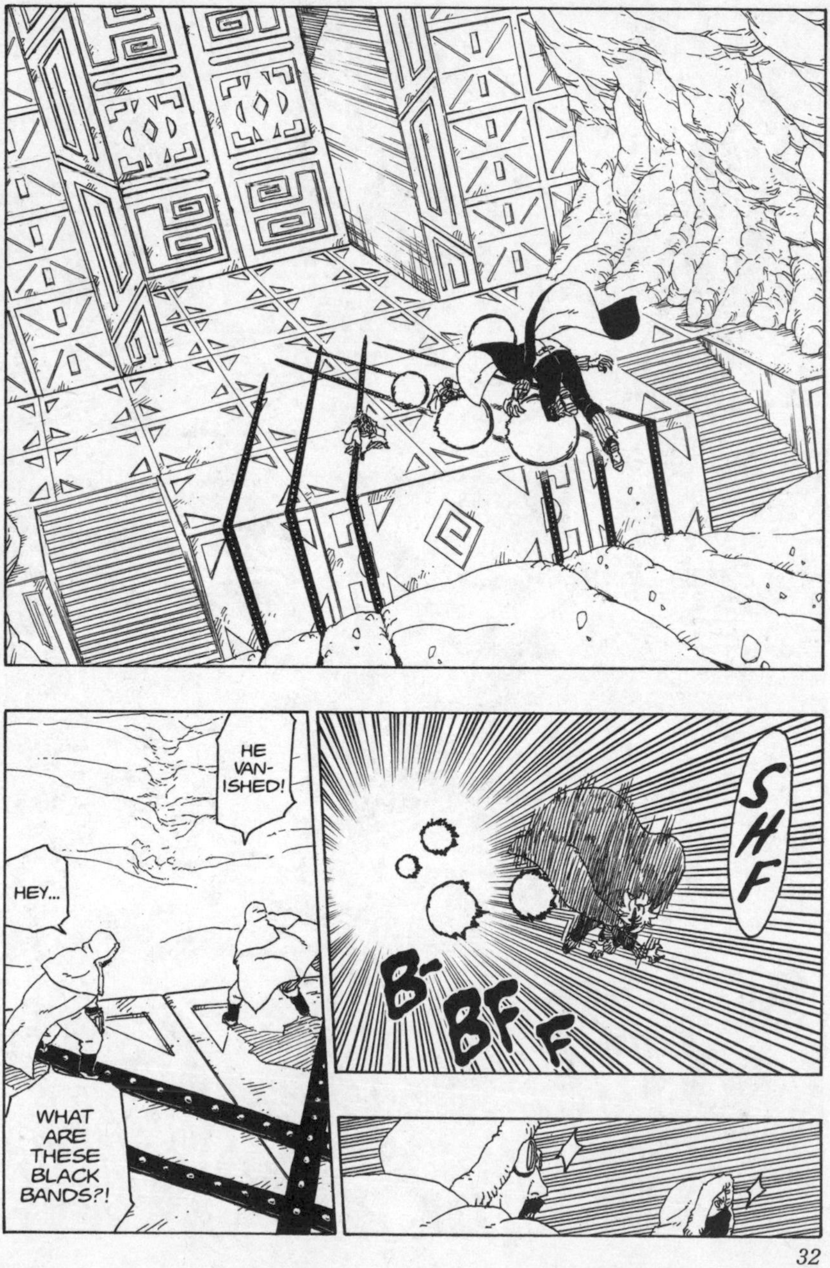
SHF
B-BFF
HE VAN-ISHED!
HEY...
WHAT ARE THESE BLACK BANDS?!

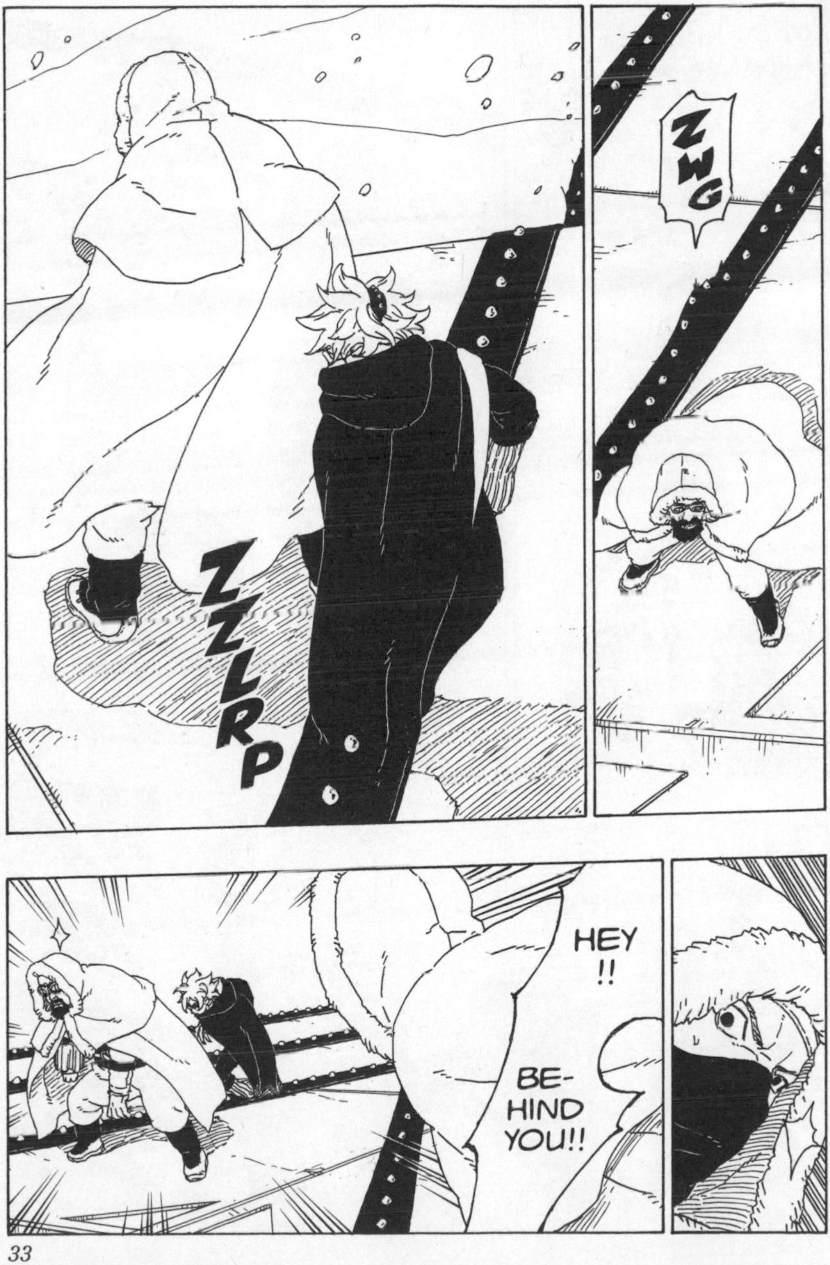
ZWG
ZZLRP
HEY!!
BE-HIND YOU!!

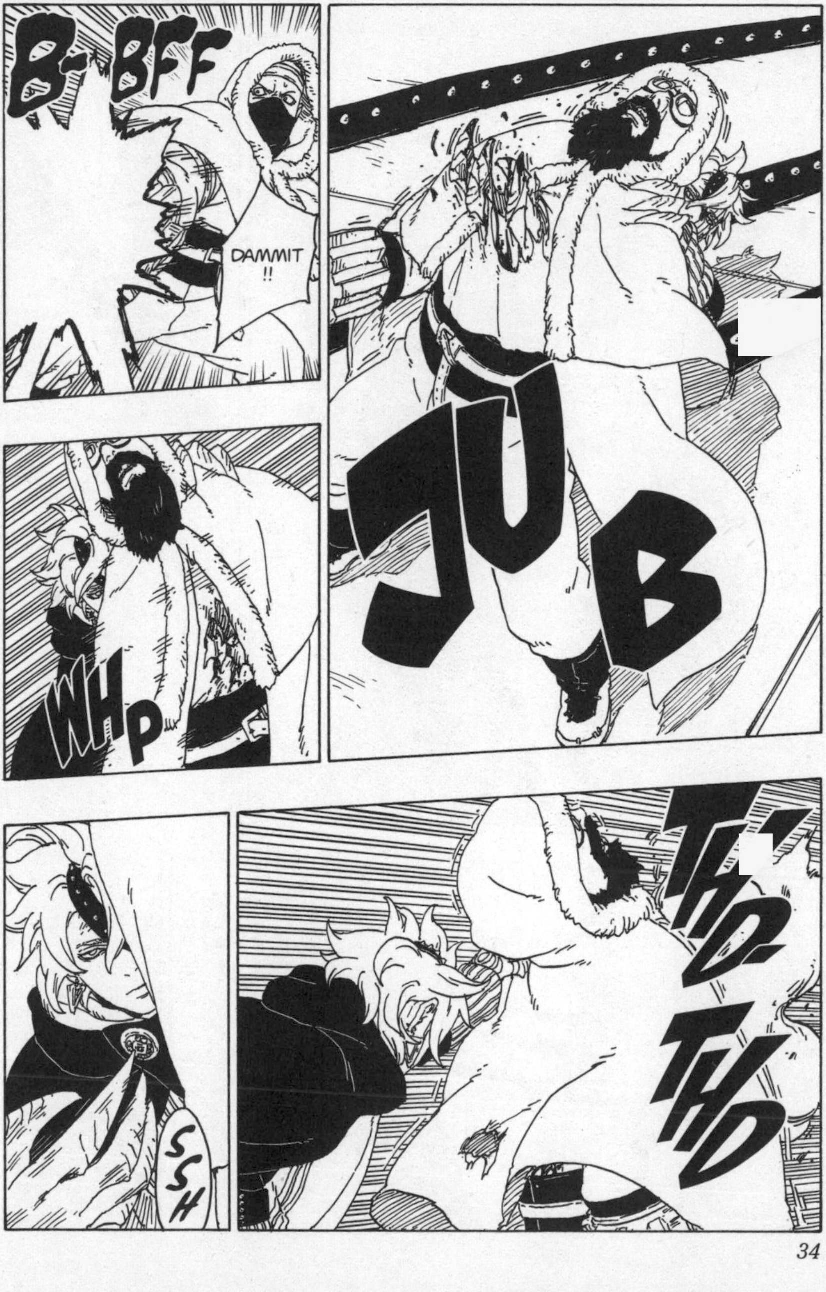
JUB
B-BFF
DAMMIT !!
WHP
THD-THD THD
SSH

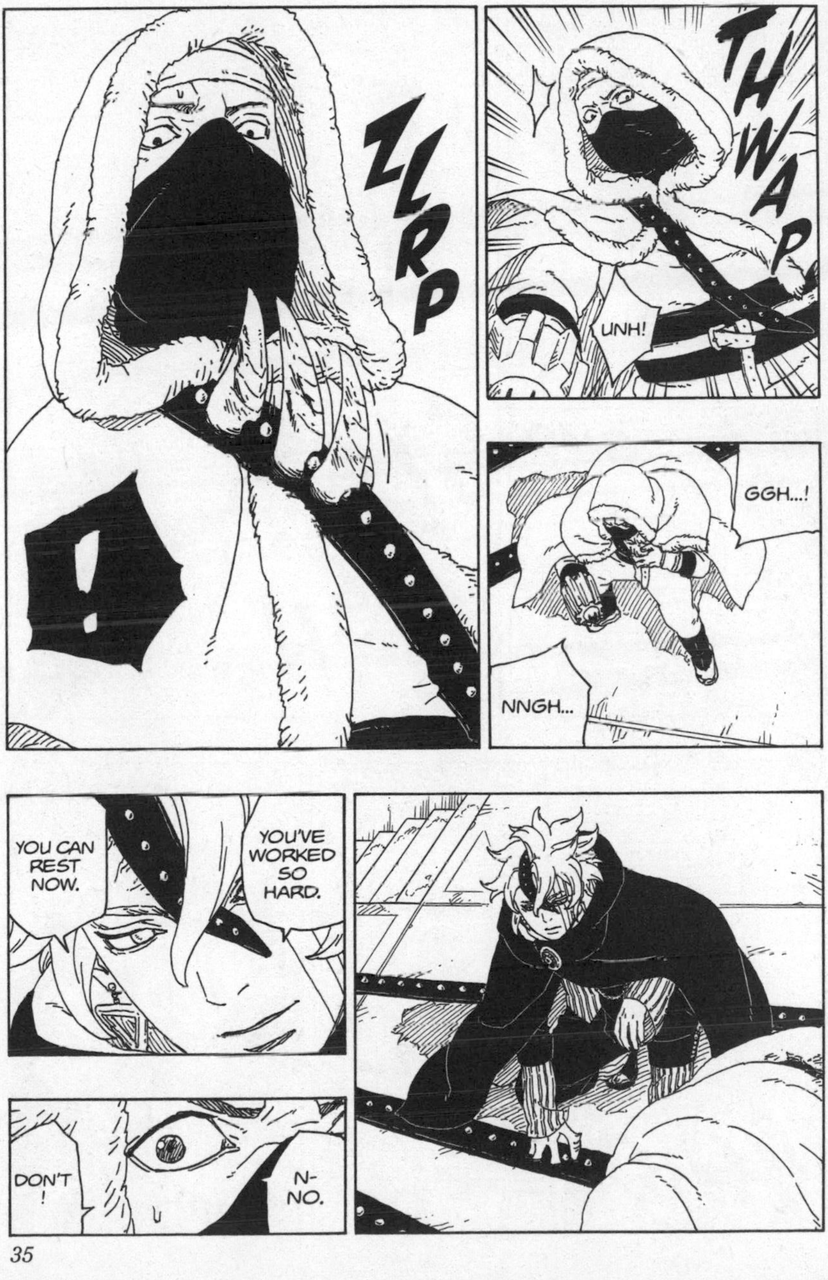
THWAP
UNH!
GGH...!
NNGH...
ZLRP
!
YOU'VE WORKED SO HARD.
YOU CAN REST NOW.
N-NO.
DON'T!

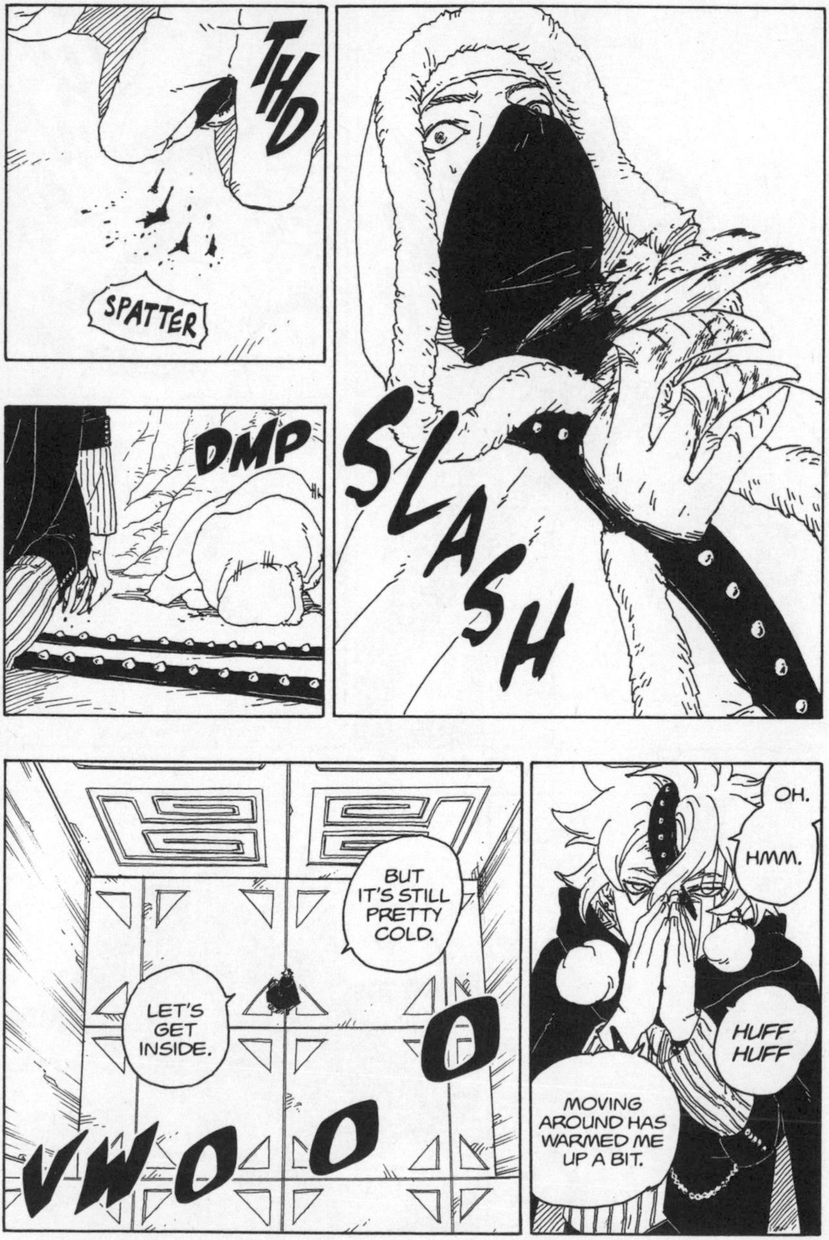
SLASH
THD
SPATTER
DMP
OH.
HMM.
HUFF HUFF
MOVING AROUND HAS WARMED ME UP A BIT.
BUT IT'S STILL PRETTY COLD.
LET'S GET INSIDE.
VWOOOO

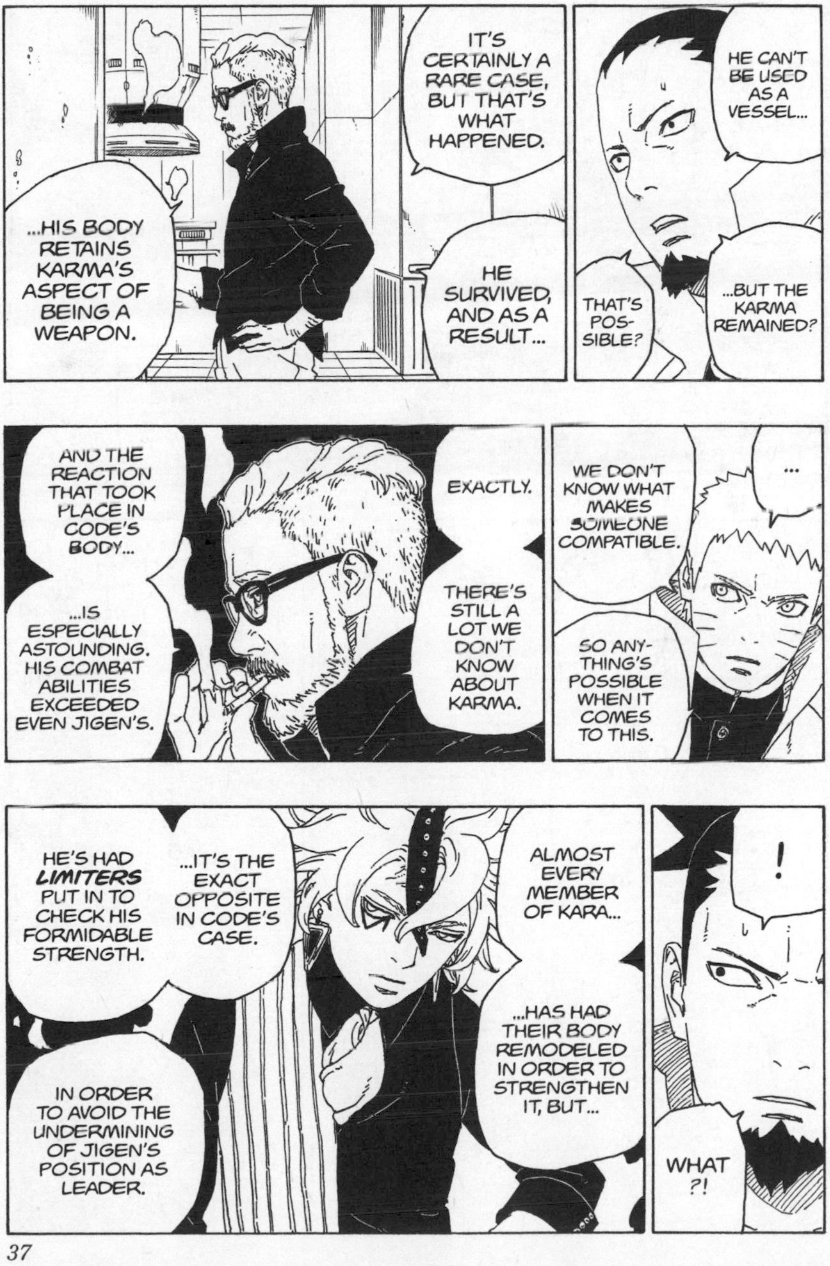
HE CAN'T BE USED AS A VESSEL...
...BUT THE KARMA REMAINED?
THAT'S POSSIBLE?
IT'S CERTAINLY A RARE CASE, BUT THAT'S WHAT HAPPENED.
HE SURVIVED, AND AS A RESULT...
...HIS BODY RETAINS KARMA'S ASPECT OF BEING A WEAPON.
...
WE DON'T KNOW WHAT MAKES SOMEONE COMPATIBLE.
SO ANYTHING'S POSSIBLE WHEN IT COMES TO THIS.
EXACTLY.
THERE'S STILL A LOT WE DON'T KNOW ABOUT KARMA.
AND THE REACTION THAT TOOK PLACE IN CODE'S BODY...
...IS ESPECIALLY ASTOUNDING. HIS COMBAT ABILITIES EXCEEDED EVEN JIGEN'S.
!
WHAT?!
ALMOST EVERY MEMBER OF KARA...
...HAS HAD THEIR BODY REMODELED IN ORDER TO STRENGTHEN IT, BUT...
...IT'S THE EXACT OPPOSITE IN CODE'S CASE.
HE'S HAD ***LIMITERS*** PUT IN TO CHECK HIS FORMIDABLE STRENGTH.
IN ORDER TO AVOID THE UNDERMINING OF JIGEN'S POSITION AS LEADER.

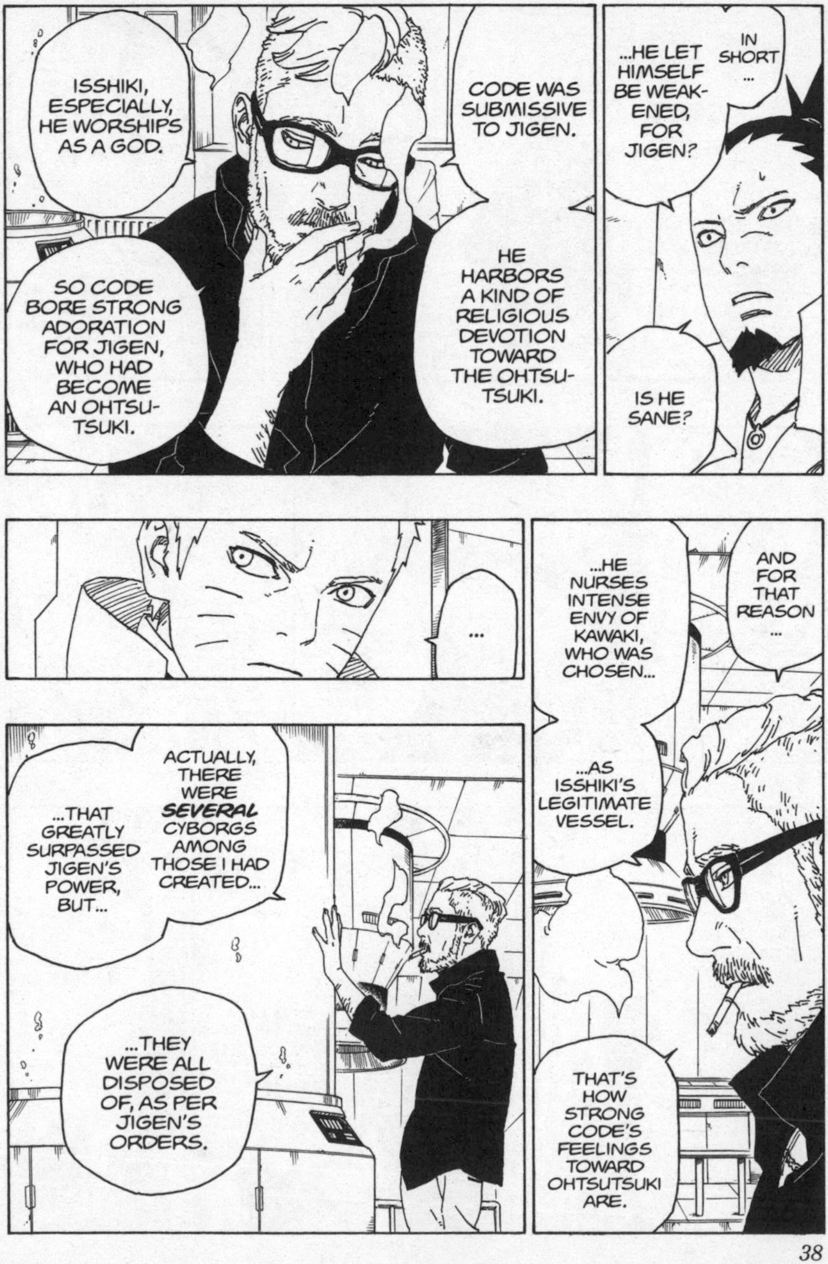
IN SHORT ...
...HE LET HIMSELF BE WEAK-ENED, FOR JIGEN?
IS HE SANE?
CODE WAS SUBMISSIVE TO JIGEN.
HE HARBORS A KIND OF RELIGIOUS DEVOTION TOWARD THE OHTSU-TSUKI.
ISSHIKI, ESPECIALLY, HE WORSHIPS AS A GOD.
SO CODE BORE STRONG ADORATION FOR JIGEN, WHO HAD BECOME AN OHTSU-TSUKI.
AND FOR THAT REASON ...
...HE NURSES INTENSE ENVY OF KAWAKI, WHO WAS CHOSEN...
...AS ISSHIKI'S LEGITIMATE VESSEL.
THAT'S HOW STRONG CODE'S FEELINGS TOWARD OHTSUTSUKI ARE.
...
ACTUALLY, THERE WERE ***SEVERAL*** CYBORGS AMONG THOSE I HAD CREATED...
...THAT GREATLY SURPASSED JIGEN'S POWER, BUT...
...THEY WERE ALL DISPOSED OF, AS PER JIGEN'S ORDERS.

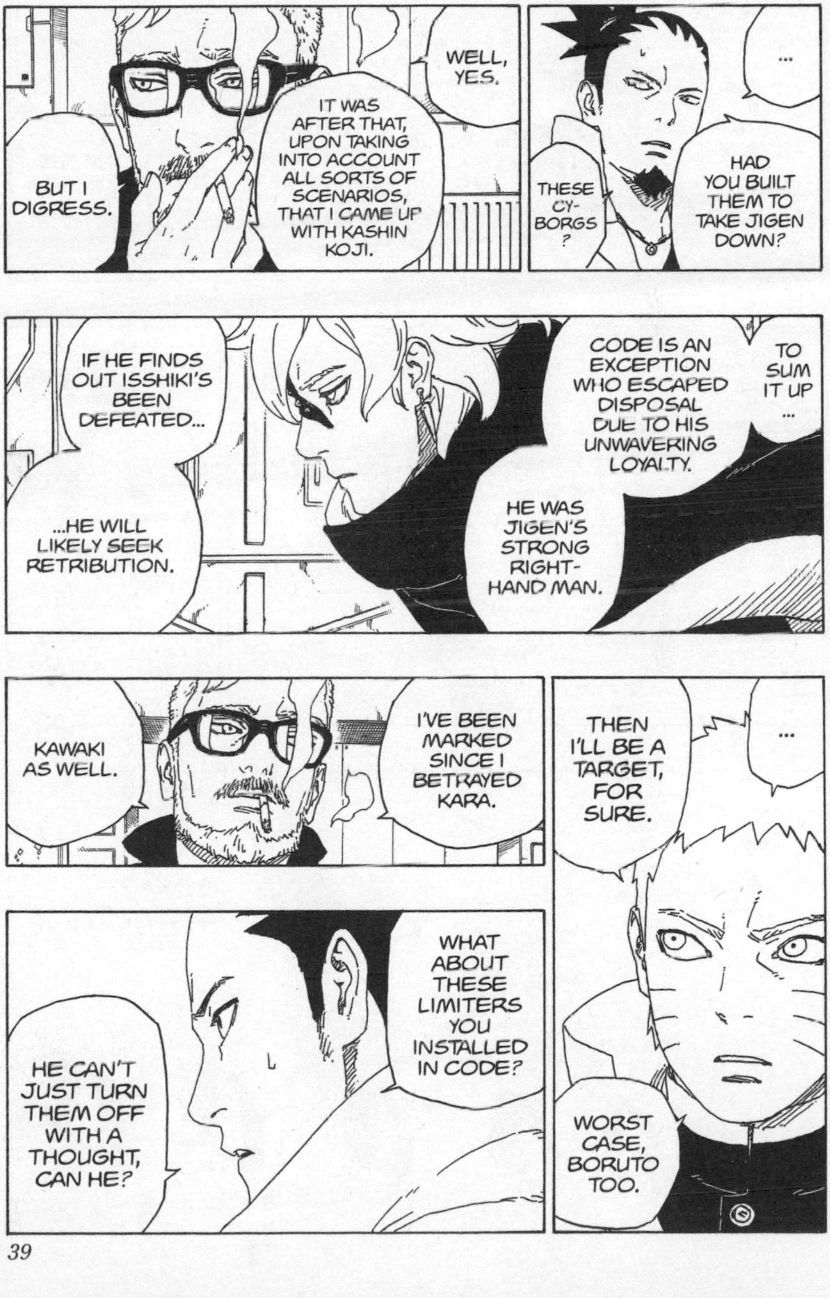
...
HAD YOU BUILT THEM TO TAKE JIGEN DOWN?
THESE CY-BORGS?
WELL, YES.
IT WAS AFTER THAT, UPON TAKING INTO ACCOUNT ALL SORTS OF SCENARIOS, THAT I CAME UP WITH KASHIN KOJI.
BUT I DIGRESS.
TO SUM IT UP...
CODE IS AN EXCEPTION WHO ESCAPED DISPOSAL DUE TO HIS UNWAVERING LOYALTY.
HE WAS JIGEN'S STRONG RIGHT-HAND MAN.
IF HE FINDS OUT ISSHIKI'S BEEN DEFEATED...
...HE WILL LIKELY SEEK RETRIBUTION.
...
THEN I'LL BE A TARGET, FOR SURE.
WORST CASE, BORUTO TOO.
I'VE BEEN MARKED SINCE I BETRAYED KARA.
KAWAKI AS WELL.
WHAT ABOUT THESE LIMITERS YOU INSTALLED IN CODE?
HE CAN'T JUST TURN THEM OFF WITH A THOUGHT, CAN HE?

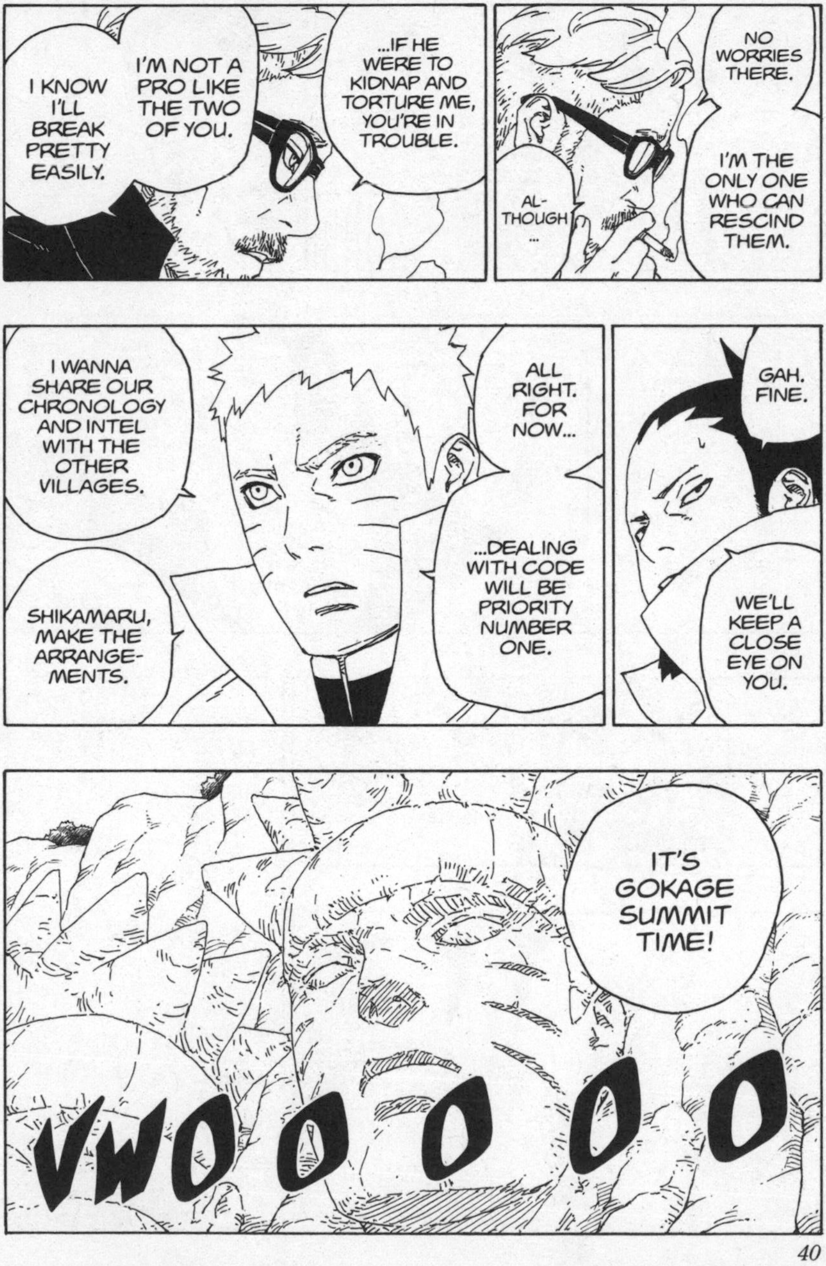
NO WORRIES THERE.
I'M THE ONLY ONE WHO CAN RESCIND THEM.
ALTHOUGH...
...IF HE WERE TO KIDNAP AND TORTURE ME, YOU'RE IN TROUBLE.
I'M NOT A PRO LIKE THE TWO OF YOU.
I KNOW I'LL BREAK PRETTY EASILY.
GAH. FINE.
WE'LL KEEP A CLOSE EYE ON YOU.
ALL RIGHT. FOR NOW...
...DEALING WITH CODE WILL BE PRIORITY NUMBER ONE.
I WANNA SHARE OUR CHRONOLOGY AND INTEL WITH THE OTHER VILLAGES.
SHIKAMARU, MAKE THE ARRANGEMENTS.
IT'S GOKAGE SUMMIT TIME!
VWOOO O O O

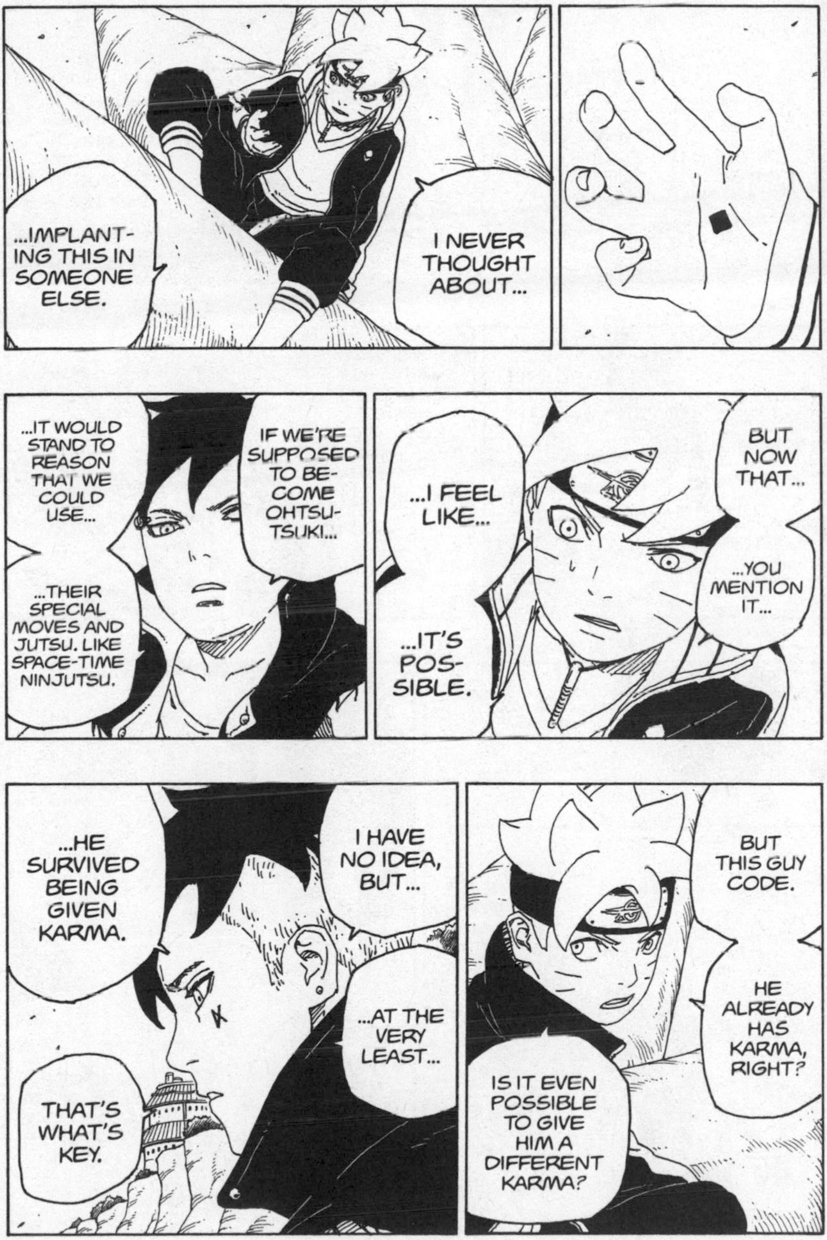

I NEVER THOUGHT ABOUT...
...IMPLANTING THIS IN SOMEONE ELSE.
BUT NOW THAT...
...YOU MENTION IT...
...I FEEL LIKE...
...IT'S POSSIBLE.
IF WE'RE SUPPOSED TO BECOME OHTSUTSUKI...
...IT WOULD STAND TO REASON THAT WE COULD USE...
...THEIR SPECIAL MOVES AND JUTSU. LIKE SPACE-TIME NINJUTSU.
BUT THIS GUY CODE.
HE ALREADY HAS KARMA, RIGHT?
IS IT EVEN POSSIBLE TO GIVE HIM A DIFFERENT KARMA?
I HAVE NO IDEA, BUT...
...HE SURVIVED BEING GIVEN KARMA.
...AT THE VERY LEAST...
THAT'S WHAT'S KEY.

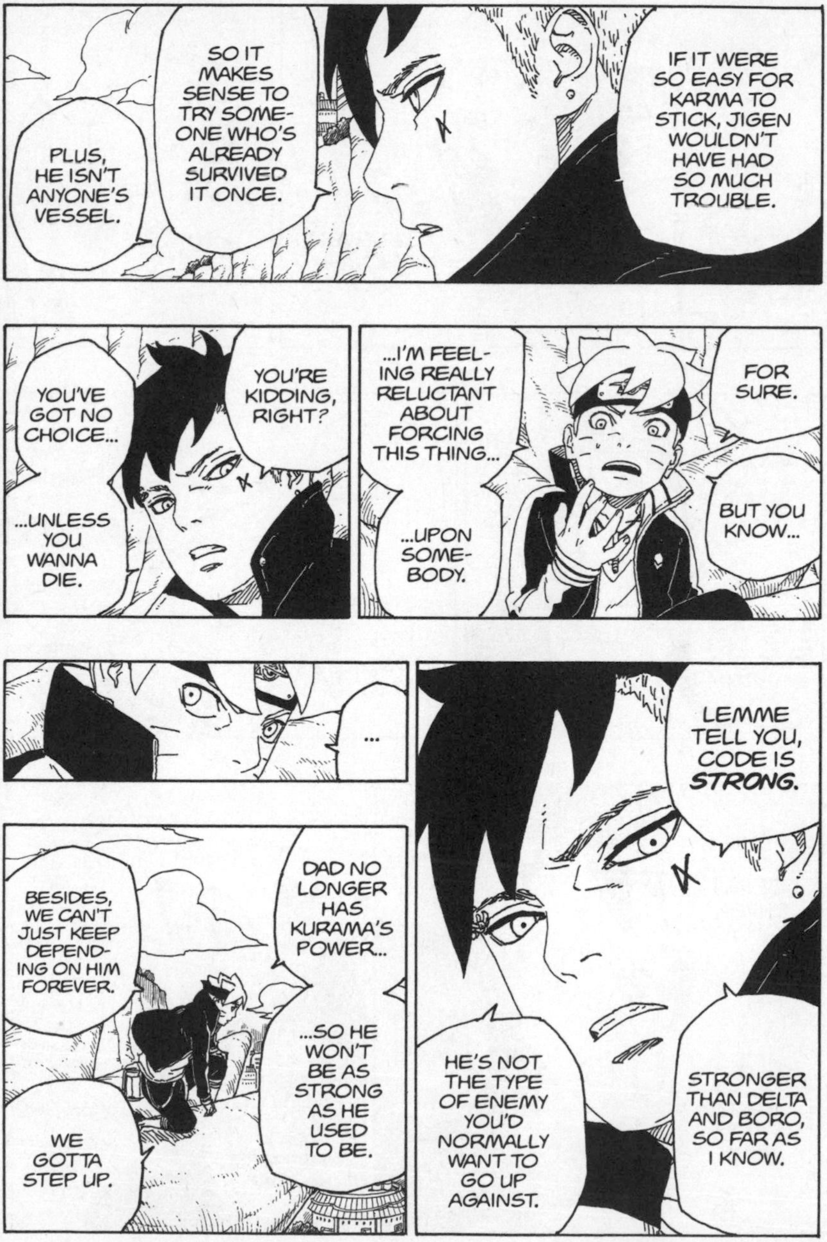
IF IT WERE SO EASY FOR KARMA TO STICK, JIGEN WOULDN'T HAVE HAD SO MUCH TROUBLE.
SO IT MAKES SENSE TO TRY SOMEONE WHO'S ALREADY SURVIVED IT ONCE.
PLUS, HE ISN'T ANYONE'S VESSEL.
FOR SURE.
BUT YOU KNOW...
...I'M FEELING REALLY RELUCTANT ABOUT FORCING THIS THING...
...UPON SOMEBODY.
YOU'RE KIDDING, RIGHT?
YOU'VE GOT NO CHOICE...
...UNLESS YOU WANNA DIE.
LEMME TELL YOU, CODE IS ***STRONG.***
STRONGER THAN DELTA AND BORO, SO FAR AS I KNOW.
HE'S NOT THE TYPE OF ENEMY YOU'D NORMALLY WANT TO GO UP AGAINST.
...
DAD NO LONGER HAS KURAMA'S POWER...
...SO HE WON'T BE AS STRONG AS HE USED TO BE.
BESIDES, WE CAN'T JUST KEEP DEPENDING ON HIM FOREVER.
WE GOTTA STEP UP.

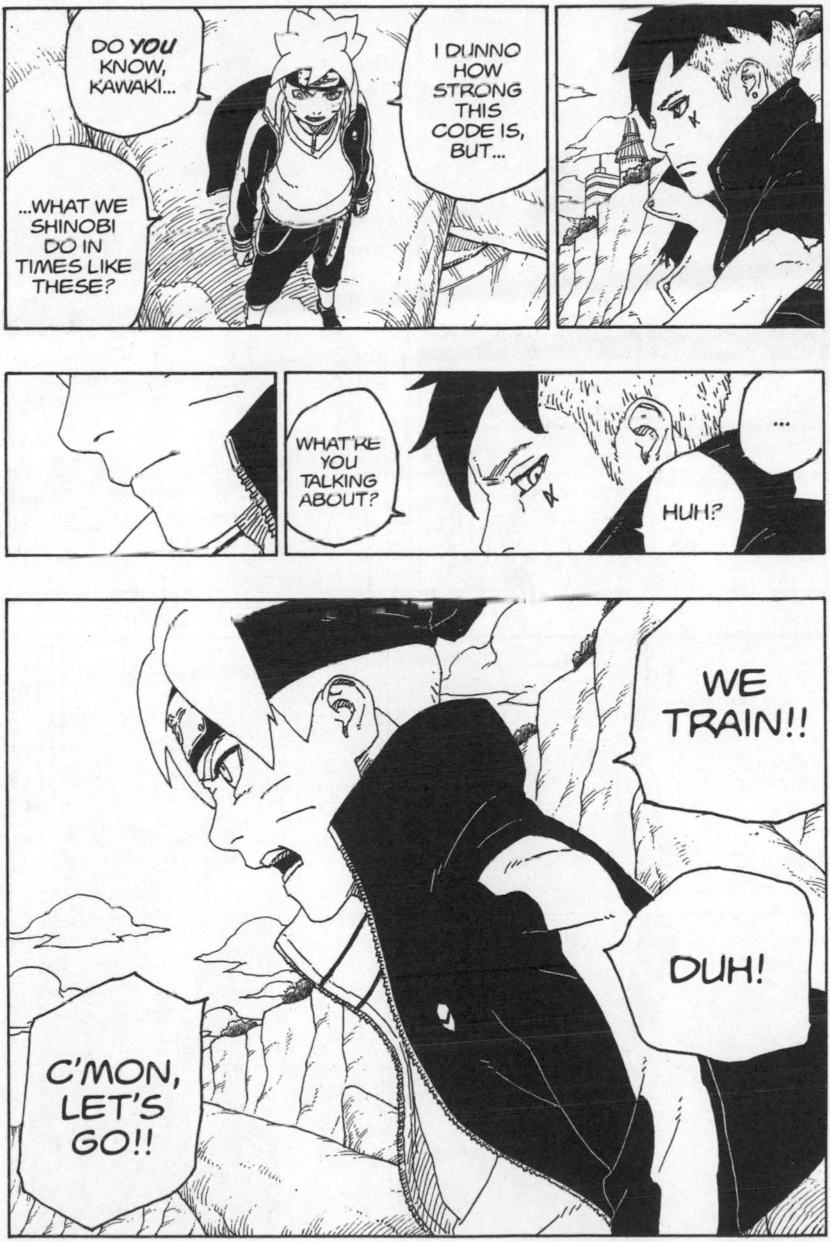
I DUNNO HOW STRONG THIS CODE IS, BUT...
DO YOU KNOW, KAWAKI...
...WHAT WE SHINOBI DO IN TIMES LIKE THESE?
...
HUH?
WHAT'RE YOU TALKING ABOUT?
WE TRAIN!!
DUH!
C'MON, LET'S GO!!

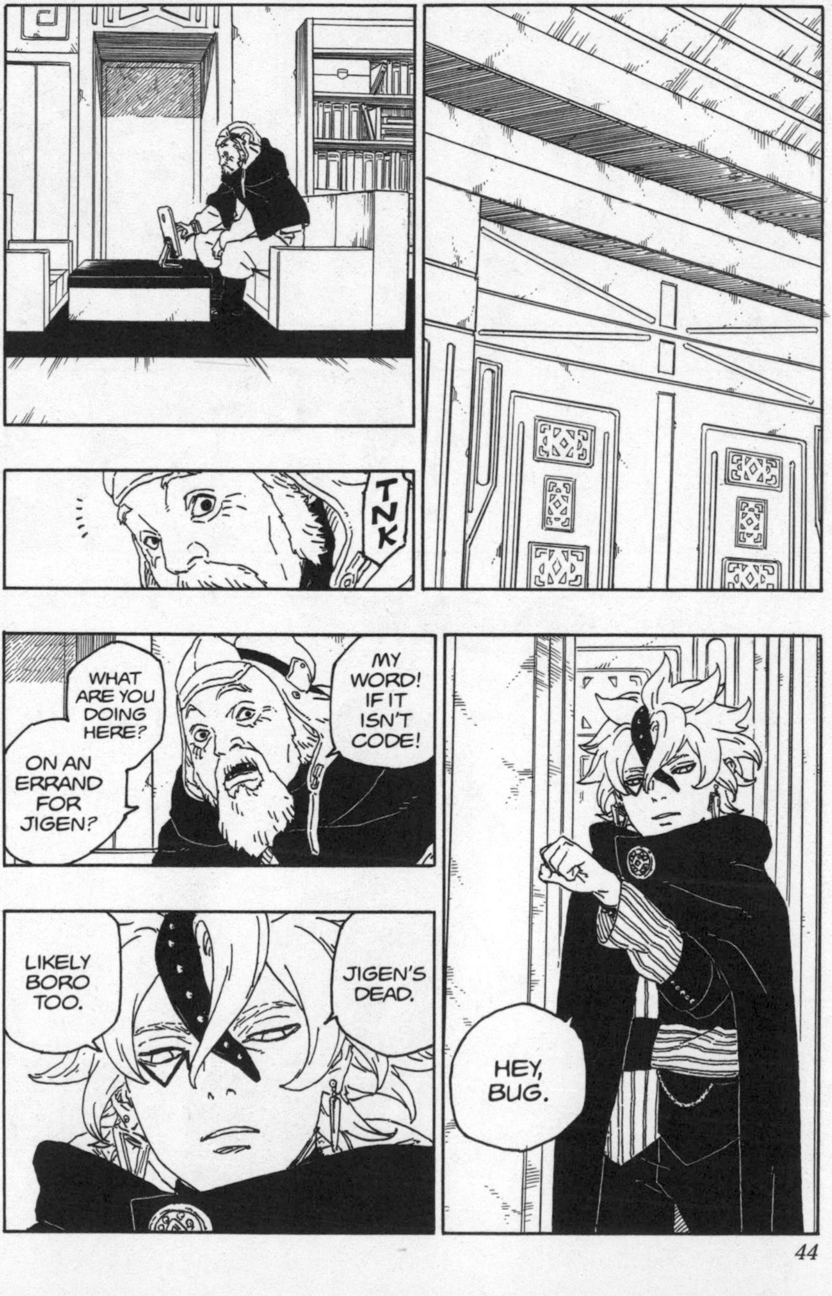
TNK
HEY, BUG.
MY WORD! IF IT ISN'T CODE!
WHAT ARE YOU DOING HERE?
ON AN ERRAND FOR JIGEN?
JIGEN'S DEAD.
LIKELY BORO TOO.

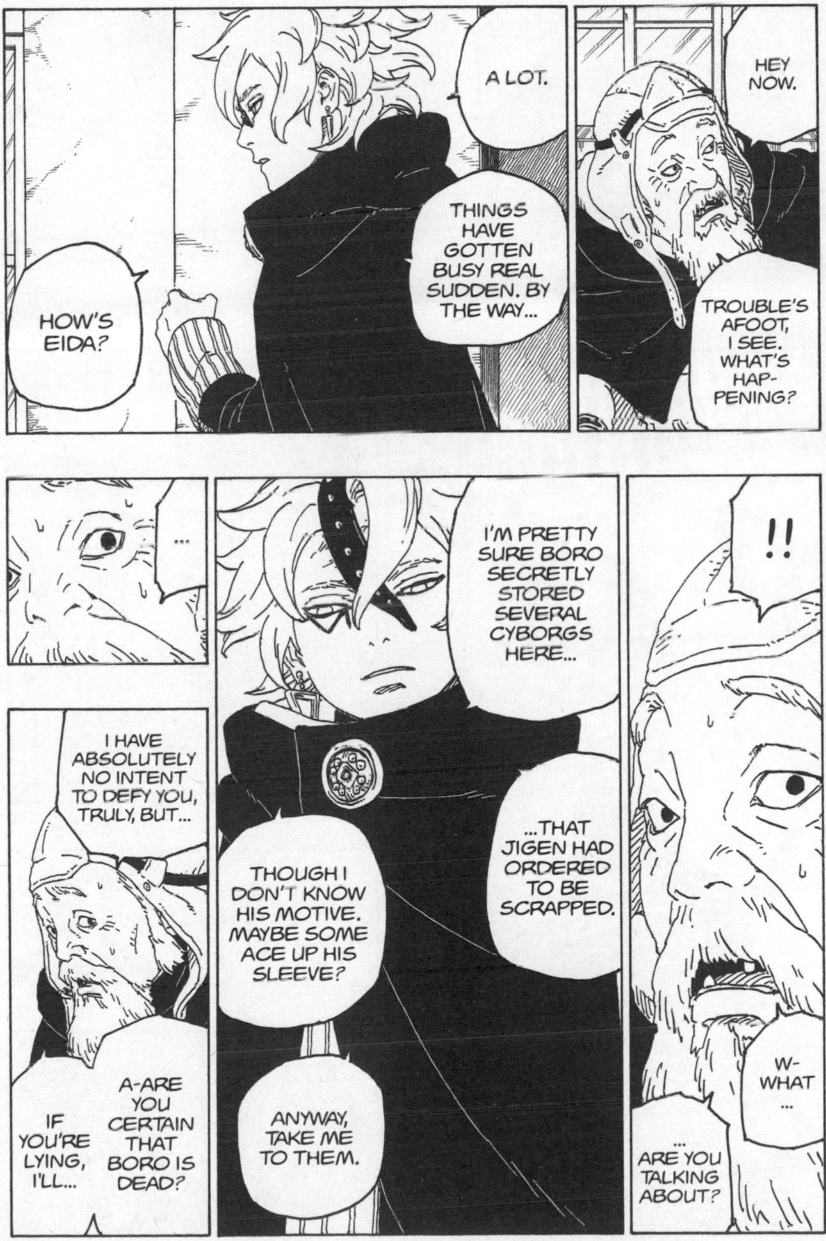
HEY NOW.
TROUBLE'S AFOOT, I SEE. WHAT'S HAP-PENING?
A LOT.
THINGS HAVE GOTTEN BUSY REAL SUDDEN. BY THE WAY...
HOW'S EIDA?
!!
W-WHAT...
...ARE YOU TALKING ABOUT?
I'M PRETTY SURE BORO SECRETLY STORED SEVERAL CYBORGS HERE...
...THAT JIGEN HAD ORDERED TO BE SCRAPPED.
THOUGH I DON'T KNOW HIS MOTIVE. MAYBE SOME ACE UP HIS SLEEVE?
ANYWAY, TAKE ME TO THEM.
...
I HAVE ABSOLUTELY NO INTENT TO DEFY YOU, TRULY, BUT...
A-ARE YOU CERTAIN THAT BORO IS DEAD?
IF YOU'RE LYING, I'LL...

BUT IN EX-
CHANGE...

ALL
RIGHT!

...YOU'LL
PAY ME,
RIGHT?!

...

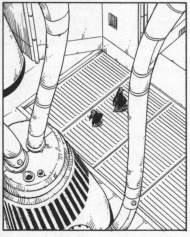

TOK

TOK

WHAT
IN THE
WORLD...

HERE
YOU
GO.

...ARE YOU
STIRRING
UP, CODE?

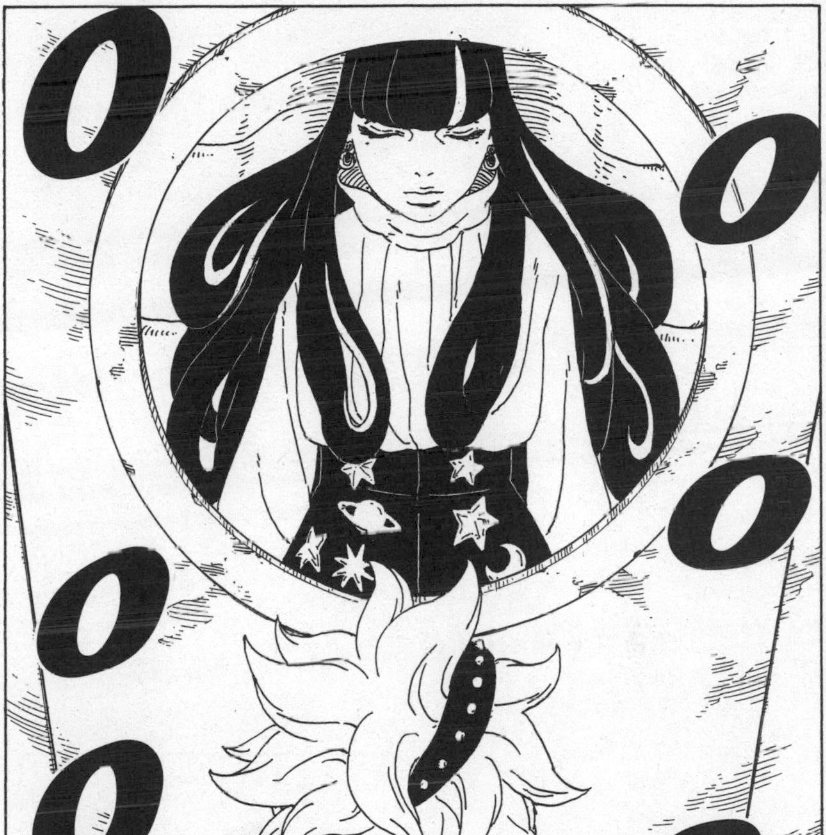
OOOOOO

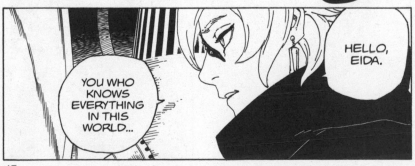

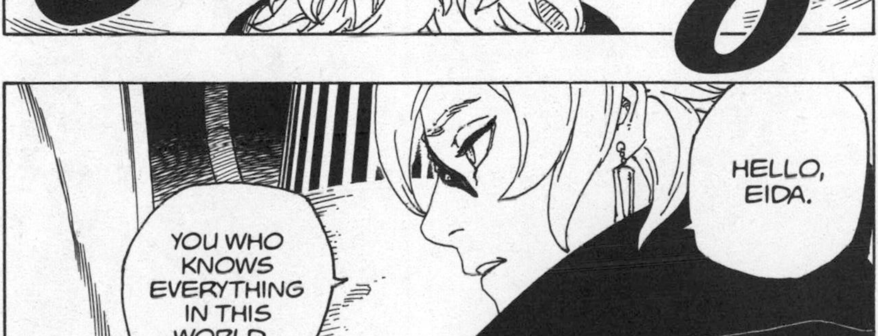
HELLO, EIDA.
YOU WHO KNOWS EVERYTHING IN THIS WORLD...

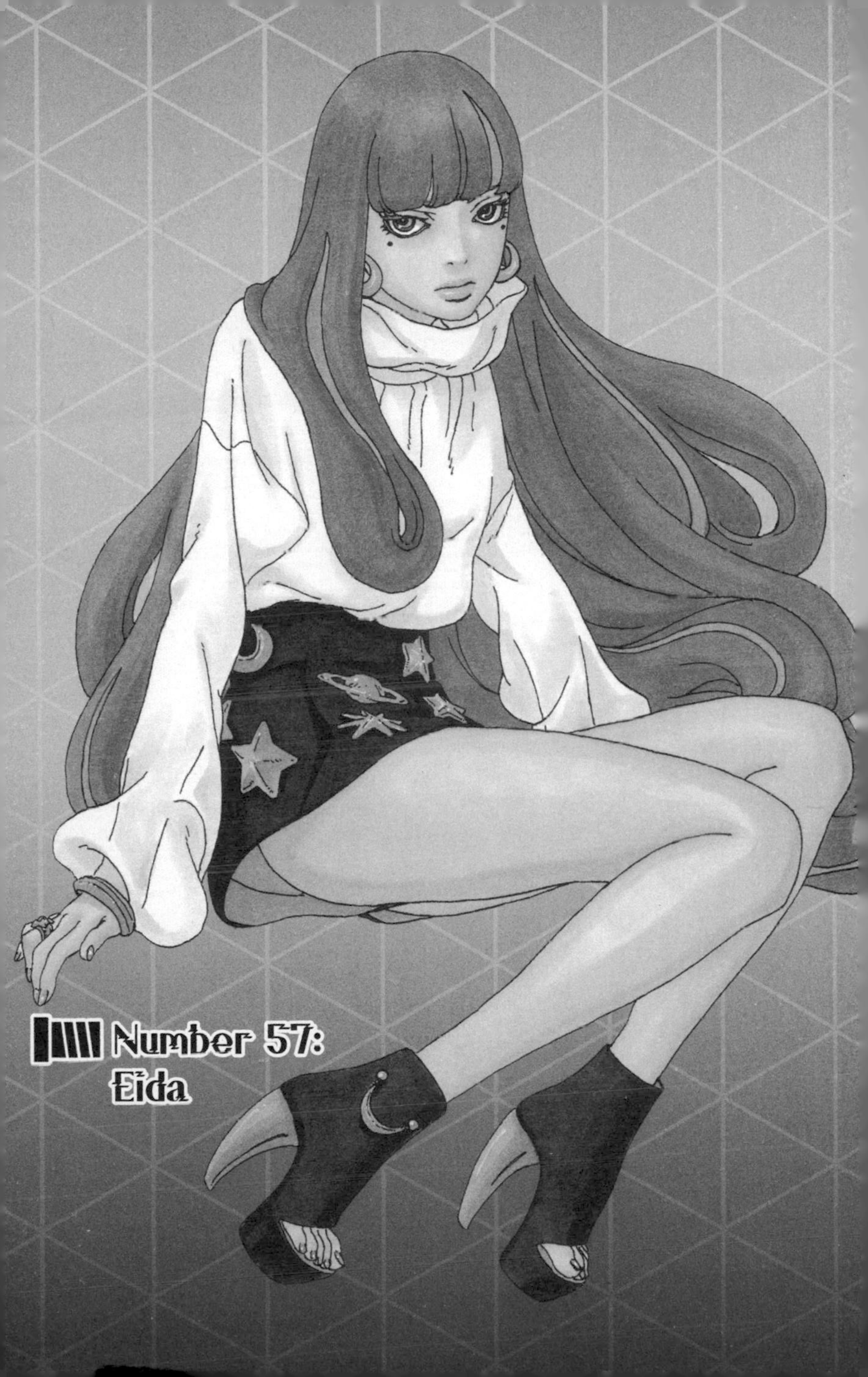

Number 57: Eida

BORUTO

-NARUTO NEXT GENERATIONS-

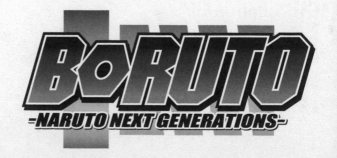

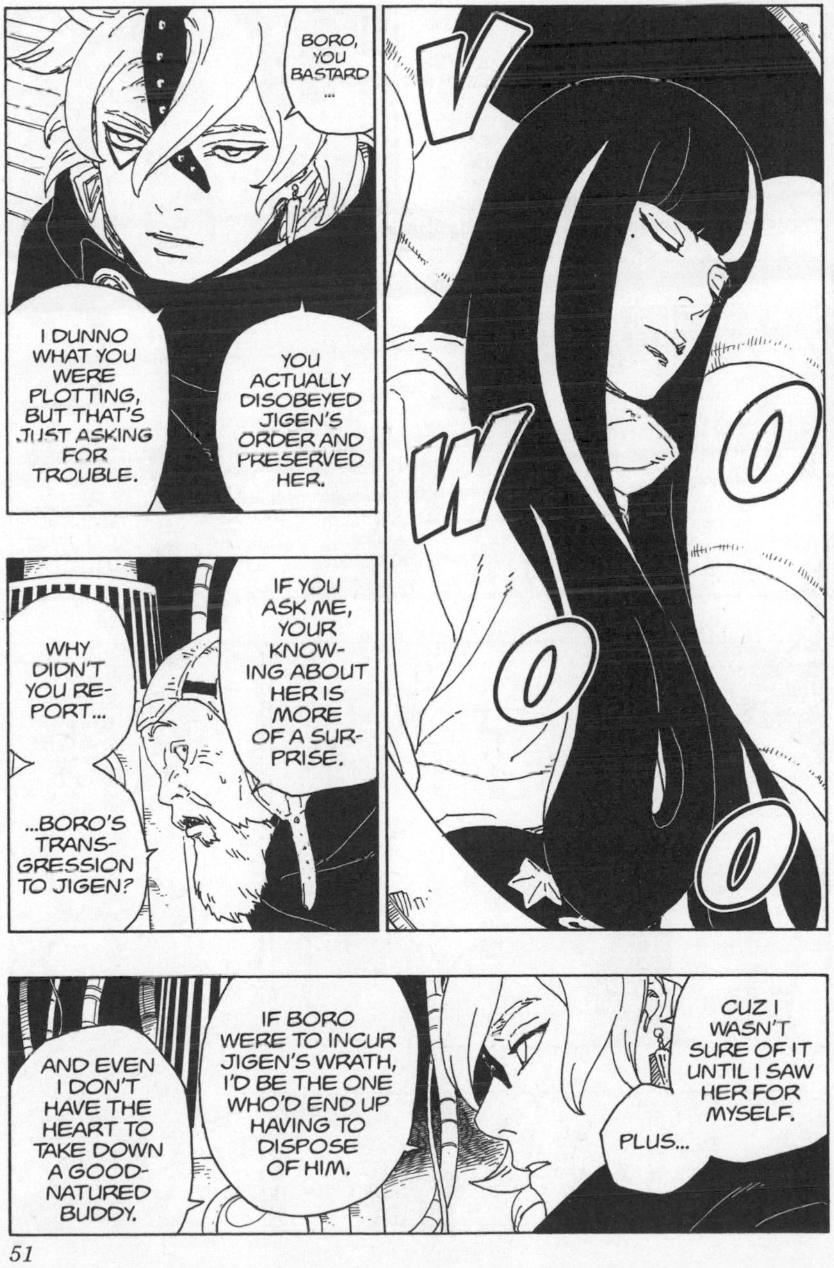
VWOOOO
BORO, YOU BASTARD ...
YOU ACTUALLY DISOBEYED JIGEN'S ORDER AND PRESERVED HER.
I DUNNO WHAT YOU WERE PLOTTING, BUT THAT'S JUST ASKING FOR TROUBLE.
IF YOU ASK ME, YOUR KNOWING ABOUT HER IS MORE OF A SURPRISE.
WHY DIDN'T YOU REPORT...
...BORO'S TRANSGRESSION TO JIGEN?
CUZ I WASN'T SURE OF IT UNTIL I SAW HER FOR MYSELF.
PLUS...
IF BORO WERE TO INCUR JIGEN'S WRATH, I'D BE THE ONE WHO'D END UP HAVING TO DISPOSE OF HIM.
AND EVEN I DON'T HAVE THE HEART TO TAKE DOWN A GOOD-NATURED BUDDY.

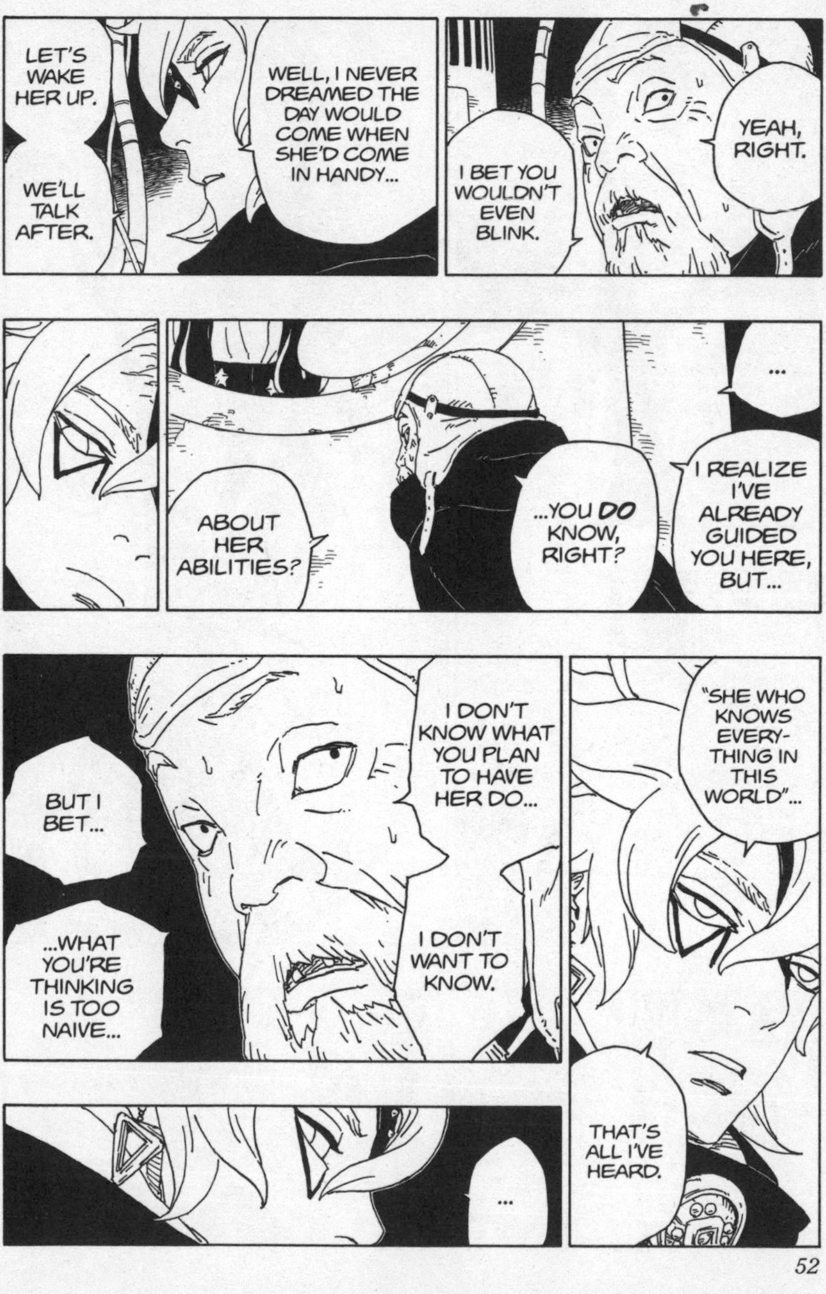
YEAH, RIGHT.
I BET YOU WOULDN'T EVEN BLINK.
WELL, I NEVER DREAMED THE DAY WOULD COME WHEN SHE'D COME IN HANDY...
LET'S WAKE HER UP.
WE'LL TALK AFTER.
...
I REALIZE I'VE ALREADY GUIDED YOU HERE, BUT...
...YOU **DO** KNOW, RIGHT?
ABOUT HER ABILITIES?
"SHE WHO KNOWS EVERY-THING IN THIS WORLD"...
THAT'S ALL I'VE HEARD.
I DON'T KNOW WHAT YOU PLAN TO HAVE HER DO...
I DON'T WANT TO KNOW.
BUT I BET...
...WHAT YOU'RE THINKING IS TOO NAIVE...
...

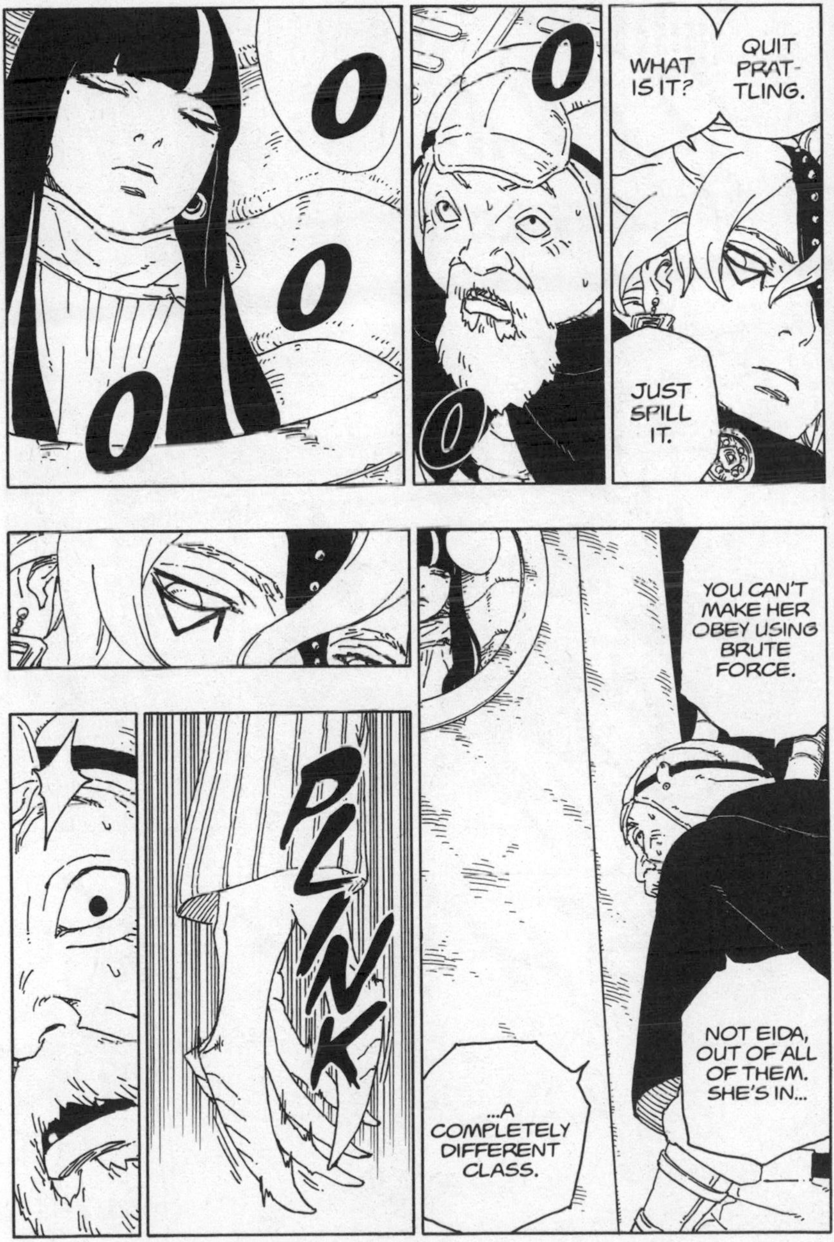
QUIT PRAT-TLING.
WHAT IS IT?
JUST SPILL IT.
O O
O O O
YOU CAN'T MAKE HER OBEY USING BRUTE FORCE.
NOT EIDA, OUT OF ALL OF THEM. SHE'S IN...
...A COMPLETELY DIFFERENT CLASS.
PLINK

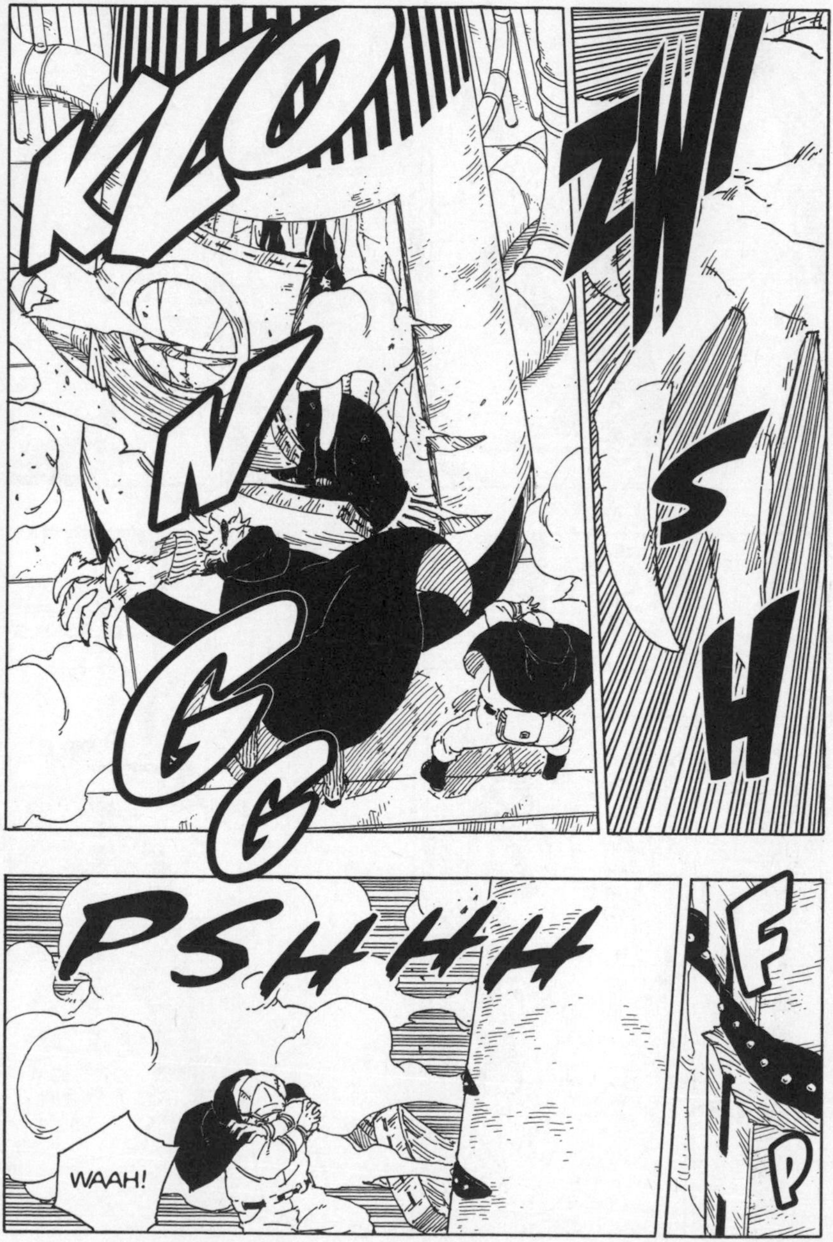
ZWISH
KLONG
FIP
PSHHH
WAAH!

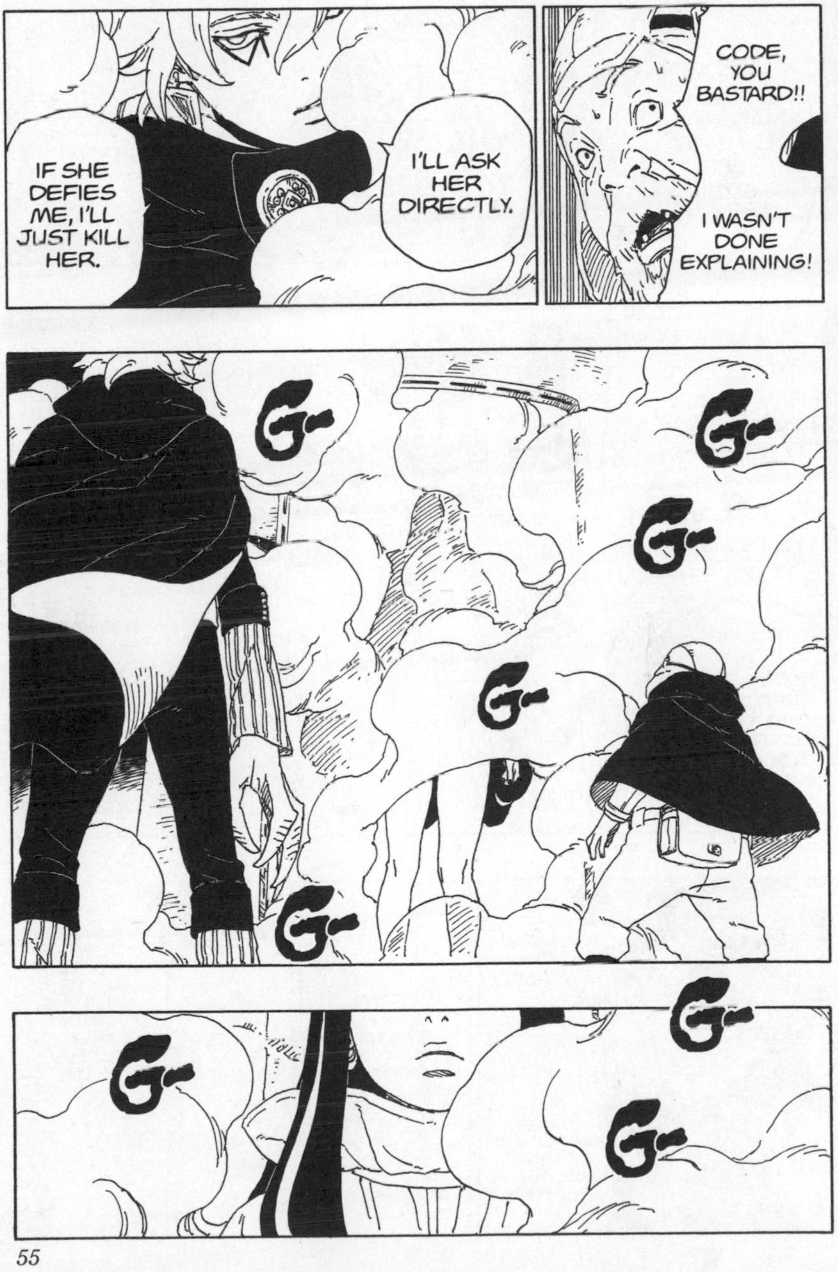
CODE, YOU BASTARD!!
I WASN'T DONE EXPLAINING!
I'LL ASK HER DIRECTLY.
IF SHE DEFIES ME, I'LL JUST KILL HER.

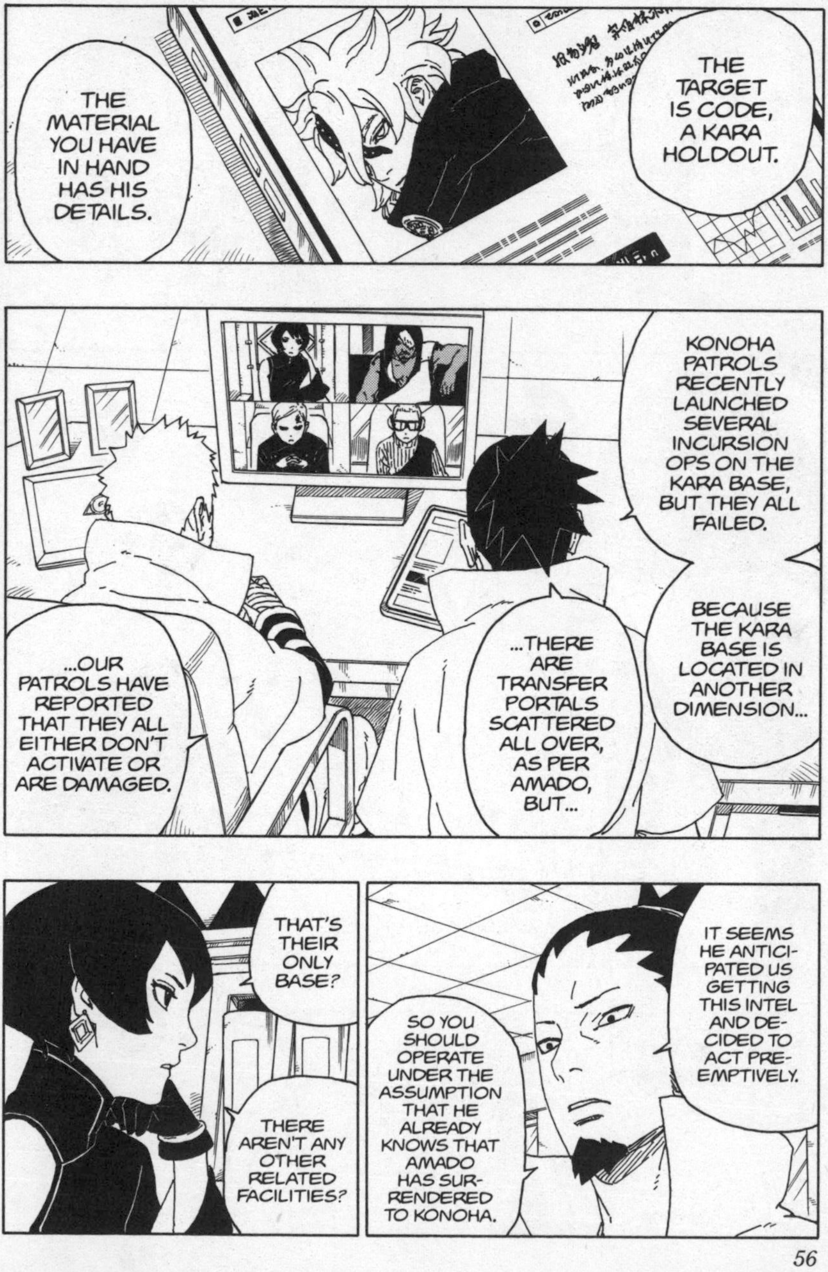
THE TARGET IS CODE, A KARA HOLDOUT.
THE MATERIAL YOU HAVE IN HAND HAS HIS DETAILS.
KONOHA PATROLS RECENTLY LAUNCHED SEVERAL INCURSION OPS ON THE KARA BASE, BUT THEY ALL FAILED.
BECAUSE THE KARA BASE IS LOCATED IN ANOTHER DIMENSION...
...THERE ARE TRANSFER PORTALS SCATTERED ALL OVER, AS PER AMADO, BUT...
...OUR PATROLS HAVE REPORTED THAT THEY ALL EITHER DON'T ACTIVATE OR ARE DAMAGED.
IT SEEMS HE ANTICI-PATED US GETTING THIS INTEL AND DE-CIDED TO ACT PRE-EMPTIVELY.
SO YOU SHOULD OPERATE UNDER THE ASSUMPTION THAT HE ALREADY KNOWS THAT AMADO HAS SUR-RENDERED TO KONOHA.
THAT'S THEIR ONLY BASE?
THERE AREN'T ANY OTHER RELATED FACILITIES?

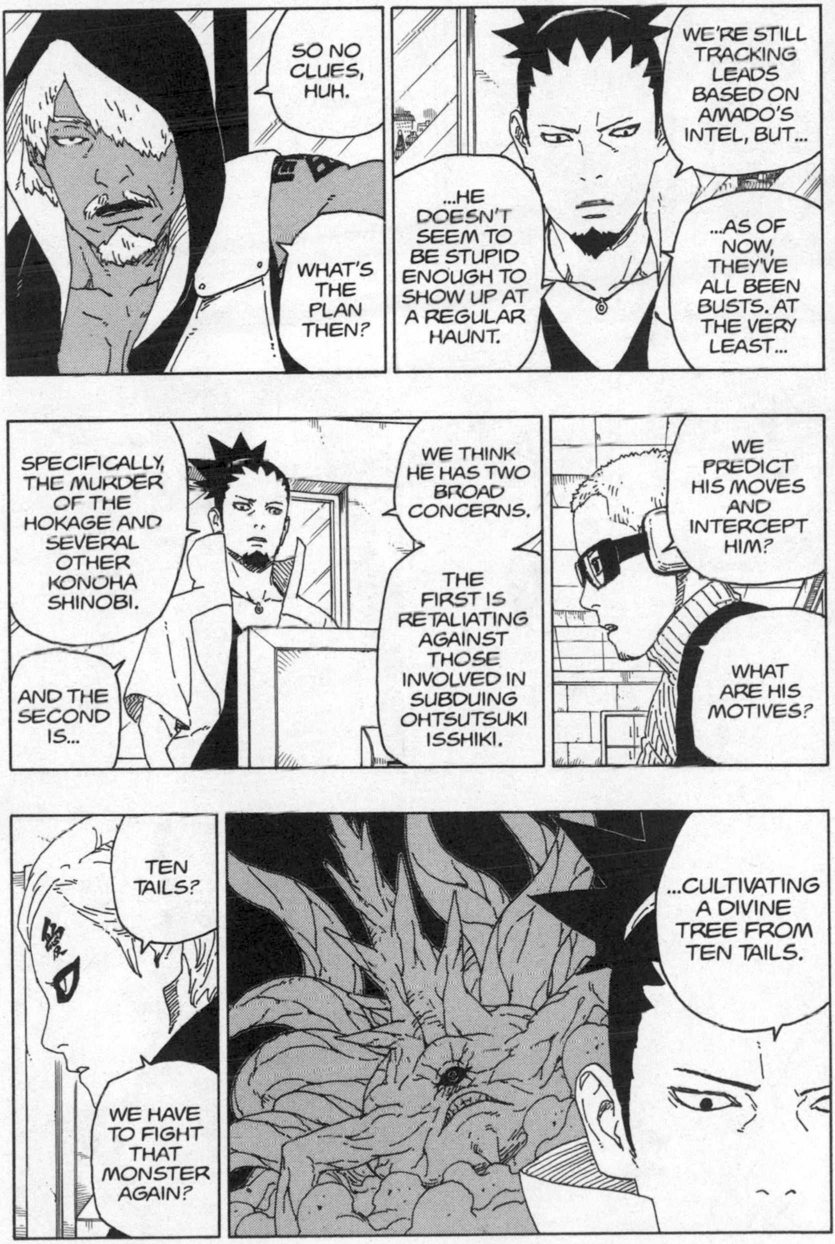
WE'RE STILL TRACKING LEADS BASED ON AMADO'S INTEL, BUT...
...AS OF NOW, THEY'VE ALL BEEN BUSTS. AT THE VERY LEAST...
...HE DOESN'T SEEM TO BE STUPID ENOUGH TO SHOW UP AT A REGULAR HAUNT.
SO NO CLUES, HUH.
WHAT'S THE PLAN THEN?
WE PREDICT HIS MOVES AND INTERCEPT HIM?
WHAT ARE HIS MOTIVES?
WE THINK HE HAS TWO BROAD CONCERNS.
THE FIRST IS RETALIATING AGAINST THOSE INVOLVED IN SUBDUING OHTSUTSUKI ISSHIKI.
SPECIFICALLY, THE MURDER OF THE HOKAGE AND SEVERAL OTHER KONOHA SHINOBI.
AND THE SECOND IS...
...CULTIVATING A DIVINE TREE FROM TEN TAILS.
TEN TAILS?
WE HAVE TO FIGHT THAT MONSTER AGAIN?

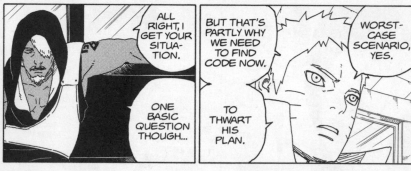

WORST-CASE SCENARIO, YES.
BUT THAT'S PARTLY WHY WE NEED TO FIND CODE NOW.
TO THWART HIS PLAN.
ALL RIGHT, I GET YOUR SITUATION.
ONE BASIC QUESTION THOUGH...
THIS SCIENTIST AMADO THAT YOU'VE GOT...
CAN WE REALLY TRUST HIM?
...
I TRUST **YOU**, KONOHA.
BUT...
THIS DEPENDENCE ON A BASTARD WHO UNTIL JUST RECENTLY BELONGED TO THE ENEMY ORGANIZATION...
YOU SURE HE'S NOT USING YOU FOR HIS OWN PURPOSES?
IF YOU WANT MY PERSONAL OPINION...
NO, I DON'T TRUST HIM 100 PERCENT.

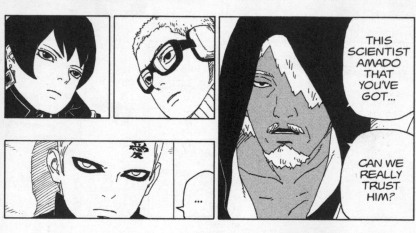

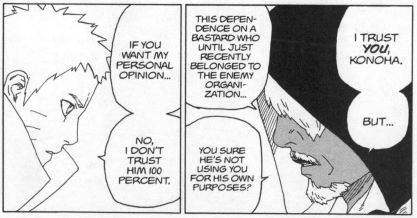

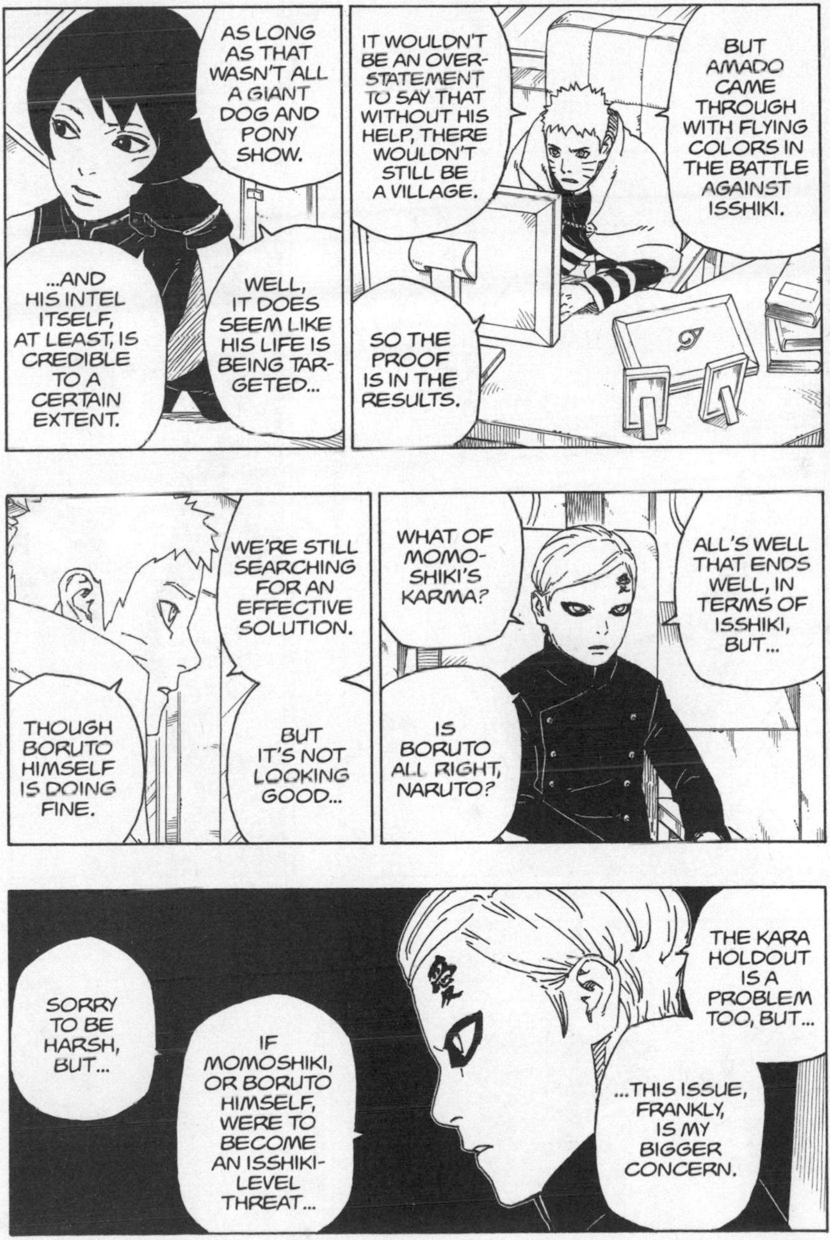
BUT AMADO CAME THROUGH WITH FLYING COLORS IN THE BATTLE AGAINST ISSHIKI.
IT WOULDN'T BE AN OVER-STATEMENT TO SAY THAT WITHOUT HIS HELP, THERE WOULDN'T STILL BE A VILLAGE.
SO THE PROOF IS IN THE RESULTS.
AS LONG AS THAT WASN'T ALL A GIANT DOG AND PONY SHOW.
WELL, IT DOES SEEM LIKE HIS LIFE IS BEING TAR-GETED...
...AND HIS INTEL ITSELF, AT LEAST, IS CREDIBLE TO A CERTAIN EXTENT.
ALL'S WELL THAT ENDS WELL, IN TERMS OF ISSHIKI, BUT...
WHAT OF MOMO-SHIKI'S KARMA?
IS BORUTO ALL RIGHT, NARUTO?
WE'RE STILL SEARCHING FOR AN EFFECTIVE SOLUTION.
BUT IT'S NOT LOOKING GOOD...
THOUGH BORUTO HIMSELF IS DOING FINE.
THE KARA HOLDOUT IS A PROBLEM TOO, BUT...
...THIS ISSUE, FRANKLY, IS MY BIGGER CONCERN.
IF MOMOSHIKI, OR BORUTO HIMSELF, WERE TO BECOME AN ISSHIKI-LEVEL THREAT...
SORRY TO BE HARSH, BUT...

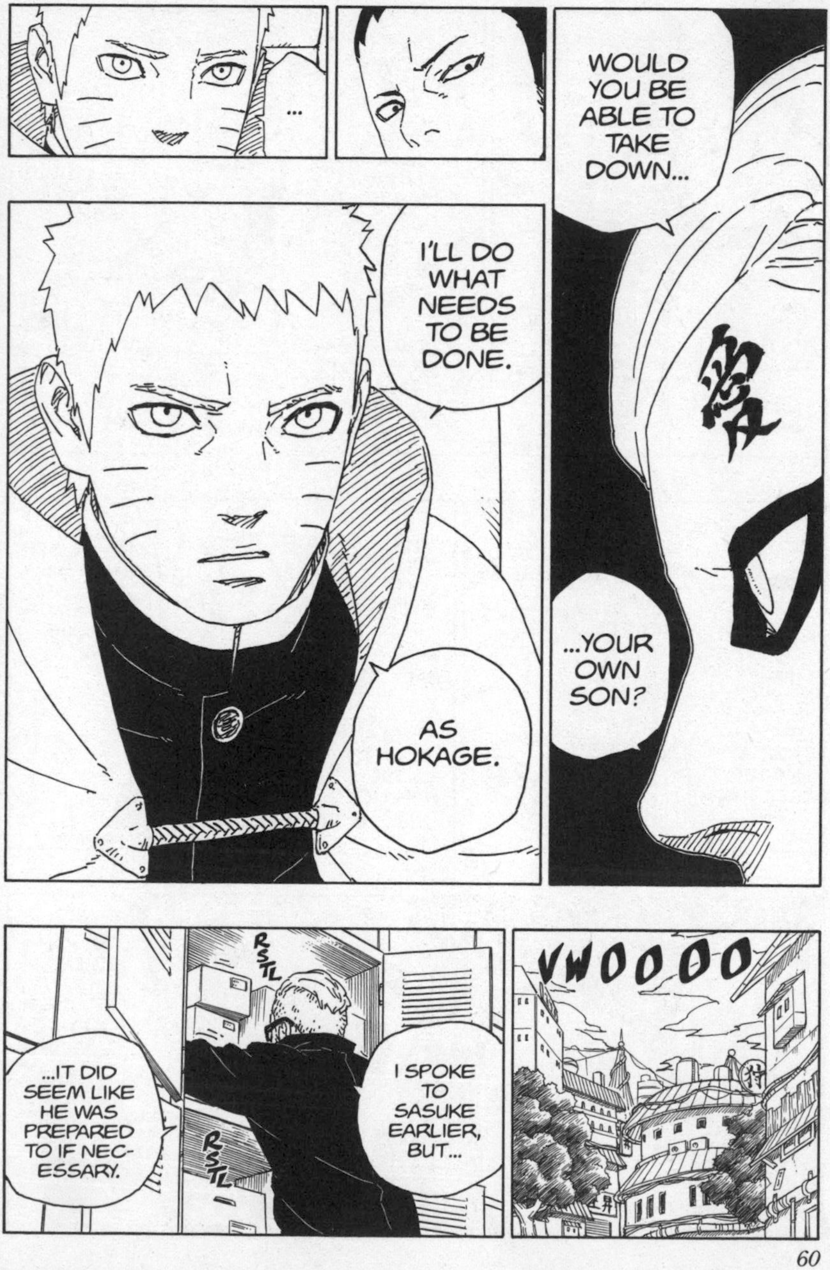
WOULD YOU BE ABLE TO TAKE DOWN...
...YOUR OWN SON?
...
I'LL DO WHAT NEEDS TO BE DONE.
AS HOKAGE.
VWOOOO
RSTL
RSTL
I SPOKE TO SASUKE EARLIER, BUT...
...IT DID SEEM LIKE HE WAS PREPARED TO IF NECESSARY.

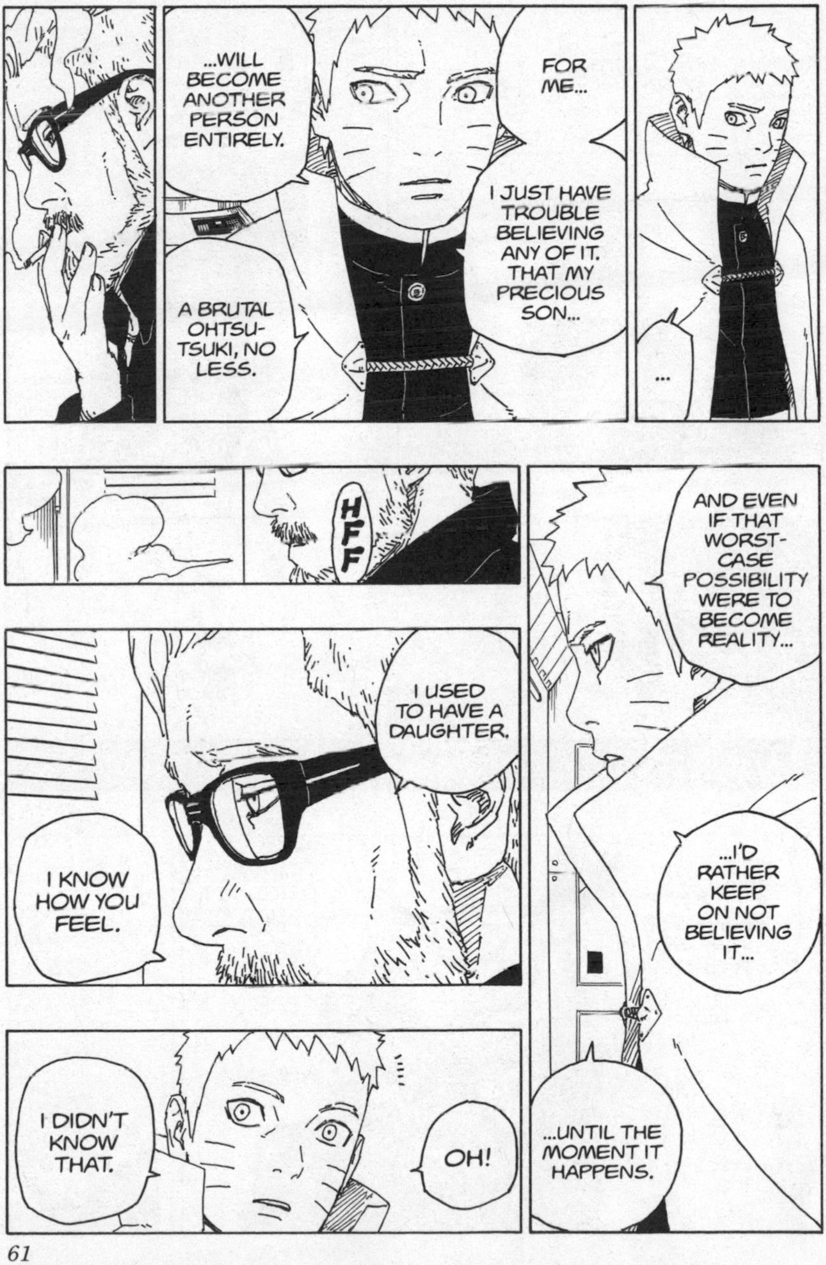
...
FOR ME...
I JUST HAVE TROUBLE BELIEVING ANY OF IT. THAT MY PRECIOUS SON...
...WILL BECOME ANOTHER PERSON ENTIRELY.
A BRUTAL OHTSUTSUKI, NO LESS.
AND EVEN IF THAT WORST-CASE POSSIBILITY WERE TO BECOME REALITY...
...I'D RATHER KEEP ON NOT BELIEVING IT...
...UNTIL THE MOMENT IT HAPPENS.
HFF
I USED TO HAVE A DAUGHTER.
I KNOW HOW YOU FEEL.
OH!
I DIDN'T KNOW THAT.

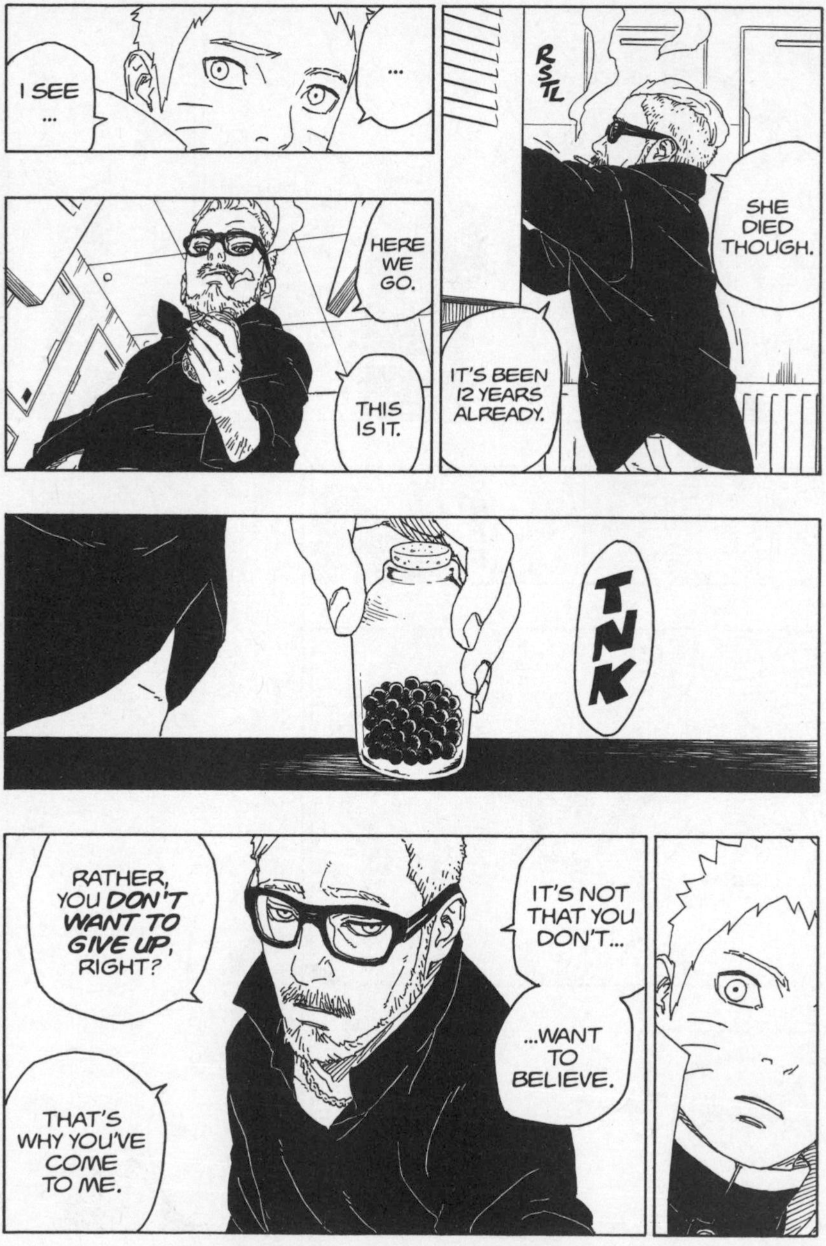
RSTL
SHE DIED THOUGH.
IT'S BEEN 12 YEARS ALREADY.
...
I SEE ...
HERE WE GO.
THIS IS IT.
TNK
IT'S NOT THAT YOU DON'T...
...WANT TO BELIEVE.
RATHER, YOU **DON'T WANT TO GIVE UP**, RIGHT?
THAT'S WHY YOU'VE COME TO ME.

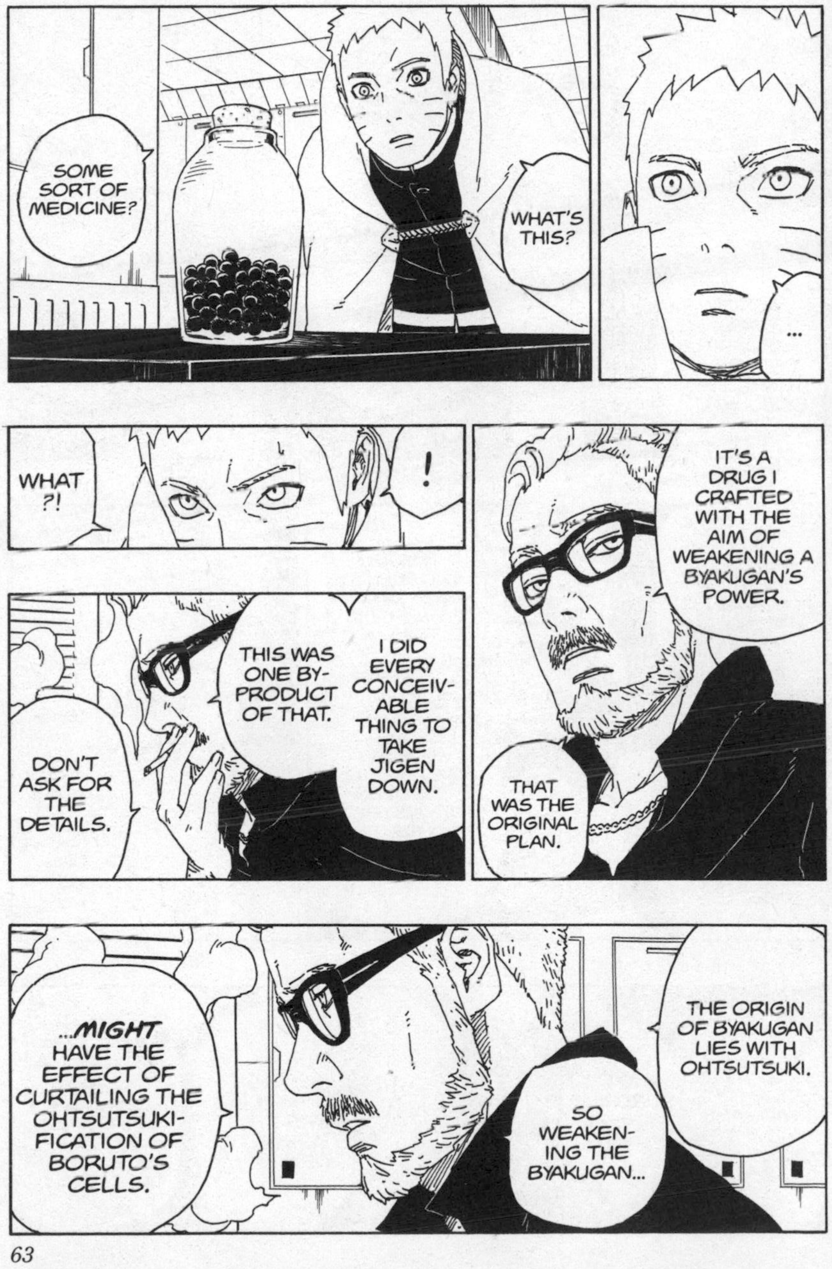
WHAT'S THIS?
...
SOME SORT OF MEDICINE?
IT'S A DRUG I CRAFTED WITH THE AIM OF WEAKENING A BYAKUGAN'S POWER.
THAT WAS THE ORIGINAL PLAN.
!
WHAT ?!
I DID EVERY CONCEIV-ABLE THING TO TAKE JIGEN DOWN.
THIS WAS ONE BY-PRODUCT OF THAT.
DON'T ASK FOR THE DETAILS.
THE ORIGIN OF BYAKUGAN LIES WITH OHTSUTSUKI.
SO WEAKEN-ING THE BYAKUGAN...
...*MIGHT* HAVE THE EFFECT OF CURTAILING THE OHTSUTSUKI-FICATION OF BORUTO'S CELLS.

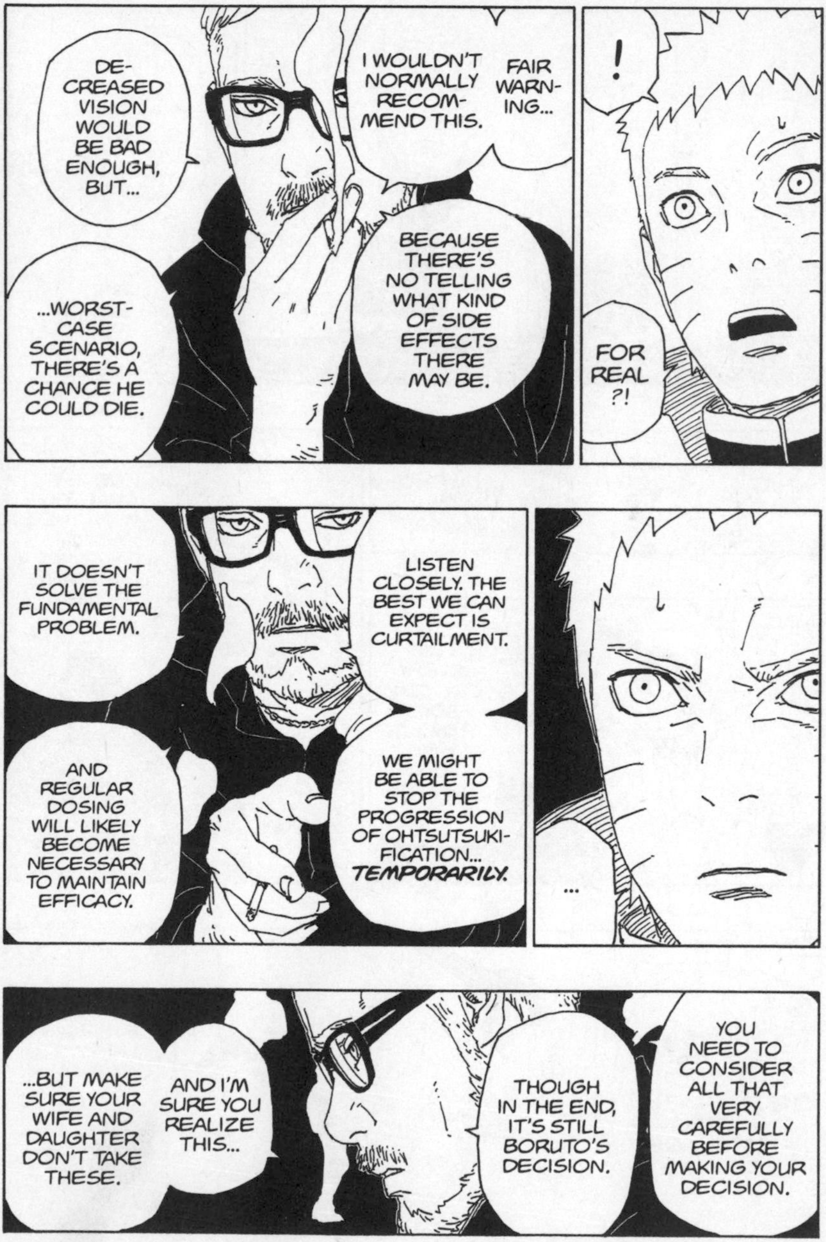
!
FOR REAL?!
FAIR WARNING...
I WOULDN'T NORMALLY RECOMMEND THIS.
BECAUSE THERE'S NO TELLING WHAT KIND OF SIDE EFFECTS THERE MAY BE.
DECREASED VISION WOULD BE BAD ENOUGH, BUT...
...WORST-CASE SCENARIO, THERE'S A CHANCE HE COULD DIE.
...
LISTEN CLOSELY. THE BEST WE CAN EXPECT IS CURTAILMENT.
IT DOESN'T SOLVE THE FUNDAMENTAL PROBLEM.
WE MIGHT BE ABLE TO STOP THE PROGRESSION OF OHTSUTSUKIFICATION... TEMPORARILY.
AND REGULAR DOSING WILL LIKELY BECOME NECESSARY TO MAINTAIN EFFICACY.
YOU NEED TO CONSIDER ALL THAT VERY CAREFULLY BEFORE MAKING YOUR DECISION.
THOUGH IN THE END, IT'S STILL BORUTO'S DECISION.
AND I'M SURE YOU REALIZE THIS...
...BUT MAKE SURE YOUR WIFE AND DAUGHTER DON'T TAKE THESE.

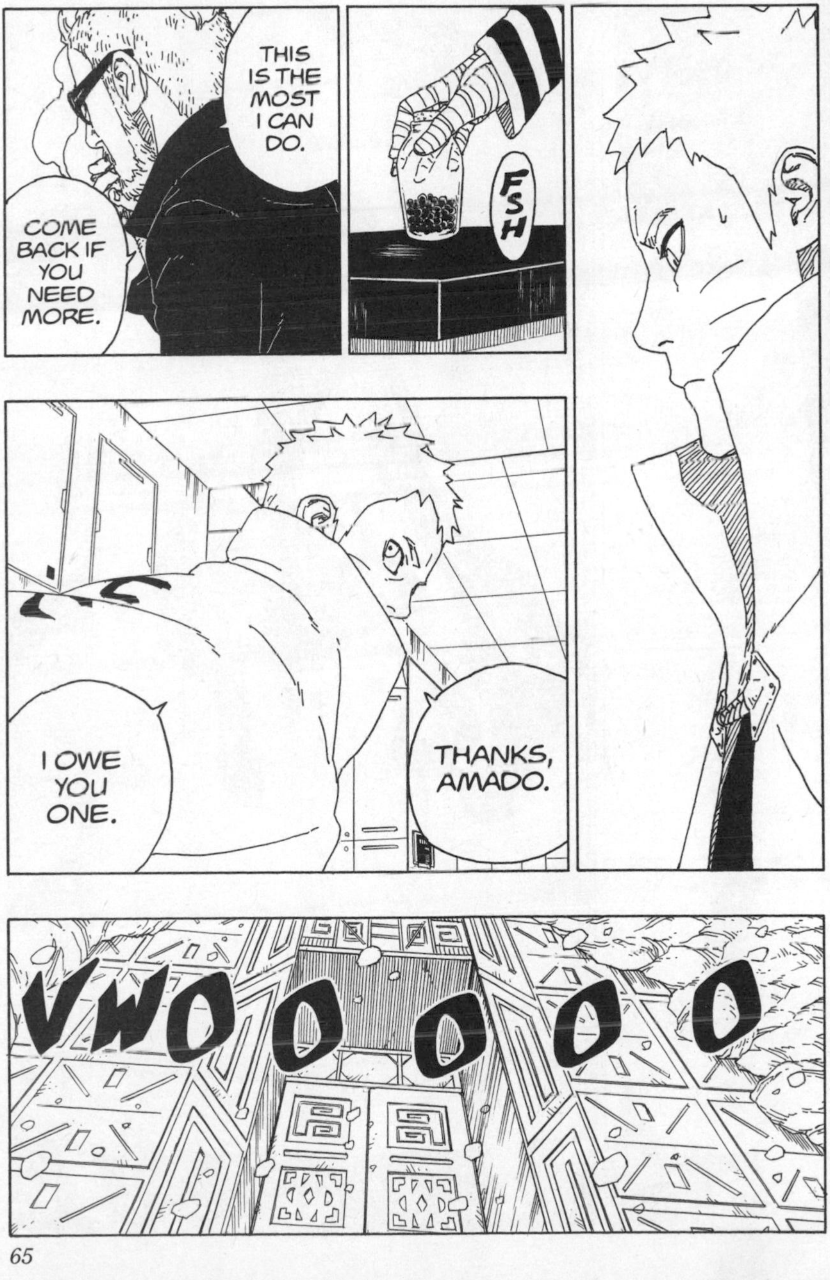
FSH
THIS IS THE MOST I CAN DO.
COME BACK IF YOU NEED MORE.
THANKS, AMADO.
I OWE YOU ONE.
VWOOOOO

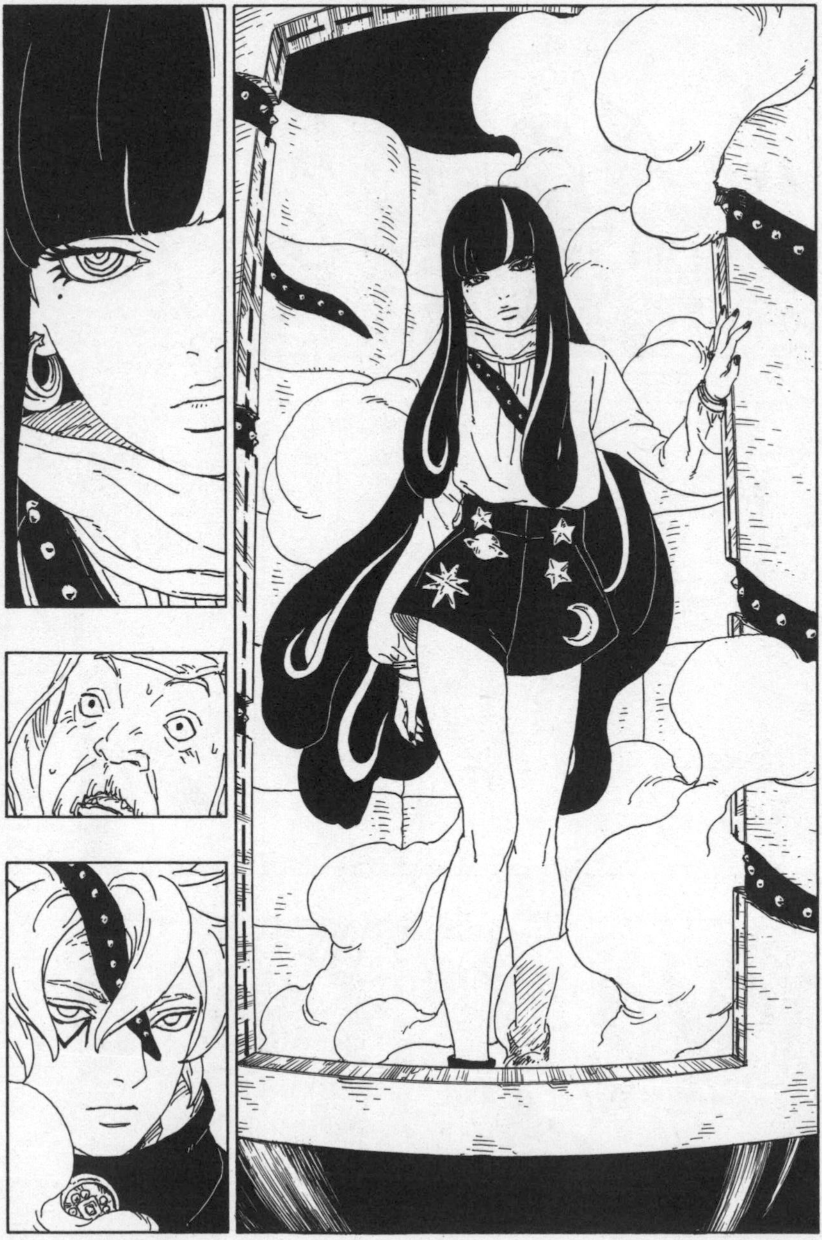

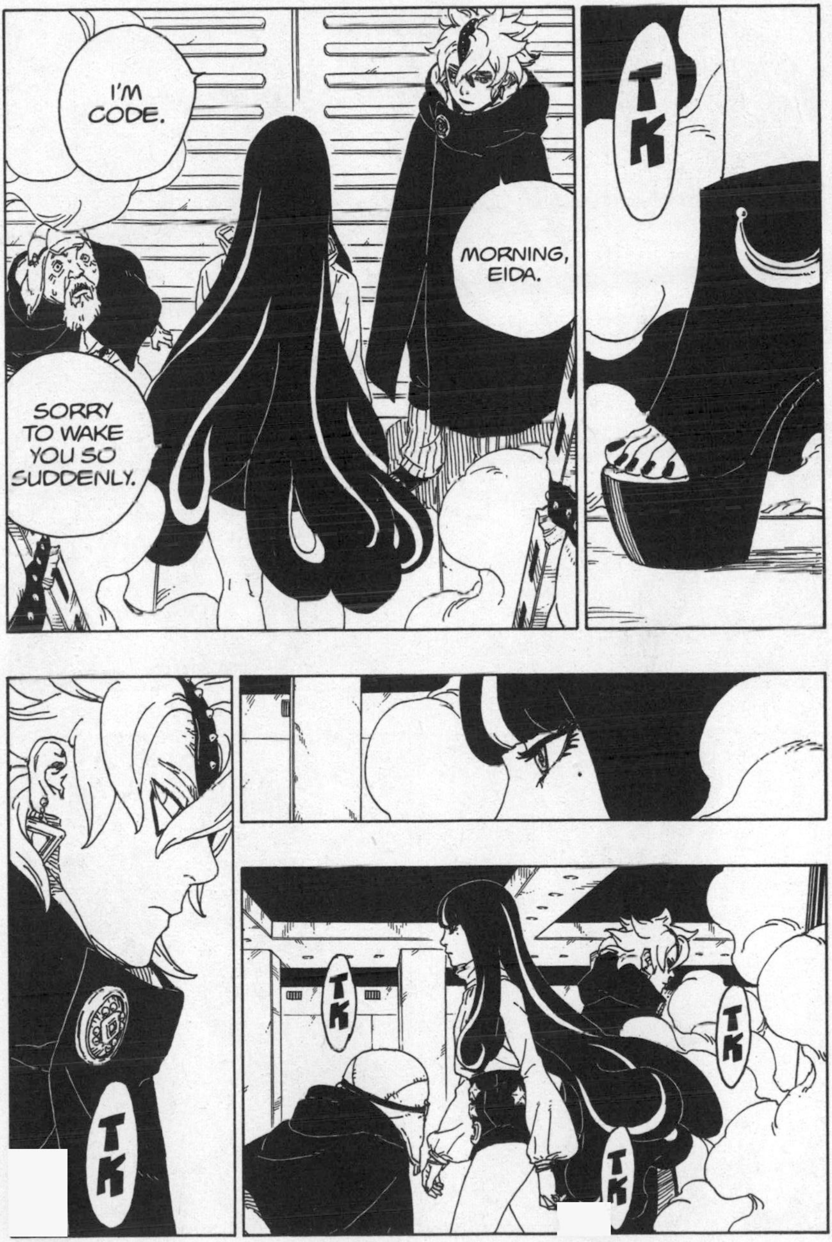
TK
MORNING, EIDA.
I'M CODE.
SORRY TO WAKE YOU SO SUDDENLY.
TK
TK
TK
TK

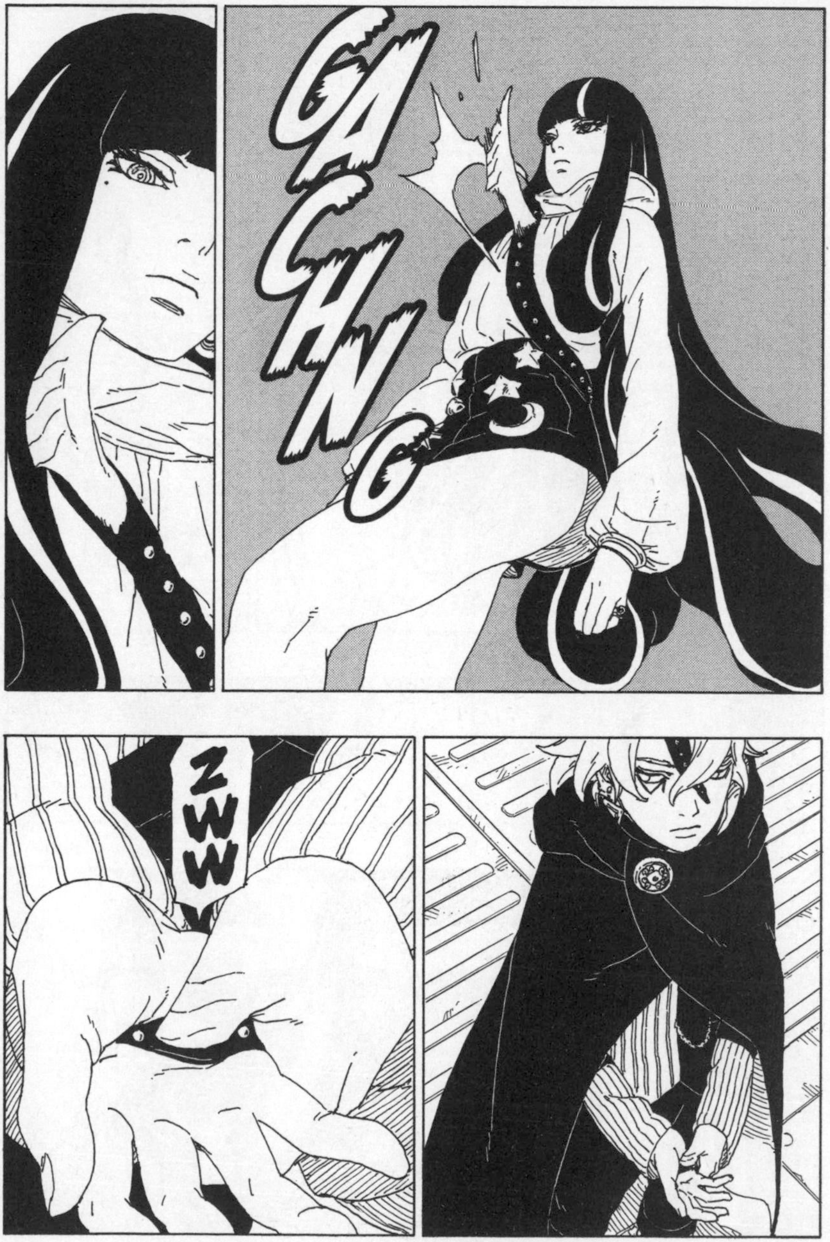
GACHNG
ZWW

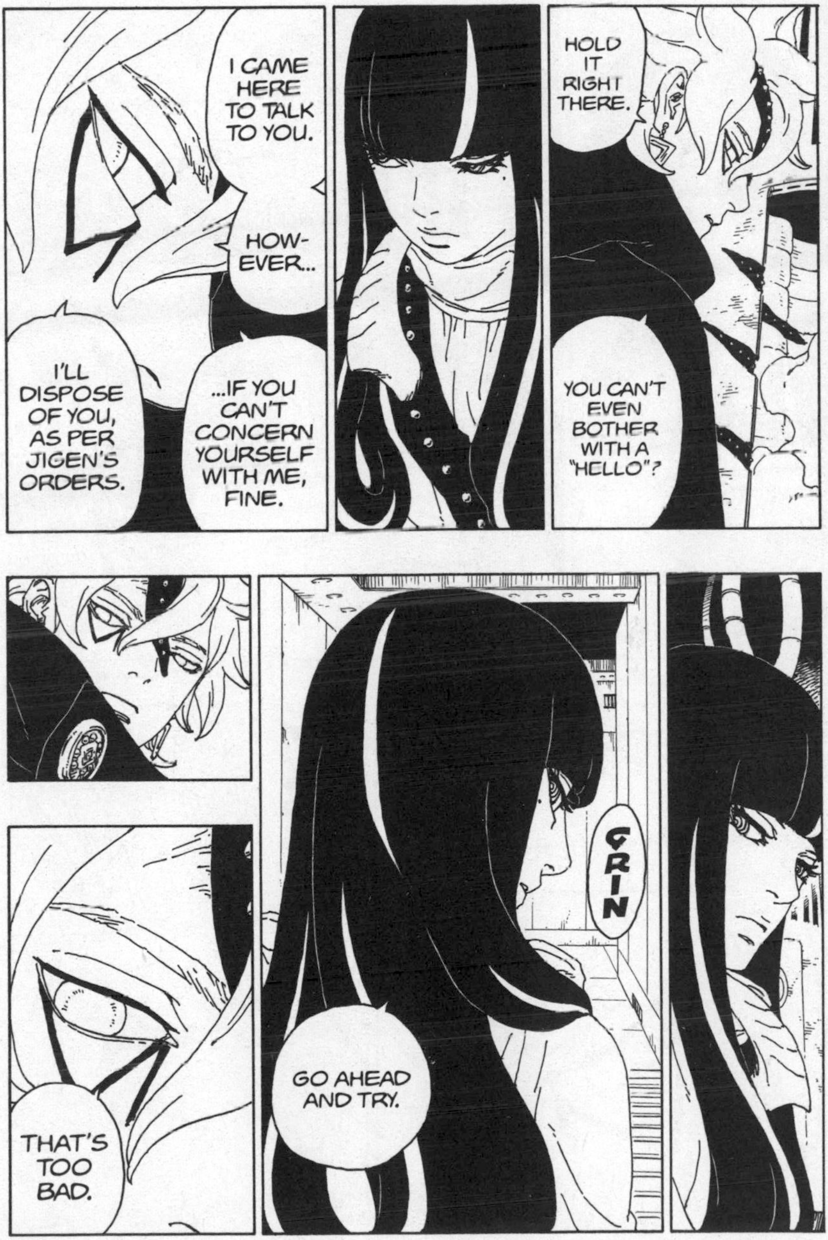

HOLD IT RIGHT THERE.
YOU CAN'T EVEN BOTHER WITH A "HELLO"?
I CAME HERE TO TALK TO YOU.
HOW-EVER...
...IF YOU CAN'T CONCERN YOURSELF WITH ME, FINE.
I'LL DISPOSE OF YOU, AS PER JIGEN'S ORDERS.
GRIN
GO AHEAD AND TRY.
THAT'S TOO BAD.

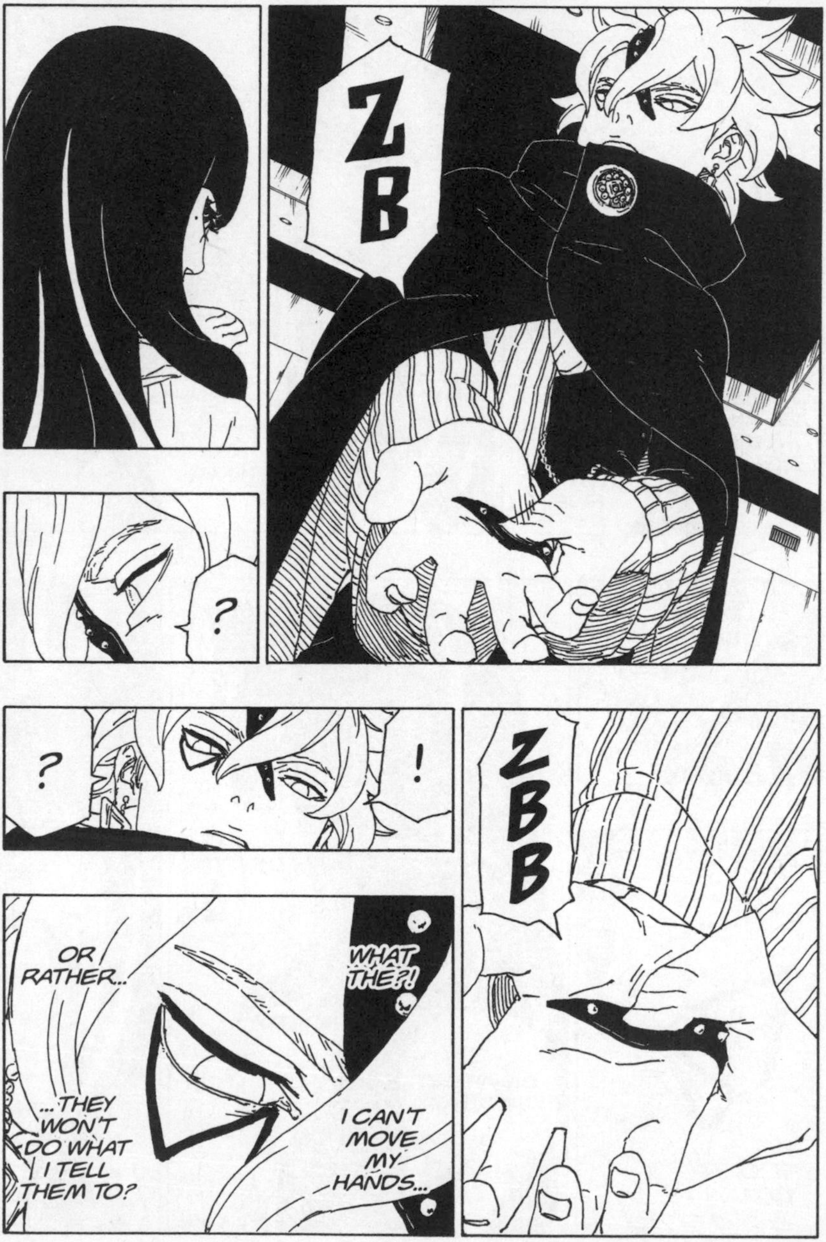
ZB
?
ZBB
?
!
WHAT THE?!
I CAN'T MOVE MY HANDS...
OR RATHER...
...THEY WON'T DO WHAT I TELL THEM TO?

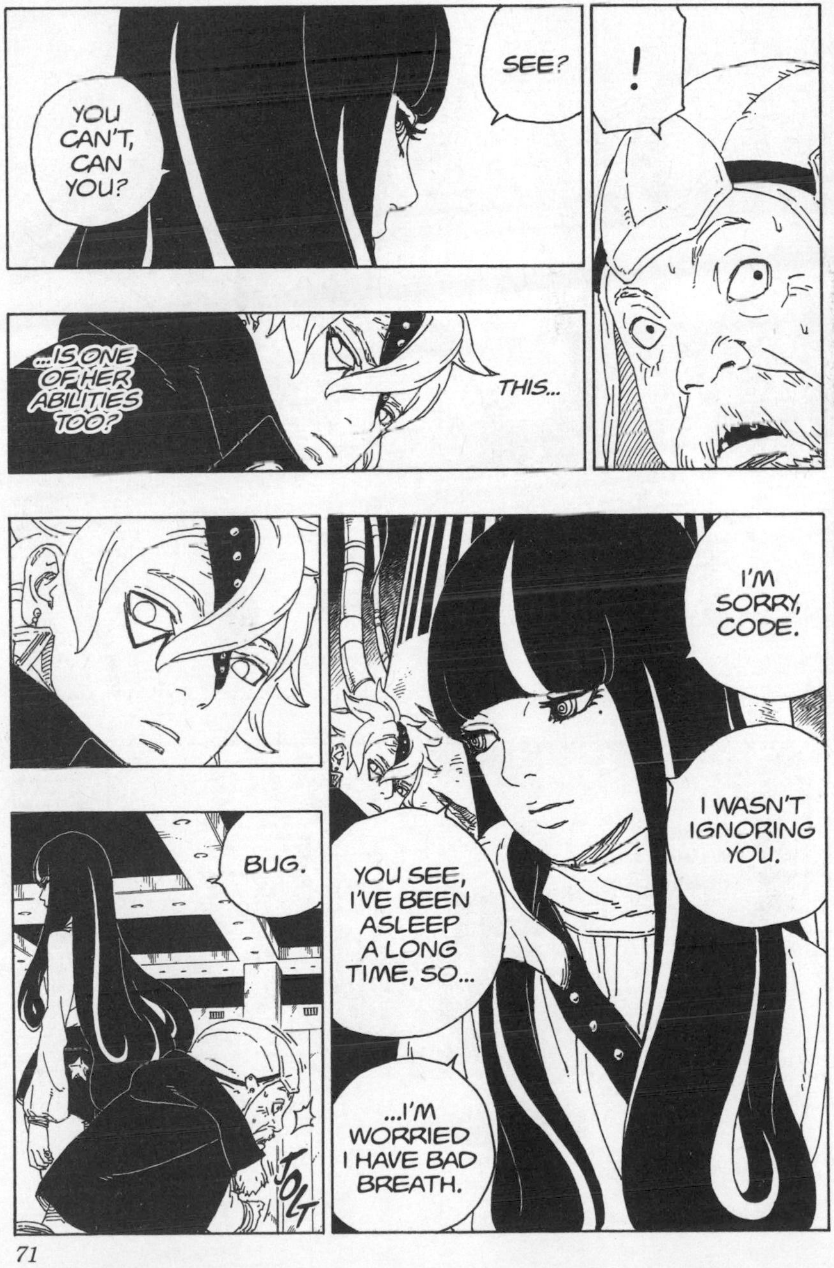
!
SEE?
YOU CAN'T, CAN YOU?
THIS...
...IS ONE OF HER ABILITIES TOO?
I'M SORRY, CODE.
I WASN'T IGNORING YOU.
YOU SEE, I'VE BEEN ASLEEP A LONG TIME, SO...
...I'M WORRIED I HAVE BAD BREATH.
BUG.
JOLT

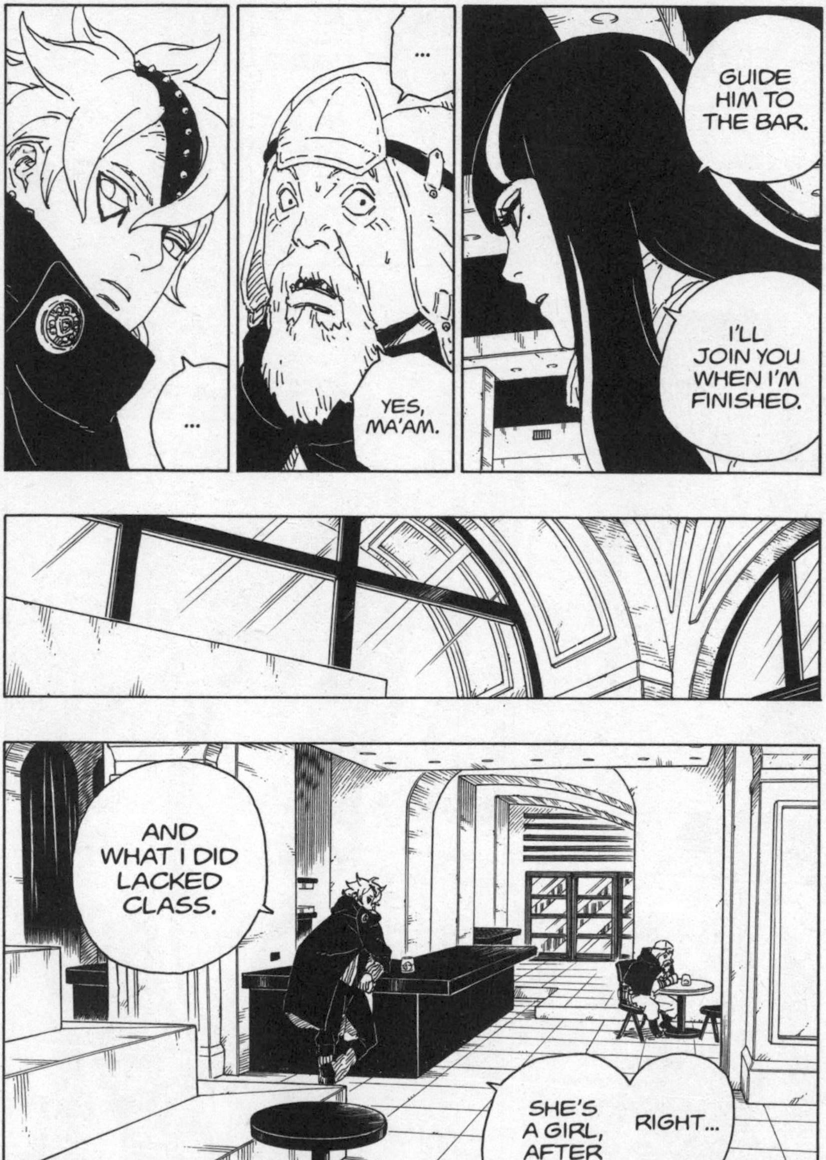
GUIDE HIM TO THE BAR.
I'LL JOIN YOU WHEN I'M FINISHED.
...
YES, MA'AM.
...
RIGHT...
SHE'S A GIRL, AFTER ALL.
AND WHAT I DID LACKED CLASS.

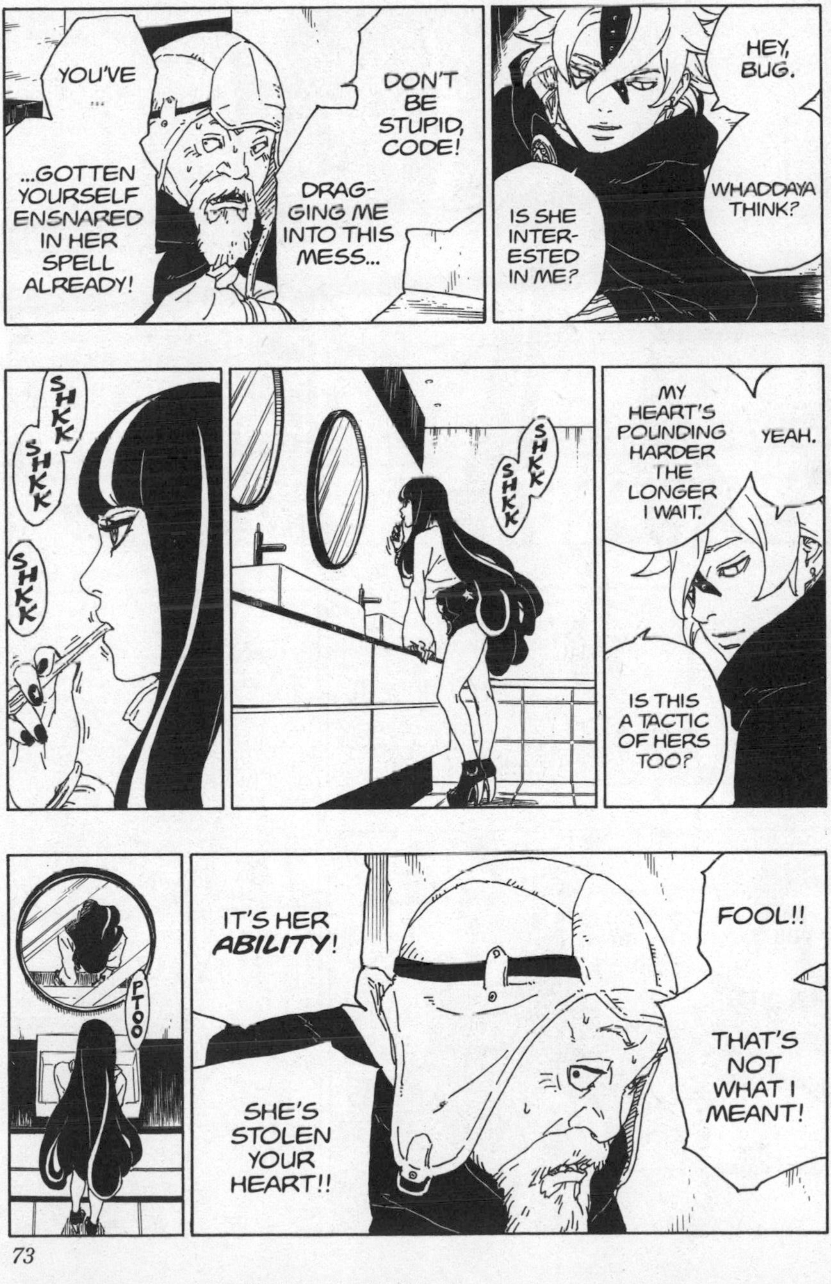
HEY, BUG.
WHADDAYA THINK?
IS SHE INTERESTED IN ME?
DON'T BE STUPID, CODE!
DRAGGING ME INTO THIS MESS...
YOU'VE
...GOTTEN YOURSELF ENSNARED IN HER SPELL ALREADY!
YEAH.
MY HEART'S POUNDING HARDER THE LONGER I WAIT.
IS THIS A TACTIC OF HERS TOO?
SHKK SHKK
SHKK SHKK
SHKK
FOOL!!
THAT'S NOT WHAT I MEANT!
IT'S HER ABILITY!
SHE'S STOLEN YOUR HEART!!
PTOO

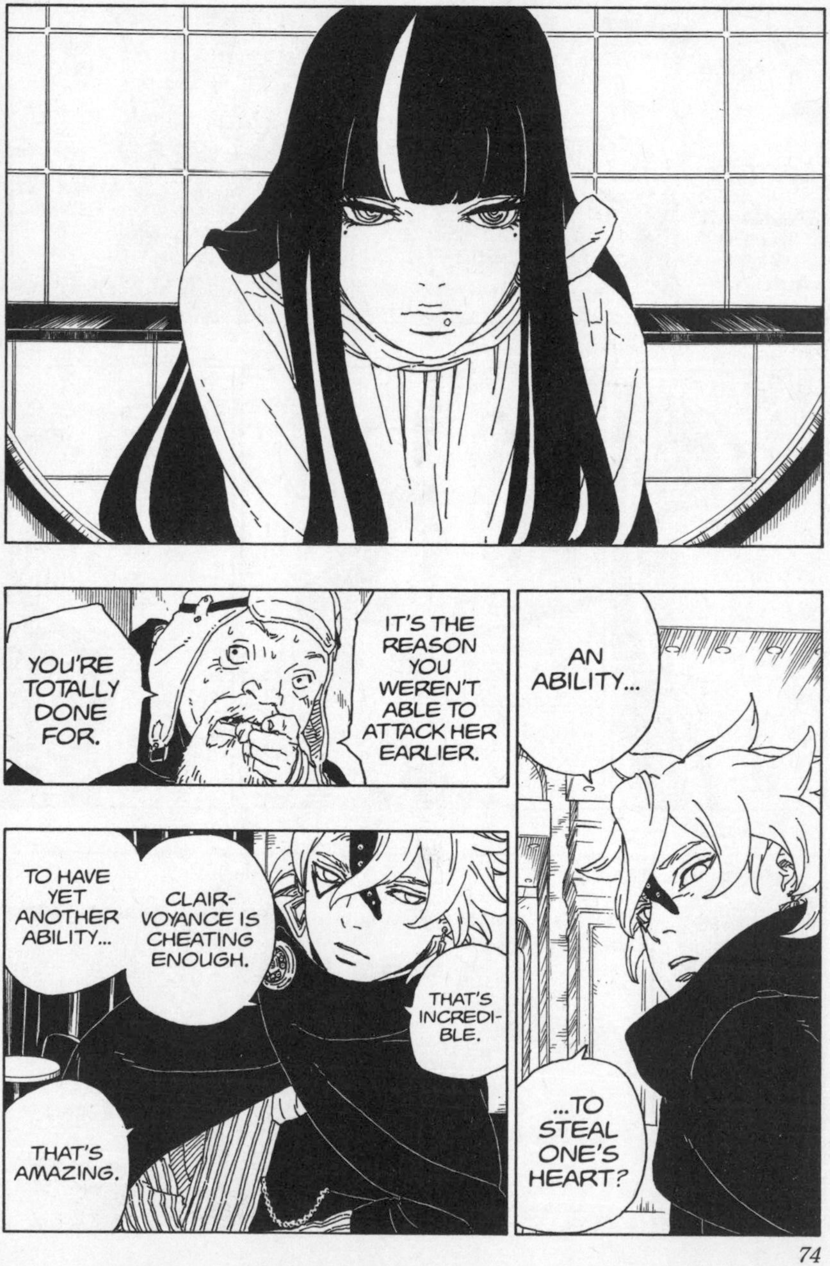
AN ABILITY...
...TO STEAL ONE'S HEART?
IT'S THE REASON YOU WEREN'T ABLE TO ATTACK HER EARLIER.
YOU'RE TOTALLY DONE FOR.
CLAIR-VOYANCE IS CHEATING ENOUGH.
TO HAVE YET ANOTHER ABILITY...
THAT'S INCREDI-BLE.
THAT'S AMAZING.

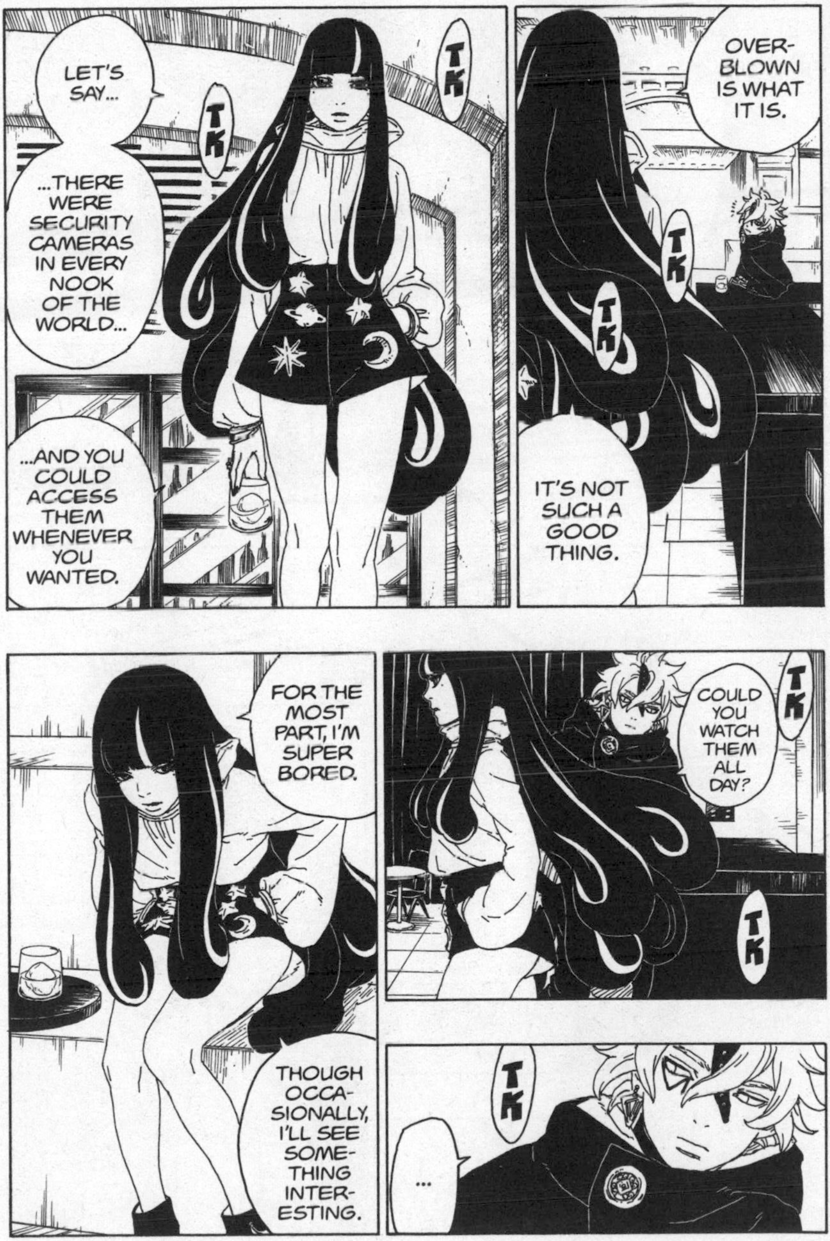
OVER-BLOWN IS WHAT IT IS.
TK
TK
IT'S NOT SUCH A GOOD THING.
TK
TK
LET'S SAY...
...THERE WERE SECURITY CAMERAS IN EVERY NOOK OF THE WORLD...
...AND YOU COULD ACCESS THEM WHENEVER YOU WANTED.
TK
COULD YOU WATCH THEM ALL DAY?
TK
TK
...
FOR THE MOST PART, I'M SUPER BORED.
THOUGH OCCASIONALLY, I'LL SEE SOMETHING INTERESTING.

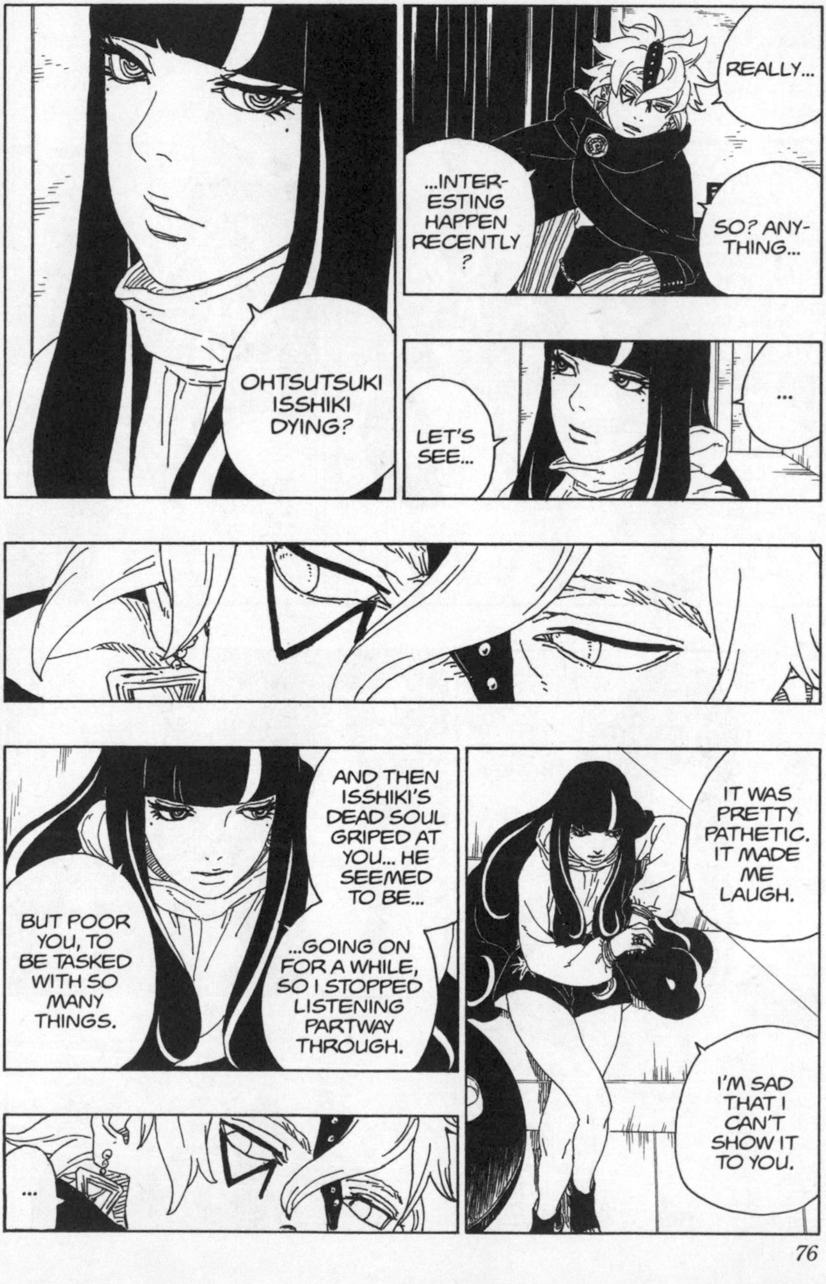
REALLY...
SO? ANY-THING...
...INTER-ESTING HAPPEN RECENTLY?
...
LET'S SEE...
OHTSUTSUKI ISSHIKI DYING?
IT WAS PRETTY PATHETIC. IT MADE ME LAUGH.
I'M SAD THAT I CAN'T SHOW IT TO YOU.
AND THEN ISSHIKI'S DEAD SOUL GRIPED AT YOU... HE SEEMED TO BE...
...GOING ON FOR A WHILE, SO I STOPPED LISTENING PARTWAY THROUGH.
BUT POOR YOU, TO BE TASKED WITH SO MANY THINGS.
...

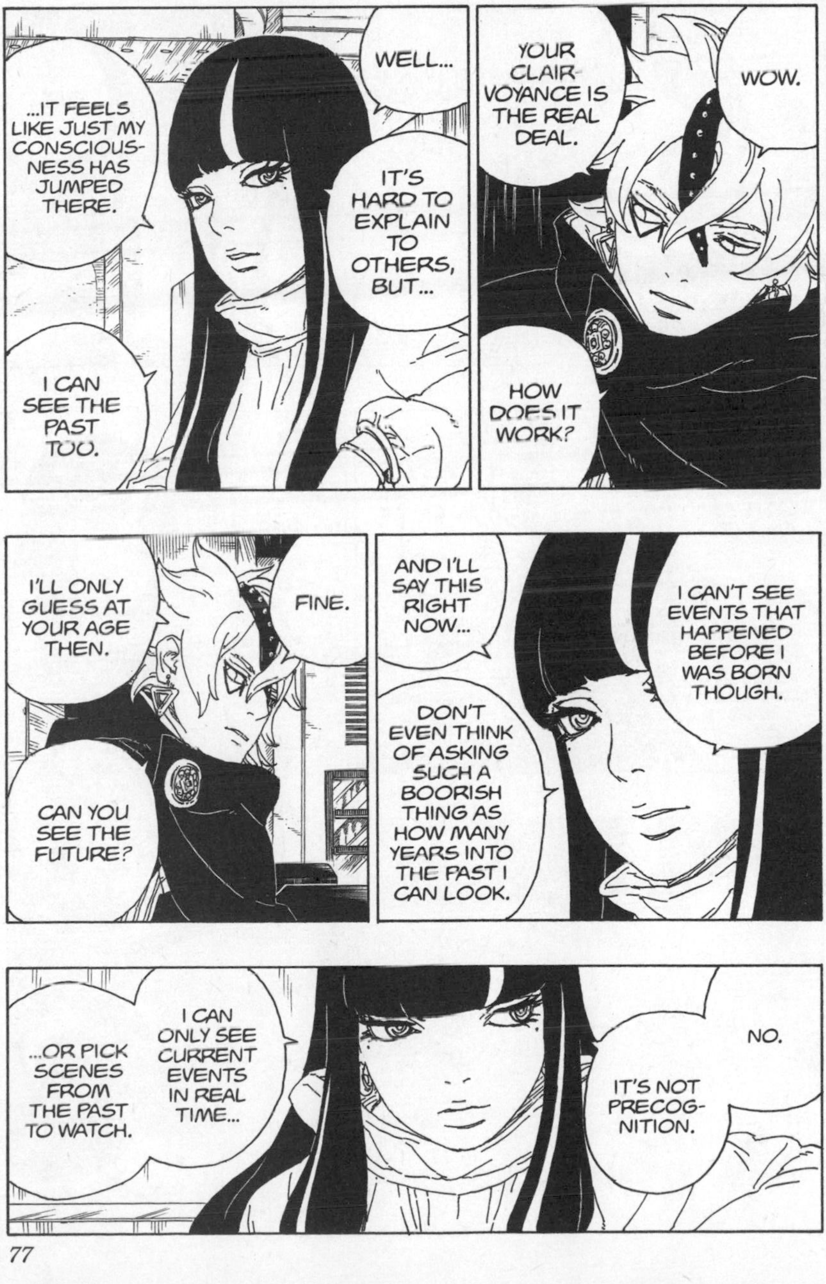
WOW.
YOUR CLAIR-VOYANCE IS THE REAL DEAL.
HOW DOES IT WORK?
WELL...
IT'S HARD TO EXPLAIN TO OTHERS, BUT...
...IT FEELS LIKE JUST MY CONSCIOUS-NESS HAS JUMPED THERE.
I CAN SEE THE PAST TOO.
I CAN'T SEE EVENTS THAT HAPPENED BEFORE I WAS BORN THOUGH.
AND I'LL SAY THIS RIGHT NOW...
DON'T EVEN THINK OF ASKING SUCH A BOORISH THING AS HOW MANY YEARS INTO THE PAST I CAN LOOK.
FINE.
I'LL ONLY GUESS AT YOUR AGE THEN.
CAN YOU SEE THE FUTURE?
NO.
IT'S NOT PRECOG-NITION.
I CAN ONLY SEE CURRENT EVENTS IN REAL TIME...
...OR PICK SCENES FROM THE PAST TO WATCH.

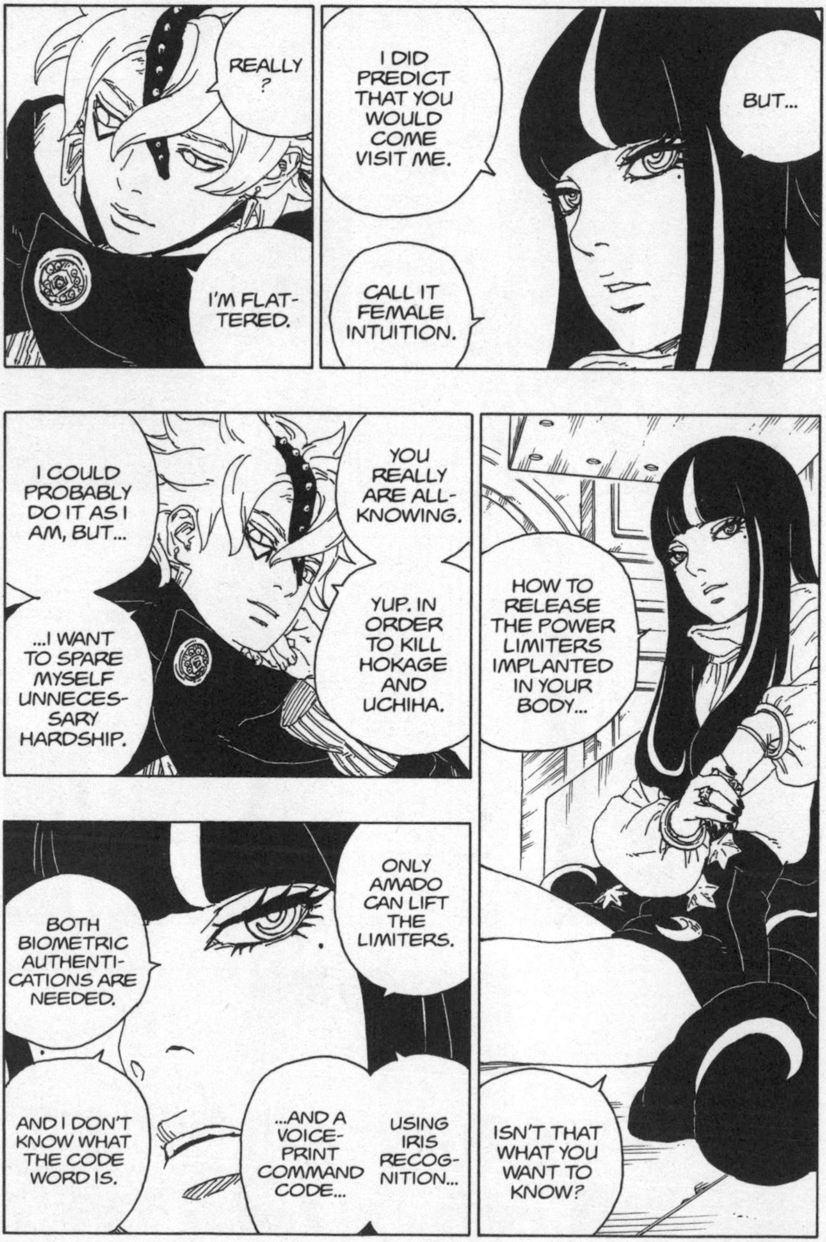
BUT...
I DID PREDICT THAT YOU WOULD COME VISIT ME.
CALL IT FEMALE INTUITION.
REALLY?
I'M FLATTERED.
HOW TO RELEASE THE POWER LIMITERS IMPLANTED IN YOUR BODY...
ISN'T THAT WHAT YOU WANT TO KNOW?
YOU REALLY ARE ALL-KNOWING.
I COULD PROBABLY DO IT AS I AM, BUT...
YUP. IN ORDER TO KILL HOKAGE AND UCHIHA.
...I WANT TO SPARE MYSELF UNNECESSARY HARDSHIP.
ONLY AMADO CAN LIFT THE LIMITERS.
BOTH BIOMETRIC AUTHENTICATIONS ARE NEEDED.
USING IRIS RECOGNITION...
...AND A VOICE-PRINT COMMAND CODE...
AND I DON'T KNOW WHAT THE CODE WORD IS.

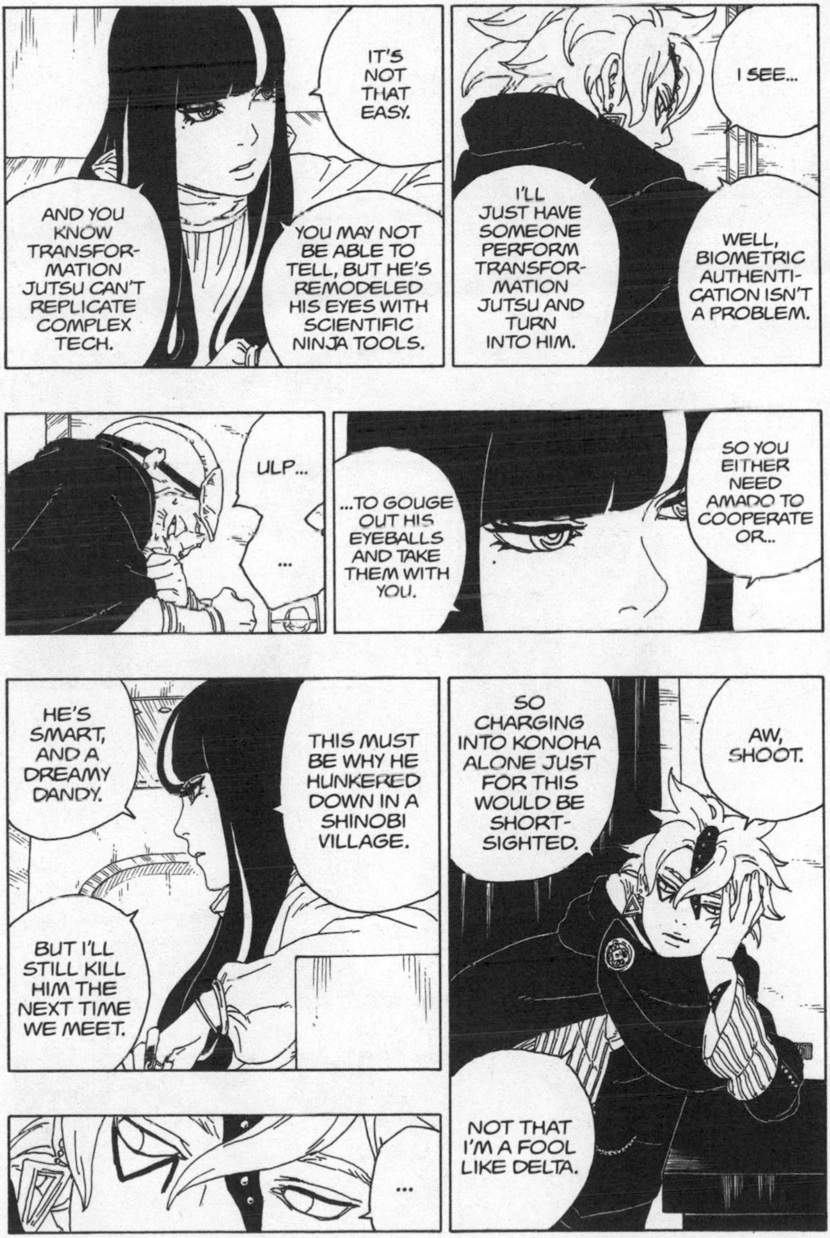
I SEE...
WELL, BIOMETRIC AUTHENTICATION ISN'T A PROBLEM.
I'LL JUST HAVE SOMEONE PERFORM TRANSFORMATION JUTSU AND TURN INTO HIM.
IT'S NOT THAT EASY.
YOU MAY NOT BE ABLE TO TELL, BUT HE'S REMODELED HIS EYES WITH SCIENTIFIC NINJA TOOLS.
AND YOU KNOW TRANSFORMATION JUTSU CAN'T REPLICATE COMPLEX TECH.
SO YOU EITHER NEED AMADO TO COOPERATE OR...
...TO GOUGE OUT HIS EYEBALLS AND TAKE THEM WITH YOU.
ULP...
...
AW, SHOOT.
SO CHARGING INTO KONOHA ALONE JUST FOR THIS WOULD BE SHORT-SIGHTED.
NOT THAT I'M A FOOL LIKE DELTA.
THIS MUST BE WHY HE HUNKERED DOWN IN A SHINOBI VILLAGE.
HE'S SMART, AND A DREAMY DANDY.
BUT I'LL STILL KILL HIM THE NEXT TIME WE MEET.
...

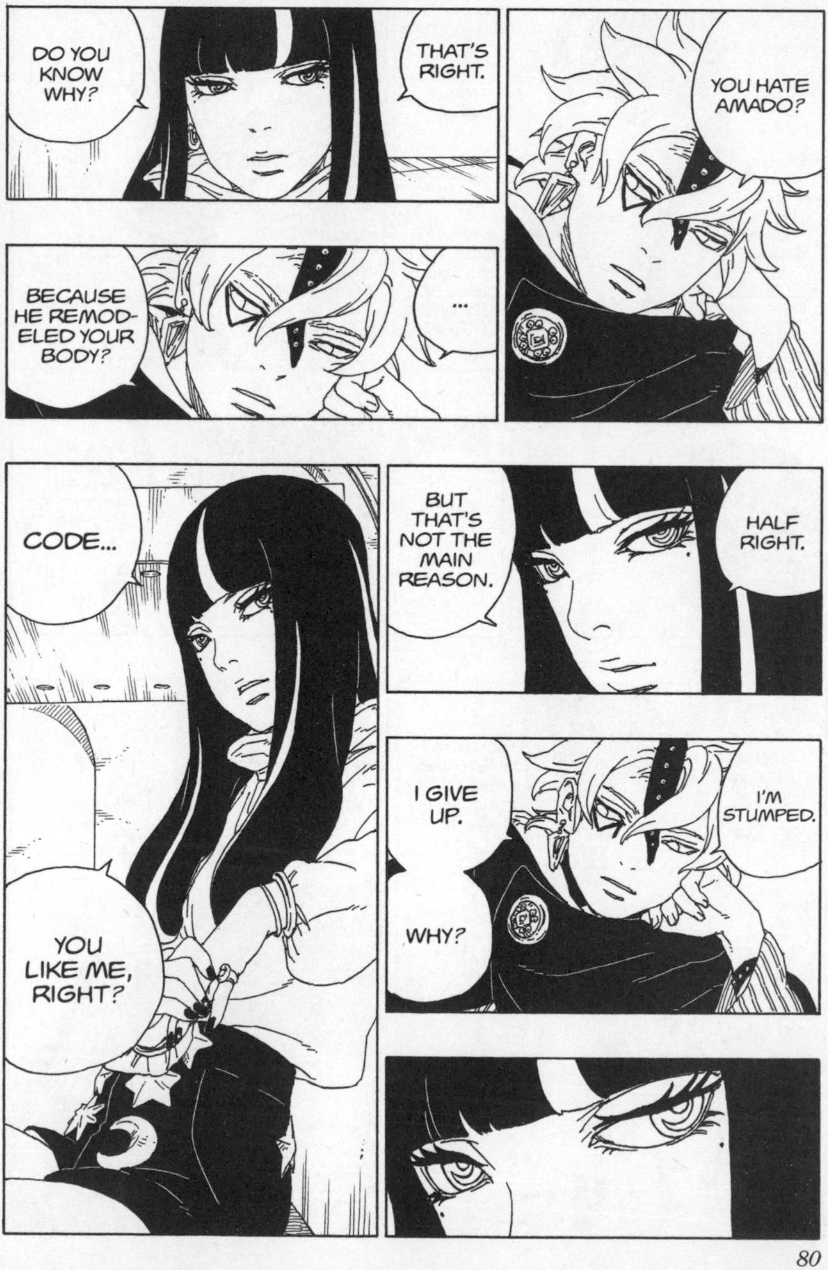
YOU HATE AMADO?
THAT'S RIGHT.
DO YOU KNOW WHY?
...
BECAUSE HE REMODELED YOUR BODY?
HALF RIGHT.
BUT THAT'S NOT THE MAIN REASON.
I'M STUMPED.
I GIVE UP.
WHY?
CODE...
YOU LIKE ME, RIGHT?

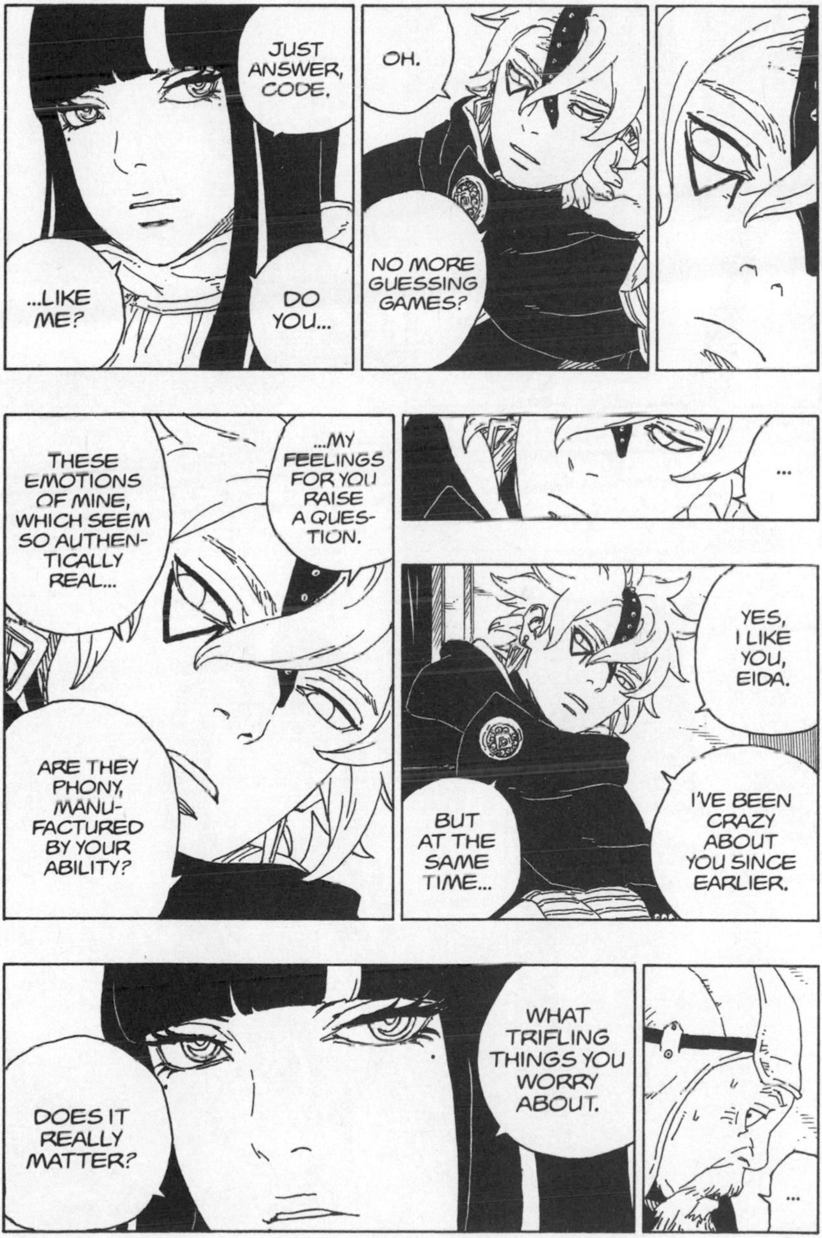
OH.
NO MORE GUESSING GAMES?
JUST ANSWER, CODE.
DO YOU...
...LIKE ME?
...
YES, I LIKE YOU, EIDA.
I'VE BEEN CRAZY ABOUT YOU SINCE EARLIER.
BUT AT THE SAME TIME...
...MY FEELINGS FOR YOU RAISE A QUESTION.
THESE EMOTIONS OF MINE, WHICH SEEM SO AUTHENTICALLY REAL...
ARE THEY PHONY, MANUFACTURED BY YOUR ABILITY?
...
WHAT TRIFLING THINGS YOU WORRY ABOUT.
DOES IT REALLY MATTER?

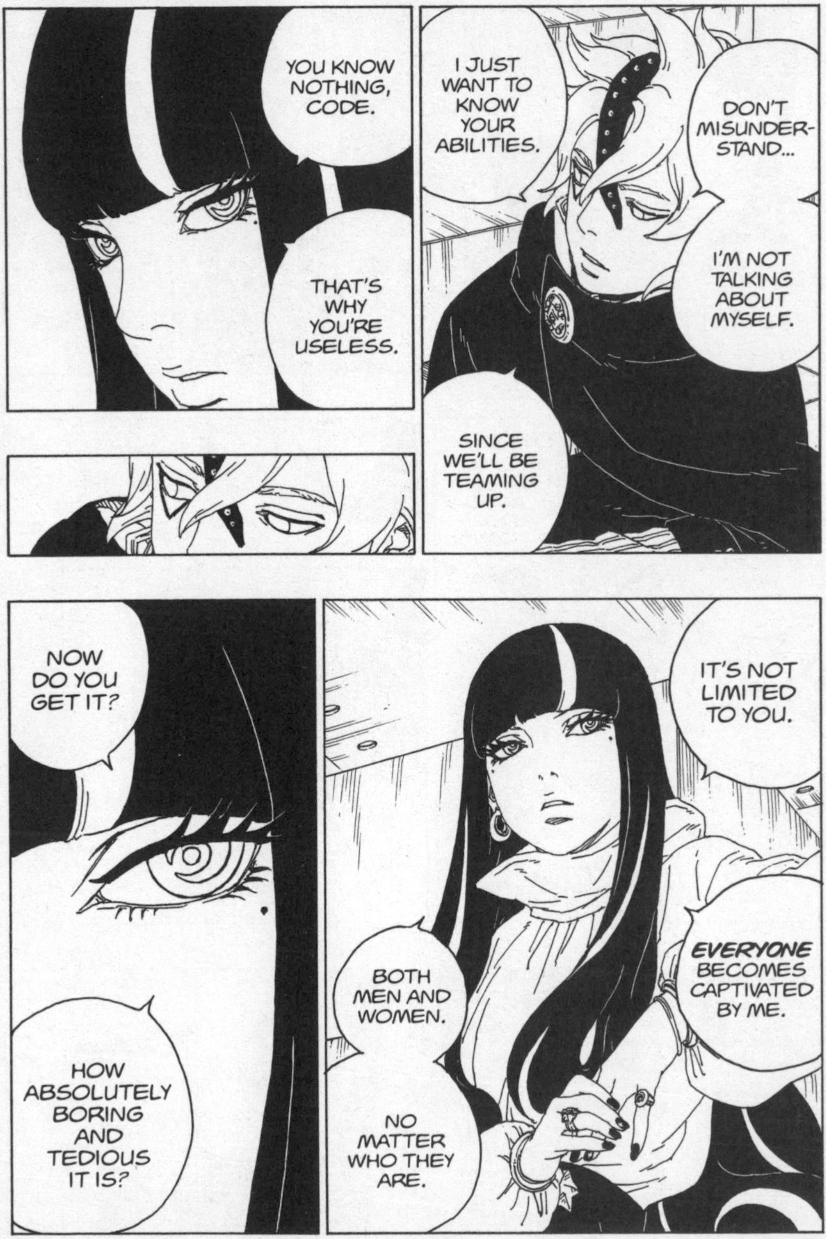

DON'T MISUNDERSTAND...
I'M NOT TALKING ABOUT MYSELF.
I JUST WANT TO KNOW YOUR ABILITIES.
SINCE WE'LL BE TEAMING UP.
YOU KNOW NOTHING, CODE.
THAT'S WHY YOU'RE USELESS.
IT'S NOT LIMITED TO YOU.
EVERYONE BECOMES CAPTIVATED BY ME.
BOTH MEN AND WOMEN.
NO MATTER WHO THEY ARE.
NOW DO YOU GET IT?
HOW ABSOLUTELY BORING AND TEDIOUS IT IS?

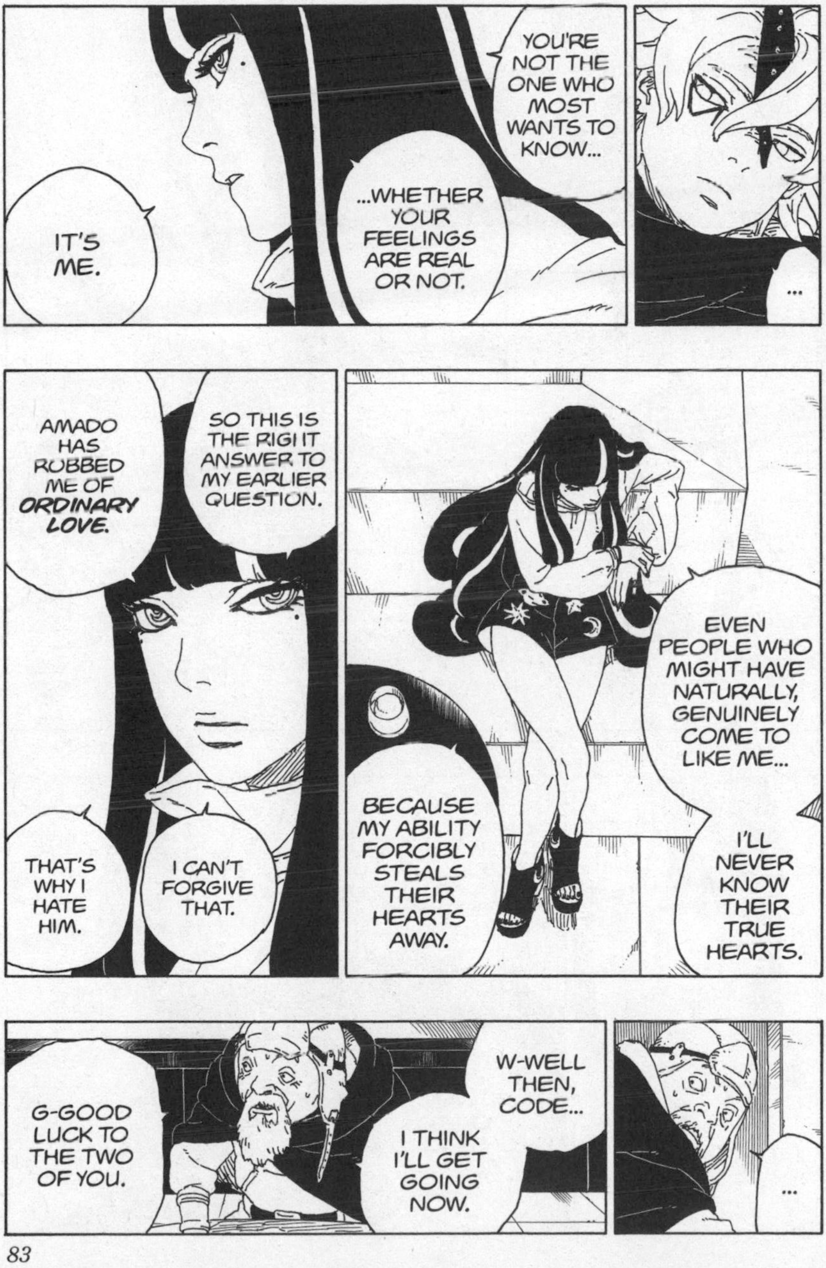
...
YOU'RE NOT THE ONE WHO MOST WANTS TO KNOW...
...WHETHER YOUR FEELINGS ARE REAL OR NOT.
IT'S ME.
EVEN PEOPLE WHO MIGHT HAVE NATURALLY, GENUINELY COME TO LIKE ME...
I'LL NEVER KNOW THEIR TRUE HEARTS.
BECAUSE MY ABILITY FORCIBLY STEALS THEIR HEARTS AWAY.
SO THIS IS THE RIGHT ANSWER TO MY EARLIER QUESTION.
AMADO HAS ROBBED ME OF ***ORDINARY LOVE.***
I CAN'T FORGIVE THAT.
THAT'S WHY I HATE HIM.
...
W-WELL THEN, CODE...
I THINK I'LL GET GOING NOW.
G-GOOD LUCK TO THE TWO OF YOU.

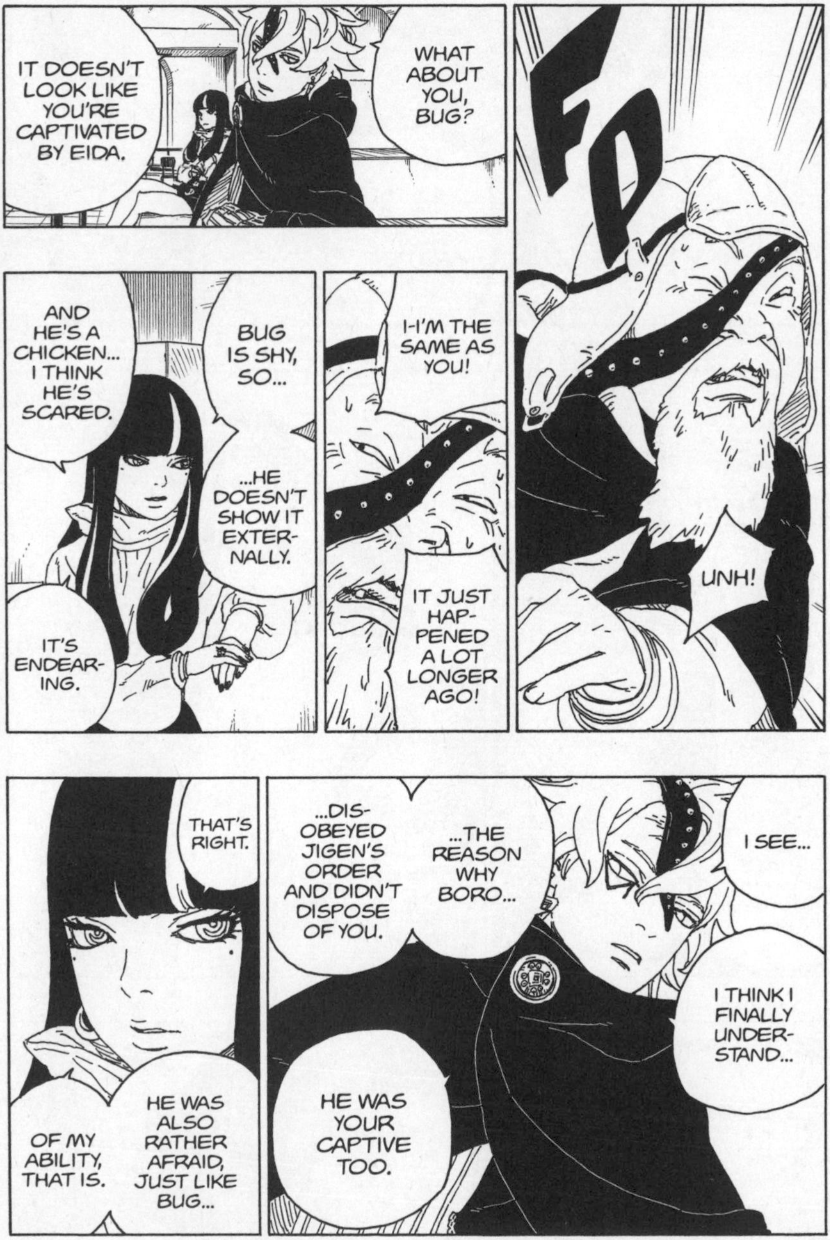
FP
UNH!
WHAT ABOUT YOU, BUG?
IT DOESN'T LOOK LIKE YOU'RE CAPTIVATED BY EIDA.
I-I'M THE SAME AS YOU!
IT JUST HAP-PENED A LOT LONGER AGO!
BUG IS SHY, SO...
...HE DOESN'T SHOW IT EXTER-NALLY.
AND HE'S A CHICKEN... I THINK HE'S SCARED.
IT'S ENDEAR-ING.
I SEE...
I THINK I FINALLY UNDER-STAND...
...THE REASON WHY BORO...
...DIS-OBEYED JIGEN'S ORDER AND DIDN'T DISPOSE OF YOU.
HE WAS YOUR CAPTIVE TOO.
THAT'S RIGHT.
HE WAS ALSO RATHER AFRAID, JUST LIKE BUG...
OF MY ABILITY, THAT IS.

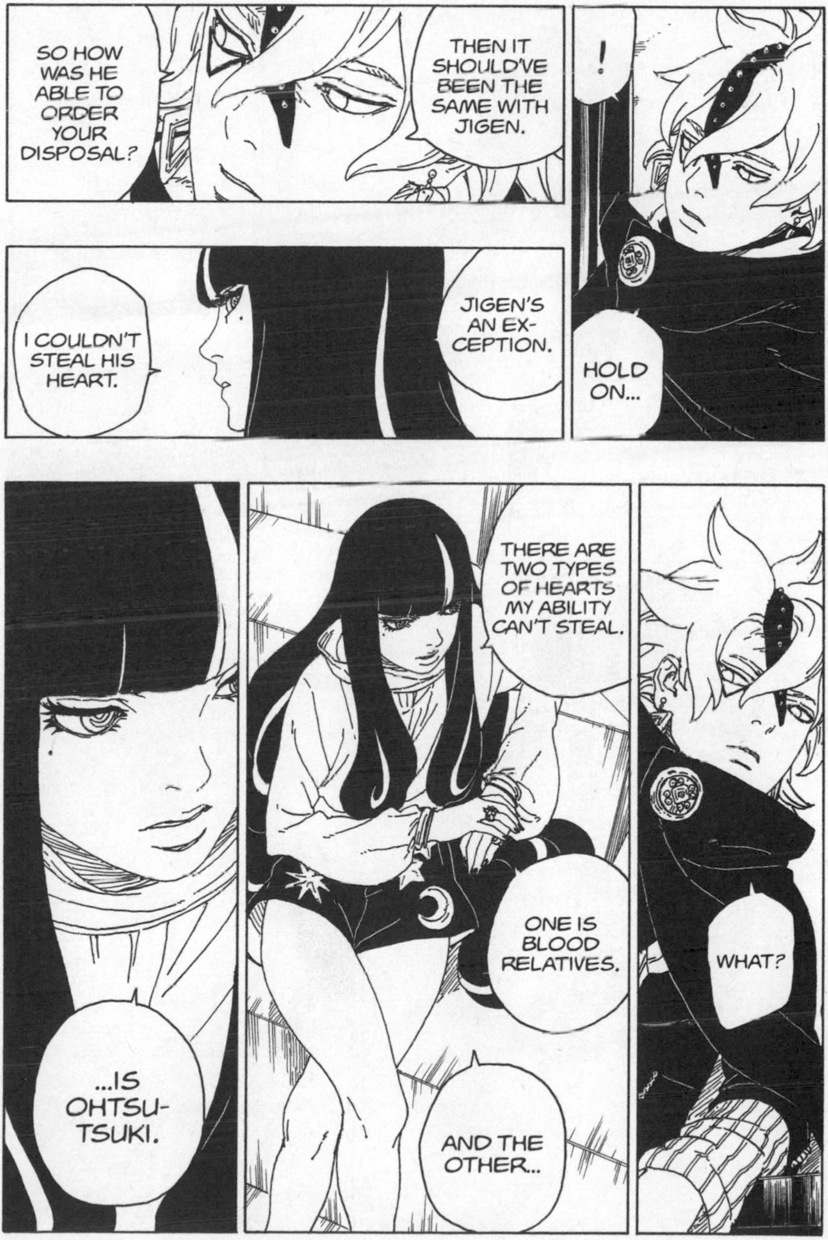
!
HOLD ON...
THEN IT SHOULD'VE BEEN THE SAME WITH JIGEN.
SO HOW WAS HE ABLE TO ORDER YOUR DISPOSAL?
JIGEN'S AN EXCEPTION.
I COULDN'T STEAL HIS HEART.
WHAT?
THERE ARE TWO TYPES OF HEARTS MY ABILITY CAN'T STEAL.
ONE IS BLOOD RELATIVES.
AND THE OTHER...
...IS OHTSUTSUKI.

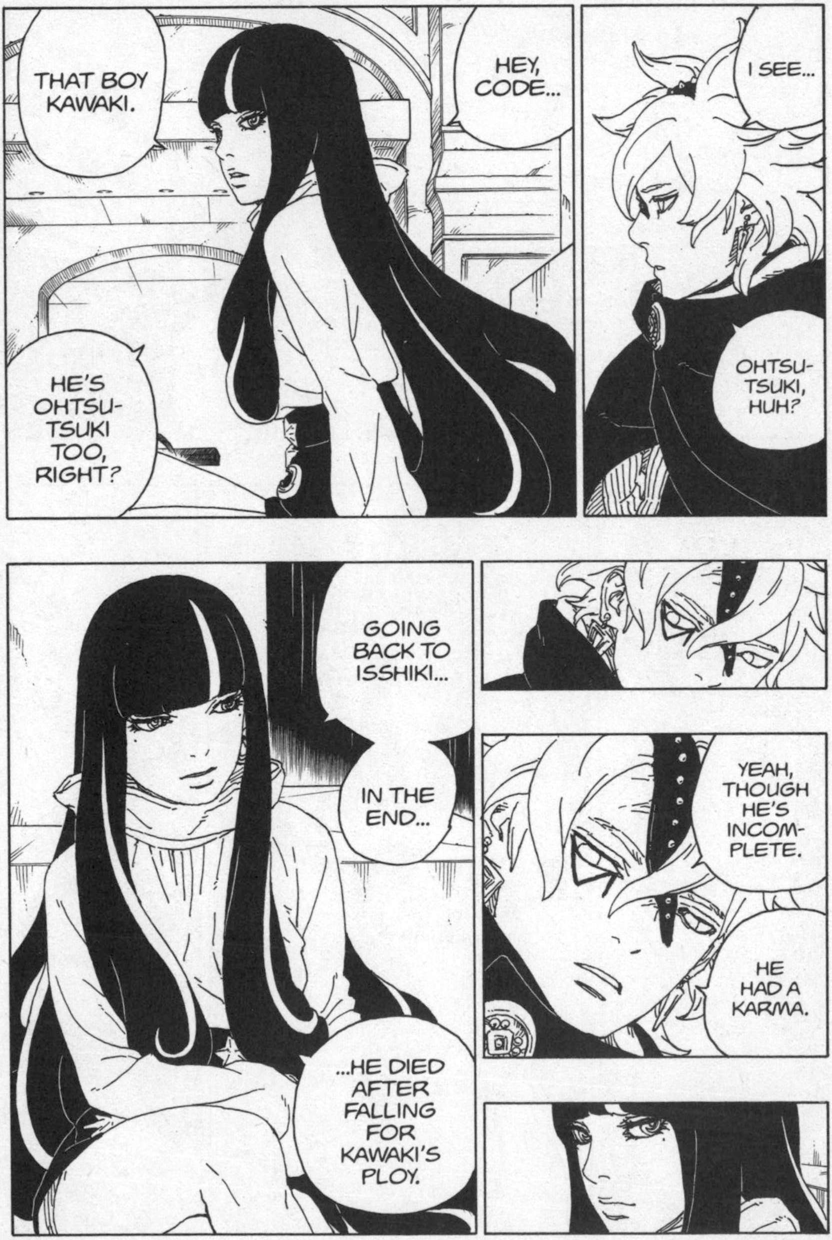
I SEE...
OHTSU-TSUKI, HUH?
HEY, CODE...
THAT BOY KAWAKI.
HE'S OHTSU-TSUKI TOO, RIGHT?
YEAH, THOUGH HE'S INCOMP-LETE.
HE HAD A KARMA.
GOING BACK TO ISSHIKI...
IN THE END...
...HE DIED AFTER FALLING FOR KAWAKI'S PLOY.

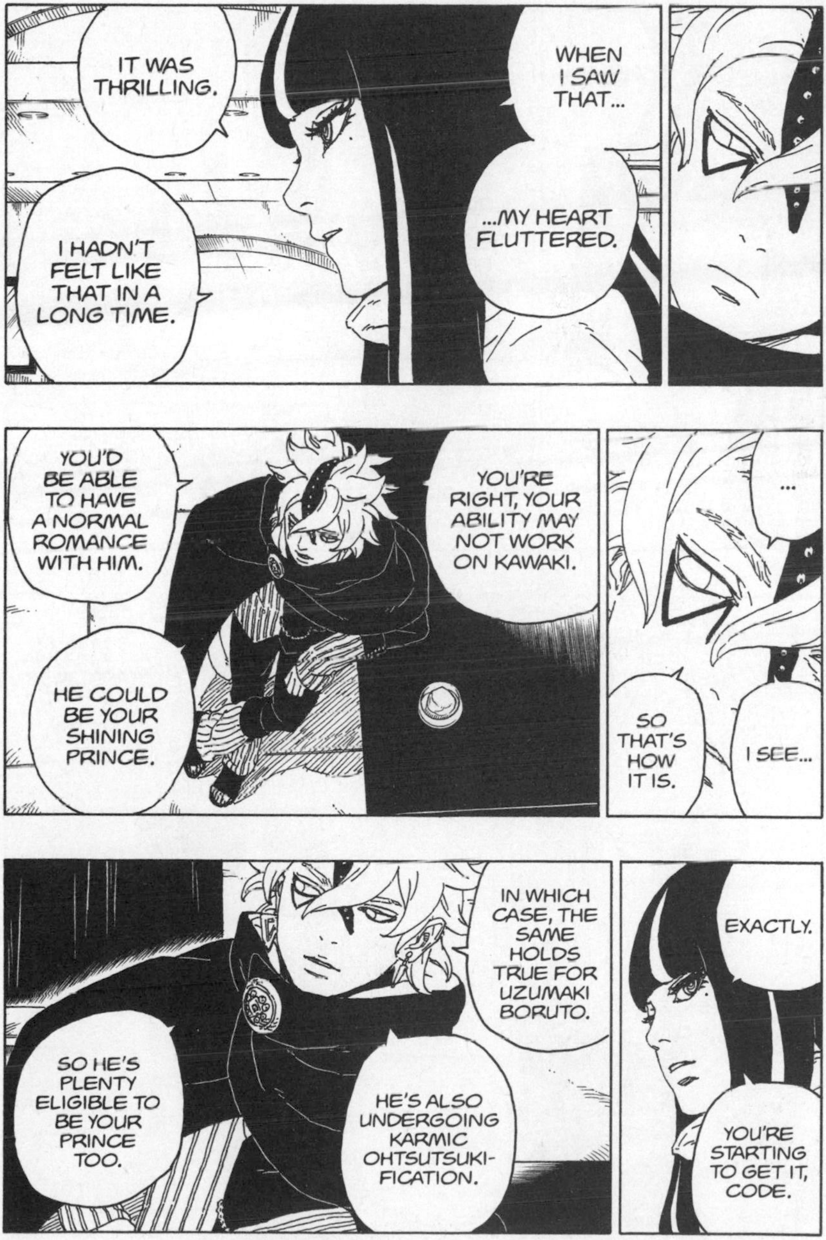
WHEN I SAW THAT...
...MY HEART FLUTTERED.
IT WAS THRILLING.
I HADN'T FELT LIKE THAT IN A LONG TIME.
...
I SEE...
SO THAT'S HOW IT IS.
YOU'RE RIGHT, YOUR ABILITY MAY NOT WORK ON KAWAKI.
YOU'D BE ABLE TO HAVE A NORMAL ROMANCE WITH HIM.
HE COULD BE YOUR SHINING PRINCE.
EXACTLY.
YOU'RE STARTING TO GET IT, CODE.
IN WHICH CASE, THE SAME HOLDS TRUE FOR UZUMAKI BORUTO.
HE'S ALSO UNDERGOING KARMIC OHTSUTSUKI-FICATION.
SO HE'S PLENTY ELIGIBLE TO BE YOUR PRINCE TOO.

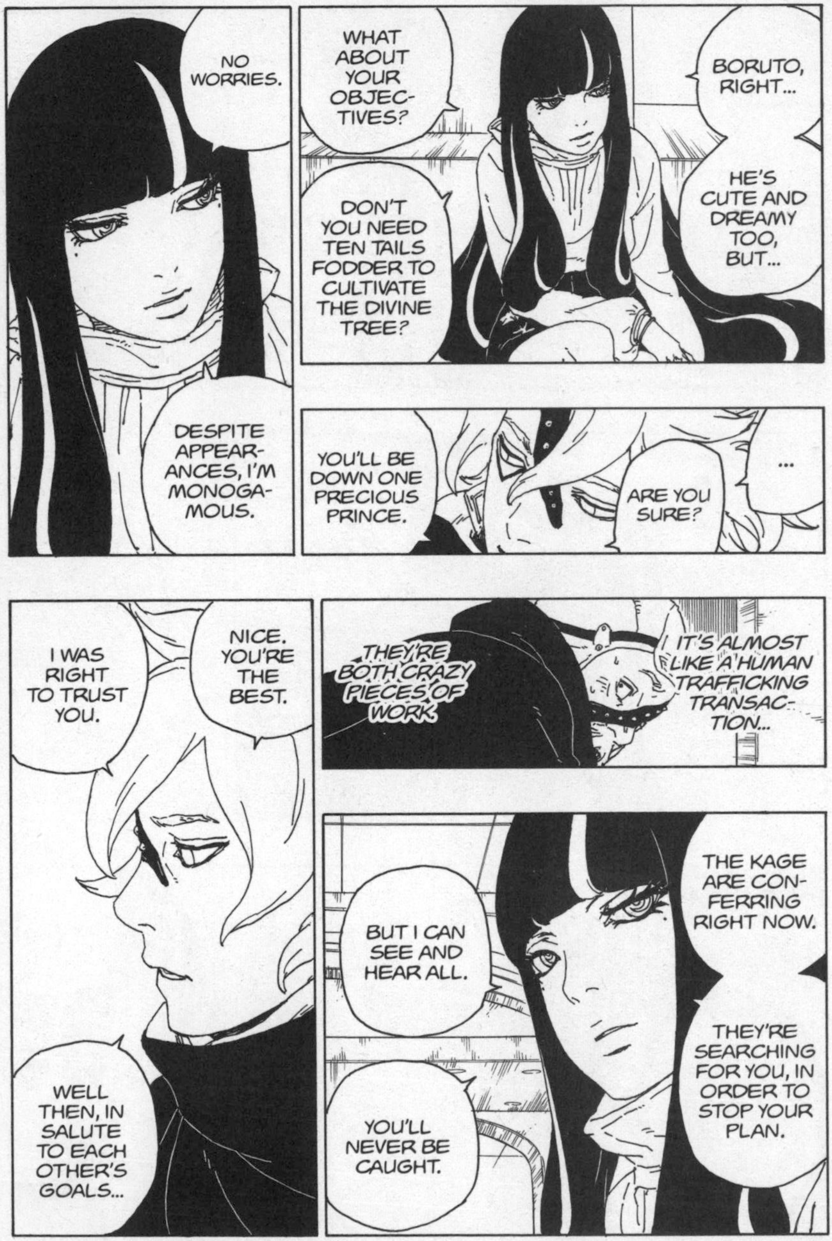
BORUTO, RIGHT...
HE'S CUTE AND DREAMY TOO, BUT...
WHAT ABOUT YOUR OBJECTIVES?
DON'T YOU NEED TEN TAILS FODDER TO CULTIVATE THE DIVINE TREE?
...
ARE YOU SURE?
YOU'LL BE DOWN ONE PRECIOUS PRINCE.
NO WORRIES.
DESPITE APPEARANCES, I'M MONOGAMOUS.
IT'S ALMOST LIKE A HUMAN TRAFFICKING TRANSACTION...
THEY'RE BOTH CRAZY PIECES OF WORK.
THE KAGE ARE CONFERRING RIGHT NOW.
BUT I CAN SEE AND HEAR ALL.
THEY'RE SEARCHING FOR YOU, IN ORDER TO STOP YOUR PLAN.
YOU'LL NEVER BE CAUGHT.
NICE. YOU'RE THE BEST.
I WAS RIGHT TO TRUST YOU.
WELL THEN, IN SALUTE TO EACH OTHER'S GOALS...

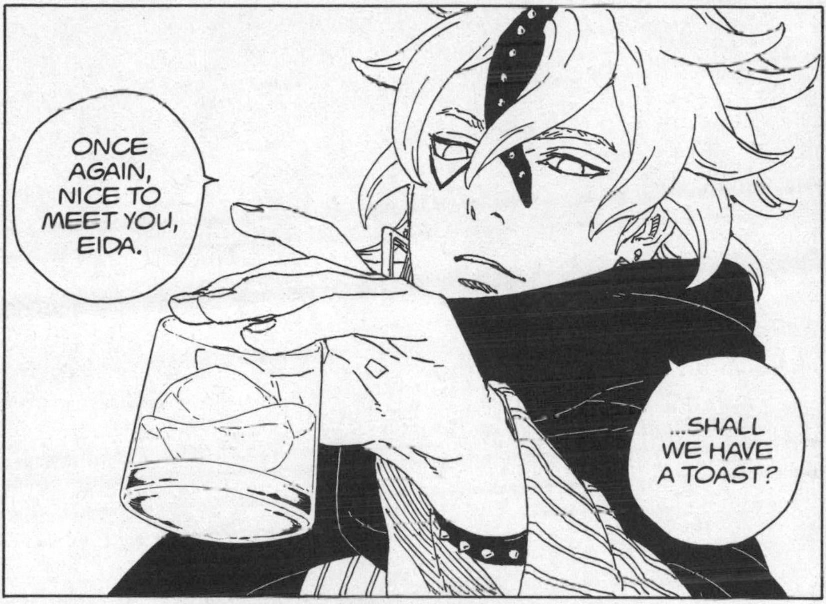
ONCE AGAIN, NICE TO MEET YOU, EIDA.
...SHALL WE HAVE A TOAST?
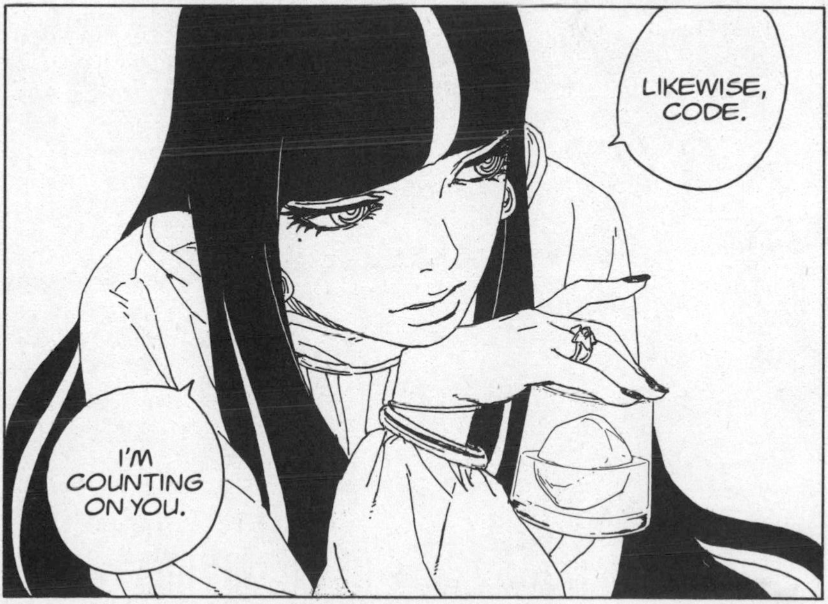
LIKEWISE, CODE.
I'M COUNTING ON YOU.

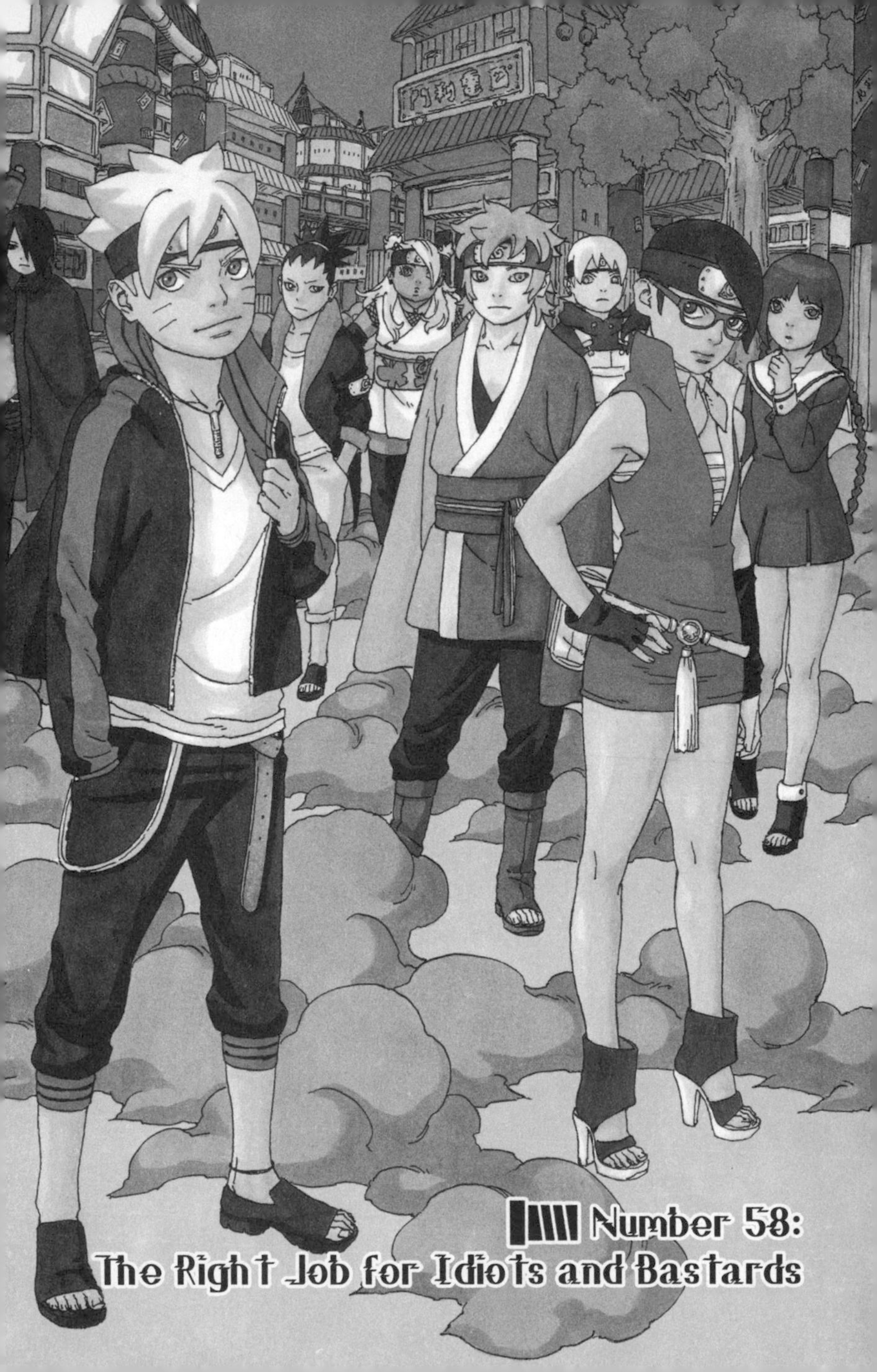
Number 58:
The Right Job for Idiots and Bastards

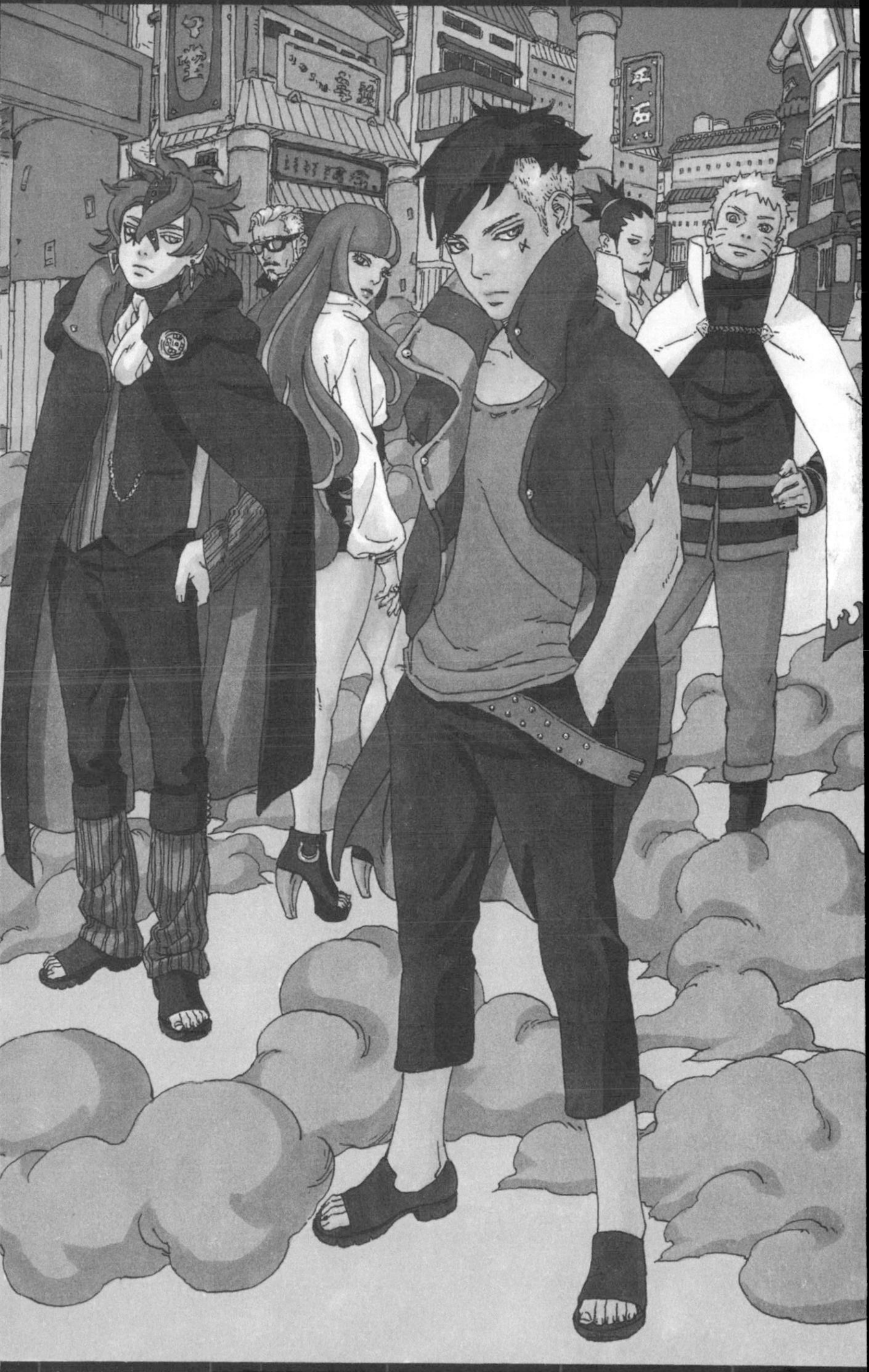

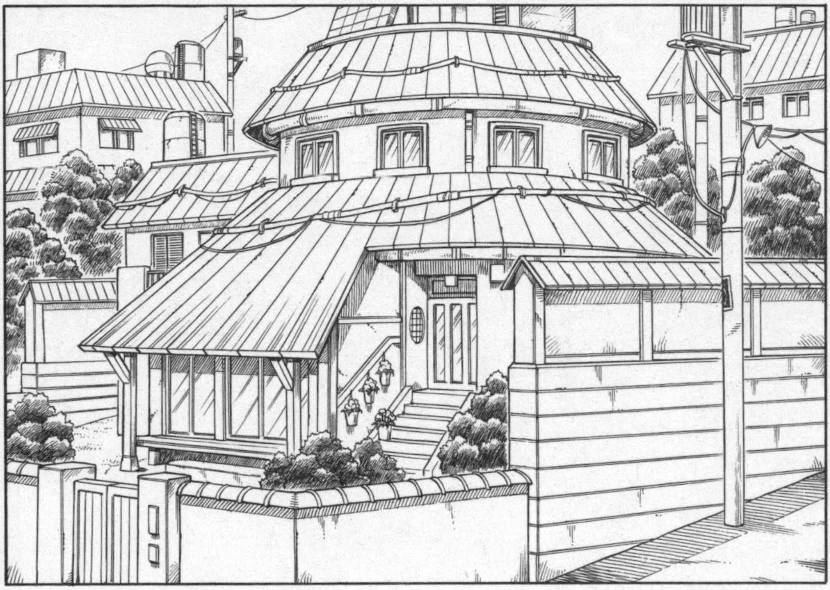

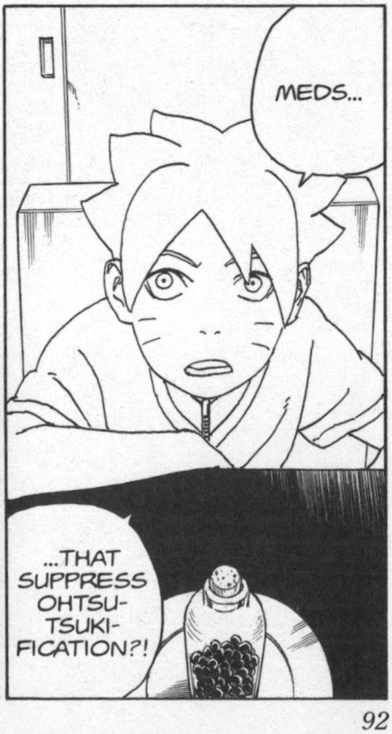
MEDS...
...THAT SUPPRESS OHTSU-TSUKI-FICATION?!

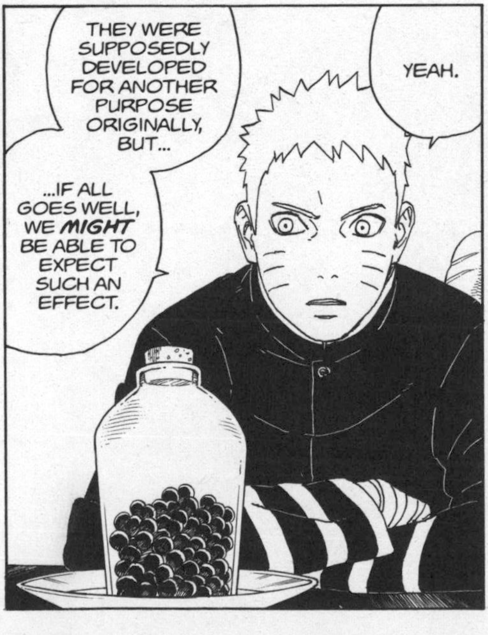
YEAH.
THEY WERE SUPPOSEDLY DEVELOPED FOR ANOTHER PURPOSE ORIGINALLY, BUT...
...IF ALL GOES WELL, WE ***MIGHT*** BE ABLE TO EXPECT SUCH AN EFFECT.

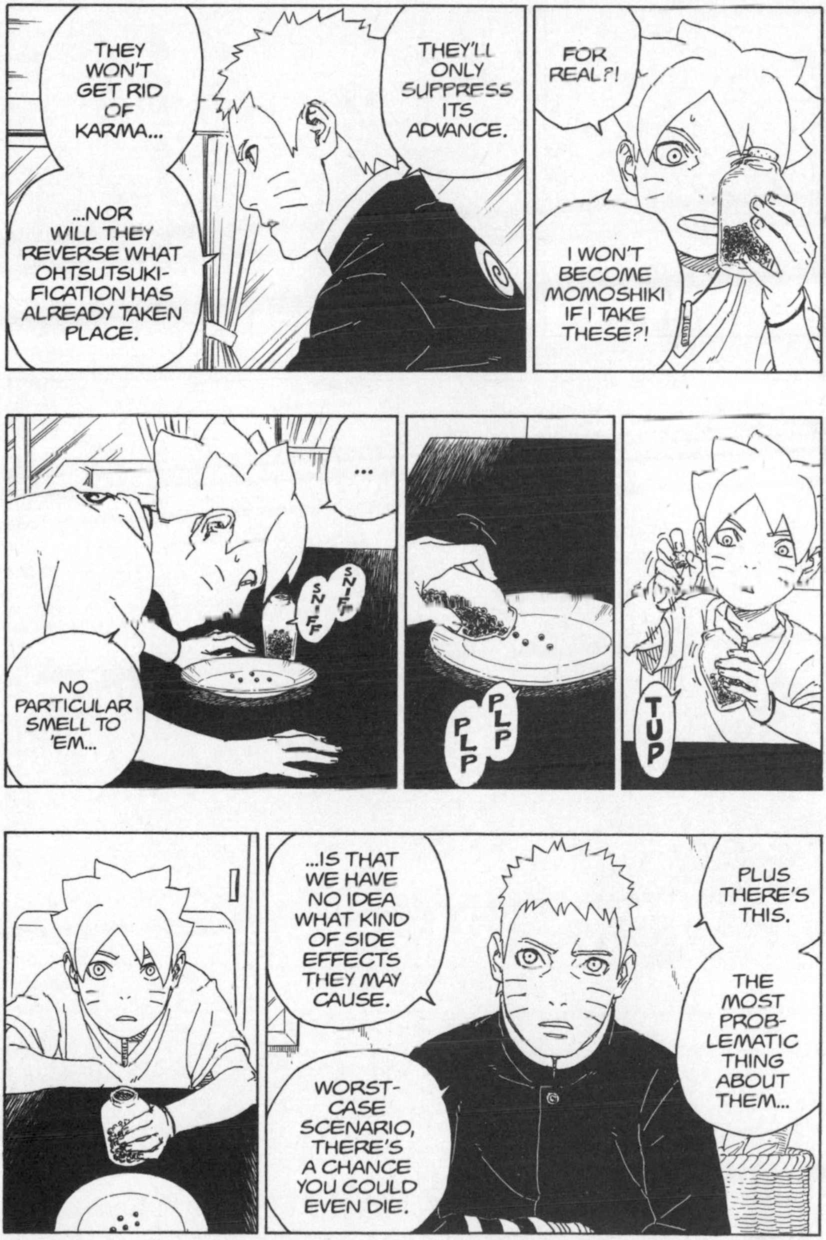
FOR REAL?!
I WON'T BECOME MOMOSHIKI IF I TAKE THESE?!
THEY WON'T GET RID OF KARMA...
...NOR WILL THEY REVERSE WHAT OHTSUTSUKI-FICATION HAS ALREADY TAKEN PLACE.
THEY'LL ONLY SUPPRESS ITS ADVANCE.
TUP
PLP PLP
...
SNIFF SNIFF
NO PARTICULAR SMELL TO 'EM...
PLUS THERE'S THIS.
THE MOST PROB-LEMATIC THING ABOUT THEM...
...IS THAT WE HAVE NO IDEA WHAT KIND OF SIDE EFFECTS THEY MAY CAUSE.
WORST-CASE SCENARIO, THERE'S A CHANCE YOU COULD EVEN DIE.

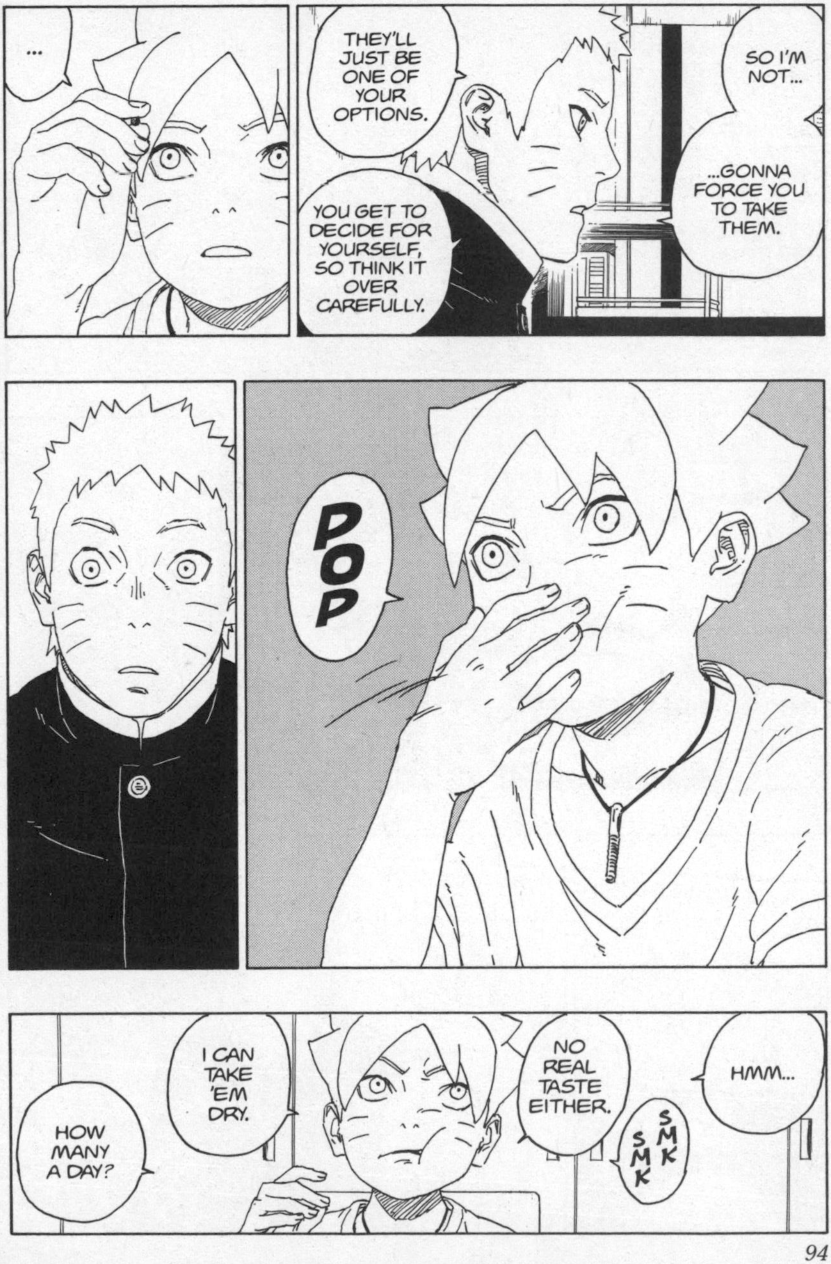
SO I'M NOT...
...GONNA FORCE YOU TO TAKE THEM.
THEY'LL JUST BE ONE OF YOUR OPTIONS.
YOU GET TO DECIDE FOR YOURSELF, SO THINK IT OVER CAREFULLY.
...
POP
HMM...
SMK SMK
NO REAL TASTE EITHER.
I CAN TAKE 'EM DRY.
HOW MANY A DAY?

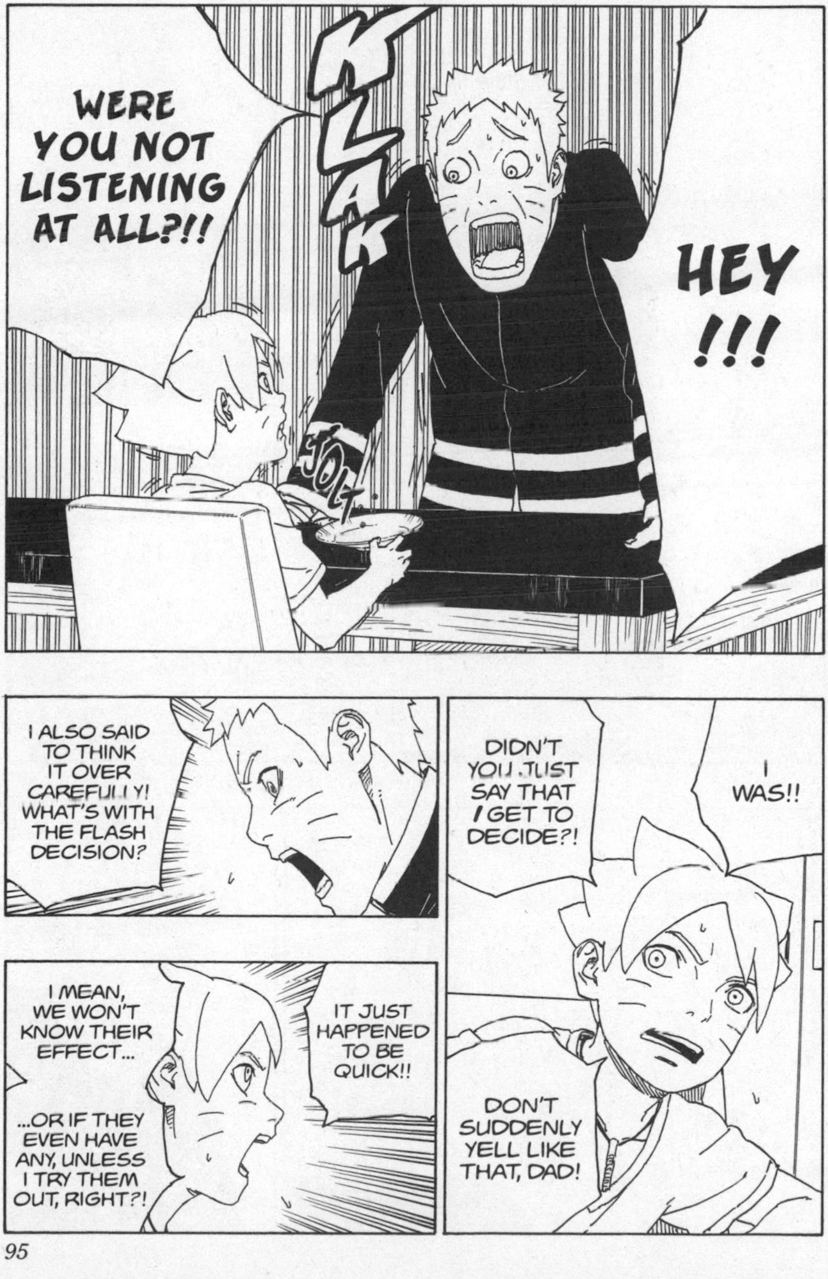
HEY!!!
KLAK
WERE YOU NOT LISTENING AT ALL?!!
JOLT
I WAS!!
DIDN'T YOU JUST SAY THAT I GET TO DECIDE?!
DON'T SUDDENLY YELL LIKE THAT, DAD!
I ALSO SAID TO THINK IT OVER CAREFULLY! WHAT'S WITH THE FLASH DECISION?
IT JUST HAPPENED TO BE QUICK!!
I MEAN, WE WON'T KNOW THEIR EFFECT...
...OR IF THEY EVEN HAVE ANY, UNLESS I TRY THEM OUT, RIGHT?!

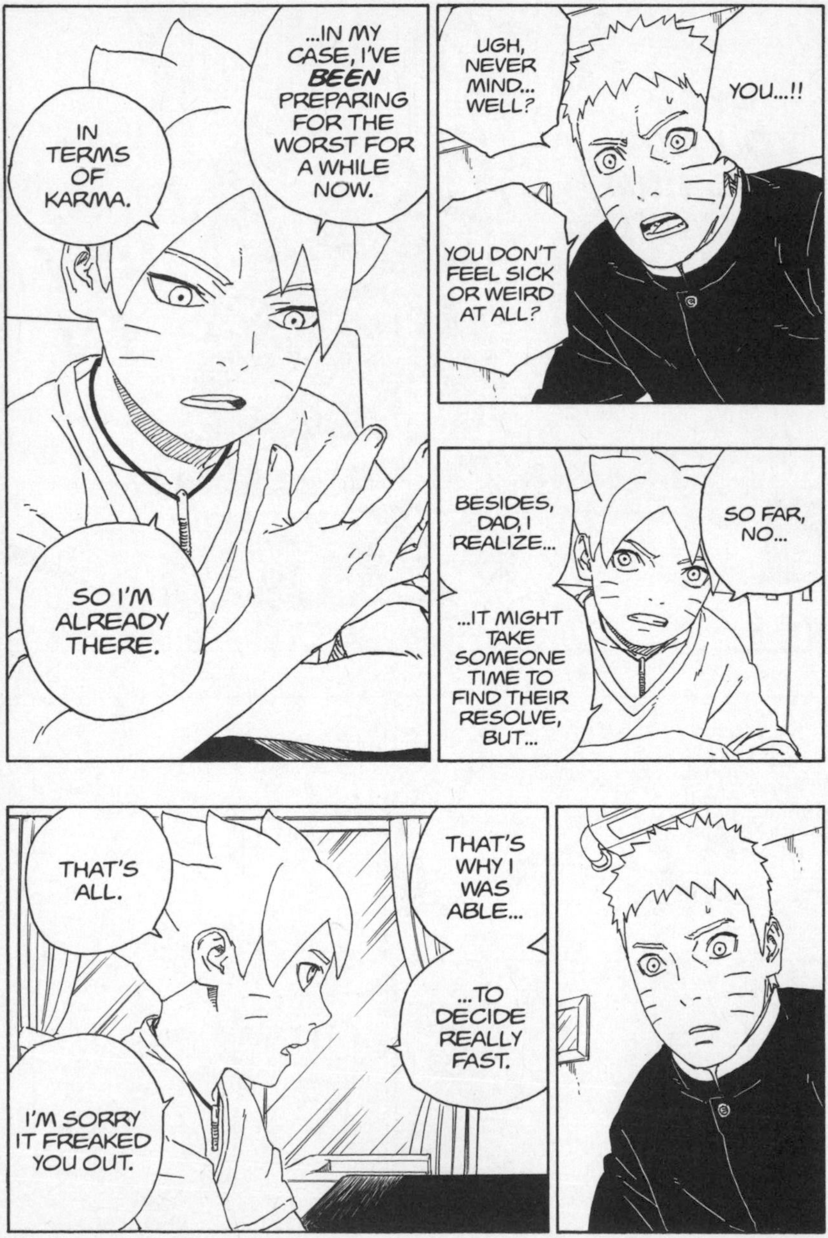
YOU...!!
UGH, NEVER MIND... WELL?
YOU DON'T FEEL SICK OR WEIRD AT ALL?
SO FAR, NO...
BESIDES, DAD, I REALIZE...
...IT MIGHT TAKE SOMEONE TIME TO FIND THEIR RESOLVE, BUT...
...IN MY CASE, I'VE *BEEN* PREPARING FOR THE WORST FOR A WHILE NOW.
IN TERMS OF KARMA.
SO I'M ALREADY THERE.
THAT'S WHY I WAS ABLE...
...TO DECIDE REALLY FAST.
THAT'S ALL.
I'M SORRY IT FREAKED YOU OUT.

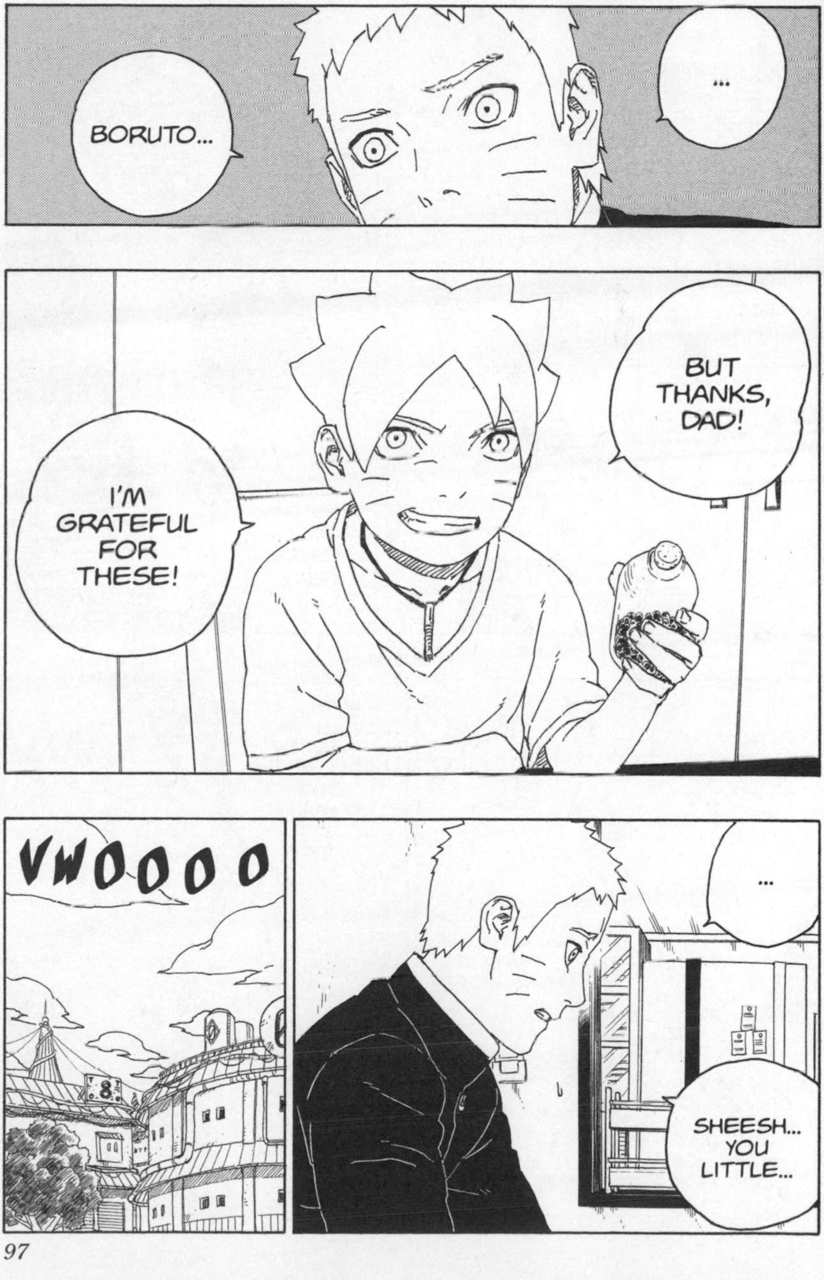
...
BORUTO...
BUT THANKS, DAD!
I'M GRATEFUL FOR THESE!
...
SHEESH... YOU LITTLE...
VWOOOO

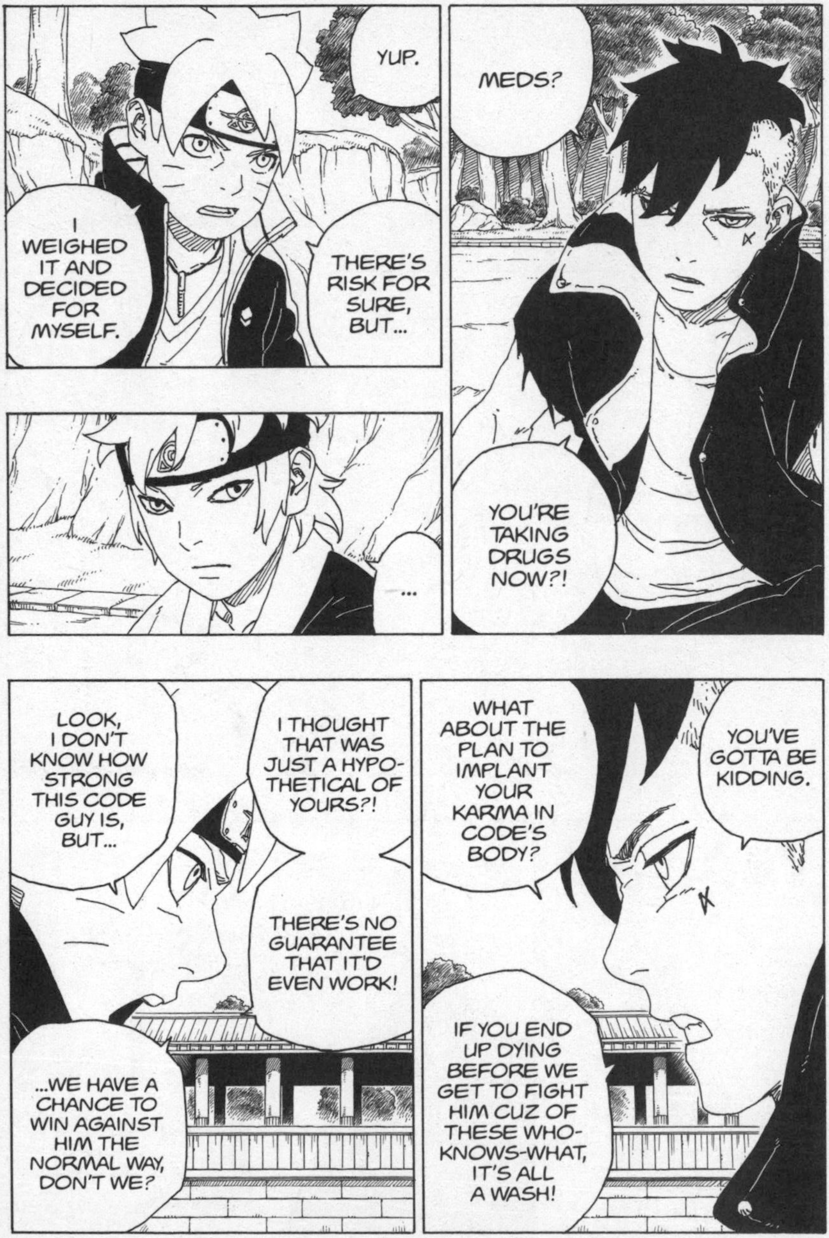
MEDS?
YOU'RE TAKING DRUGS NOW?!
YUP.
THERE'S RISK FOR SURE, BUT...
I WEIGHED IT AND DECIDED FOR MYSELF.
...
YOU'VE GOTTA BE KIDDING.
WHAT ABOUT THE PLAN TO IMPLANT YOUR KARMA IN CODE'S BODY?
IF YOU END UP DYING BEFORE WE GET TO FIGHT HIM CUZ OF THESE WHO-KNOWS-WHAT, IT'S ALL A WASH!
I THOUGHT THAT WAS JUST A HYPOTHETICAL OF YOURS?!
THERE'S NO GUARANTEE THAT IT'D EVEN WORK!
LOOK, I DON'T KNOW HOW STRONG THIS CODE GUY IS, BUT...
...WE HAVE A CHANCE TO WIN AGAINST HIM THE NORMAL WAY, DON'T WE?

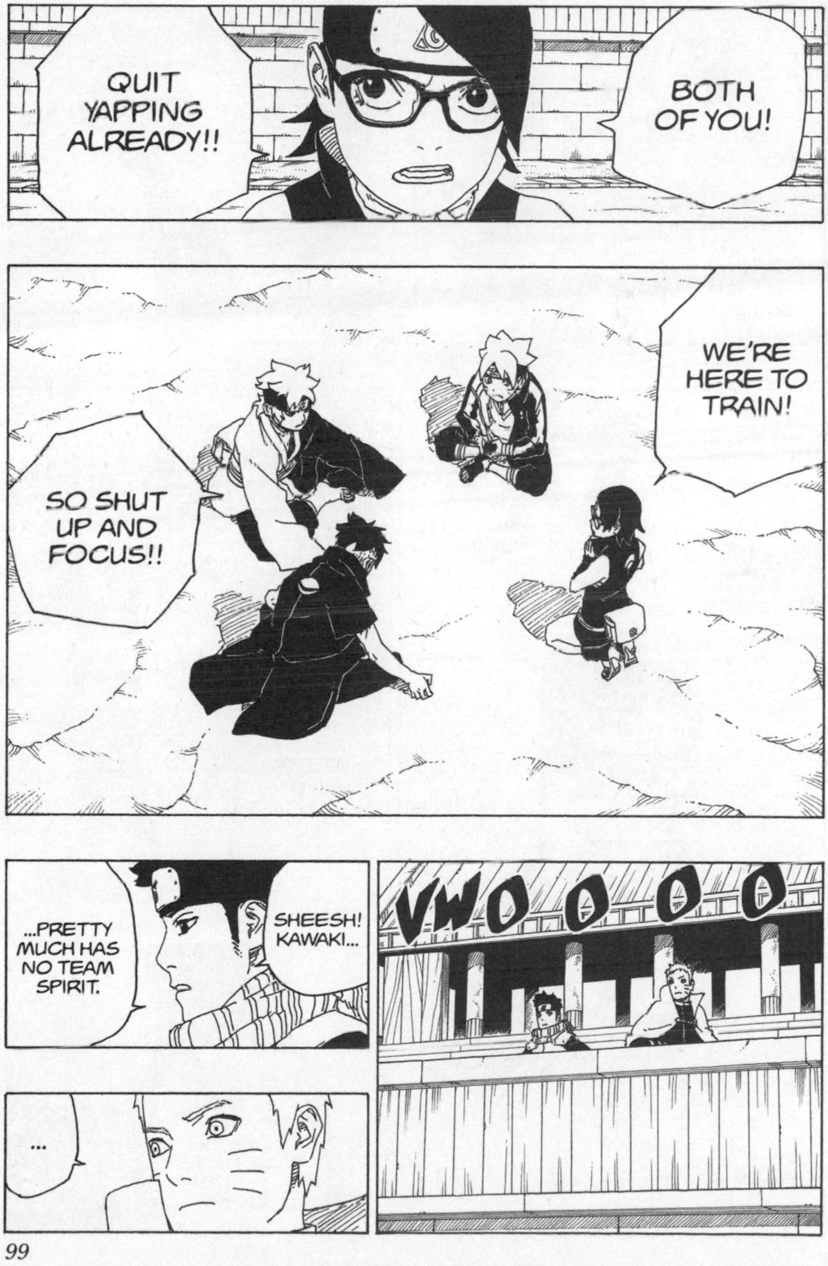
BOTH OF YOU!
QUIT YAPPING ALREADY!!
WE'RE HERE TO TRAIN!
SO SHUT UP AND FOCUS!!
VWOOOO
SHEESH! KAWAKI...
...PRETTY MUCH HAS NO TEAM SPIRIT.
...

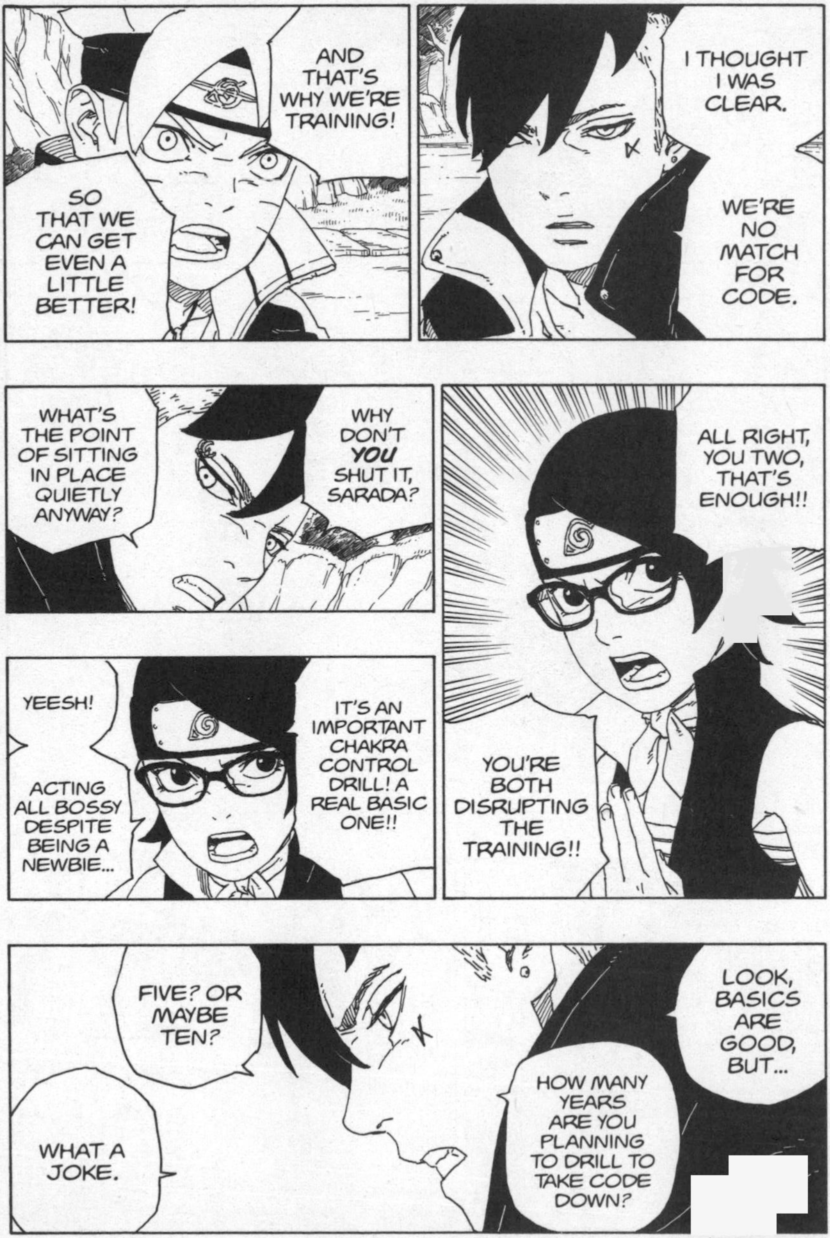
I THOUGHT I WAS CLEAR.
WE'RE NO MATCH FOR CODE.
AND THAT'S WHY WE'RE TRAINING!
SO THAT WE CAN GET EVEN A LITTLE BETTER!
ALL RIGHT, YOU TWO, THAT'S ENOUGH!!
YOU'RE BOTH DISRUPTING THE TRAINING!!
WHY DON'T *YOU* SHUT IT, SARADA?
WHAT'S THE POINT OF SITTING IN PLACE QUIETLY ANYWAY?
IT'S AN IMPORTANT CHAKRA CONTROL DRILL! A REAL BASIC ONE!!
YEESH!
ACTING ALL BOSSY DESPITE BEING A NEWBIE...
LOOK, BASICS ARE GOOD, BUT...
HOW MANY YEARS ARE YOU PLANNING TO DRILL TO TAKE CODE DOWN?
FIVE? OR MAYBE TEN?
WHAT A JOKE.

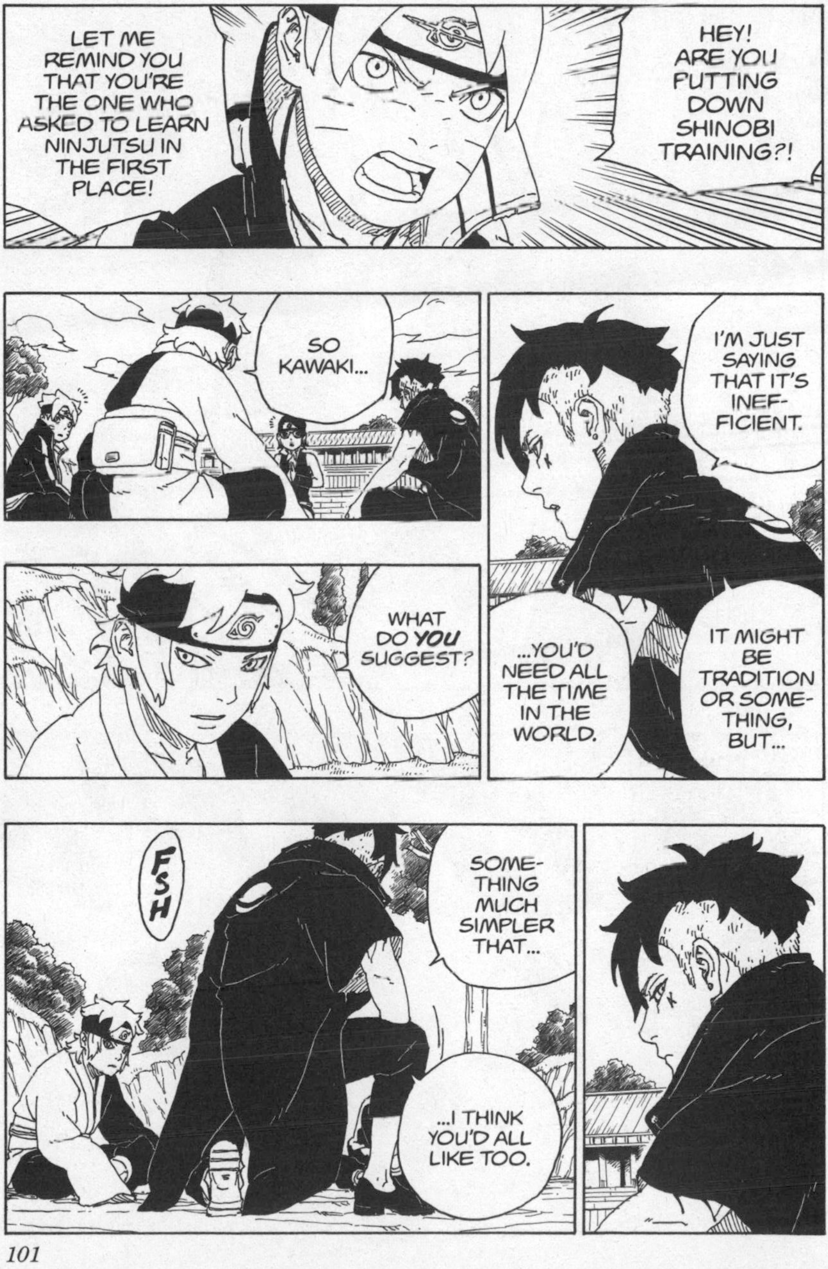
HEY! ARE YOU PUTTING DOWN SHINOBI TRAINING?!
LET ME REMIND YOU THAT YOU'RE THE ONE WHO ASKED TO LEARN NINJUTSU IN THE FIRST PLACE!
I'M JUST SAYING THAT IT'S INEF-FICIENT.
IT MIGHT BE TRADITION OR SOME-THING, BUT...
...YOU'D NEED ALL THE TIME IN THE WORLD.
SO KAWAKI...
WHAT DO ***YOU*** SUGGEST?
SOME-THING MUCH SIMPLER THAT...
FSH
...I THINK YOU'D ALL LIKE TOO.

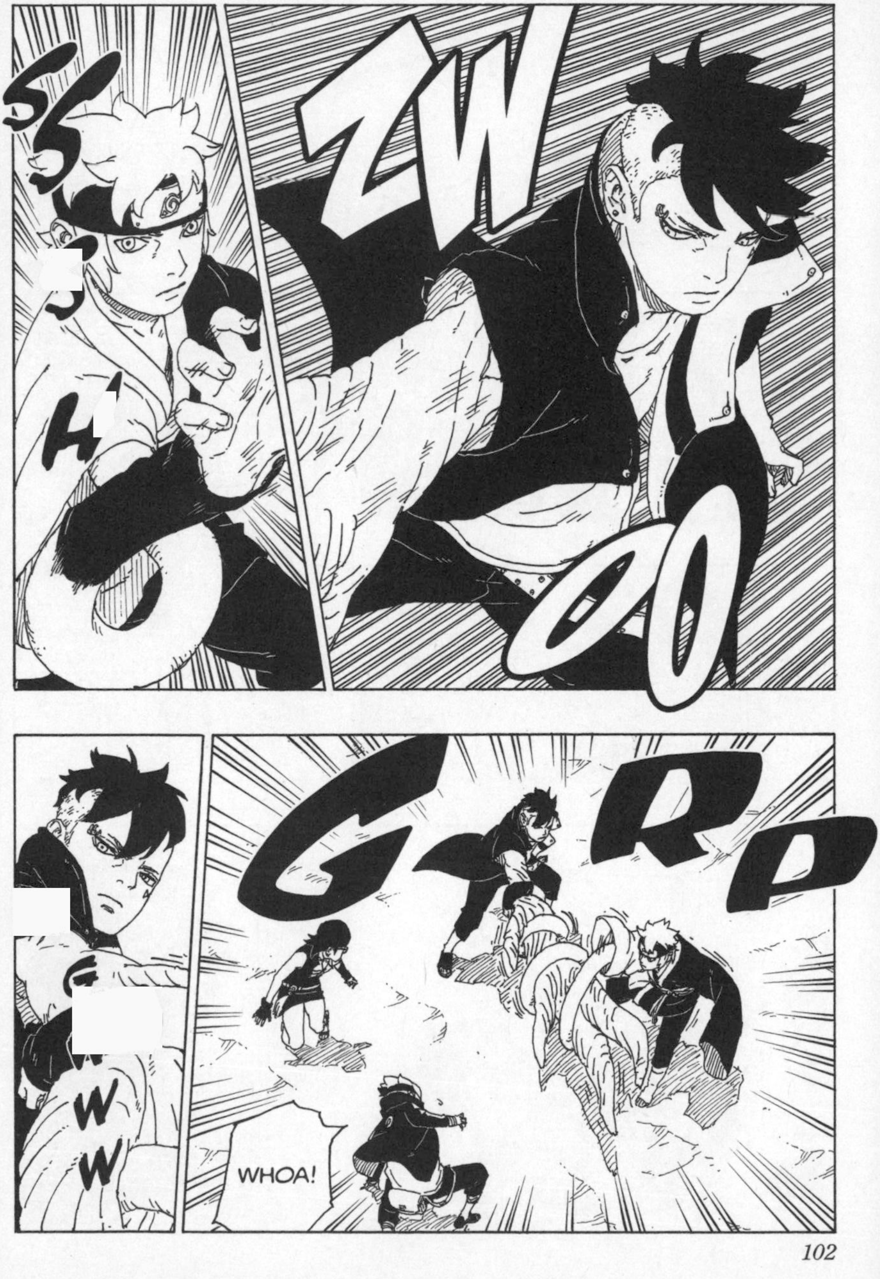
ZWOO
GRP
WHOA!

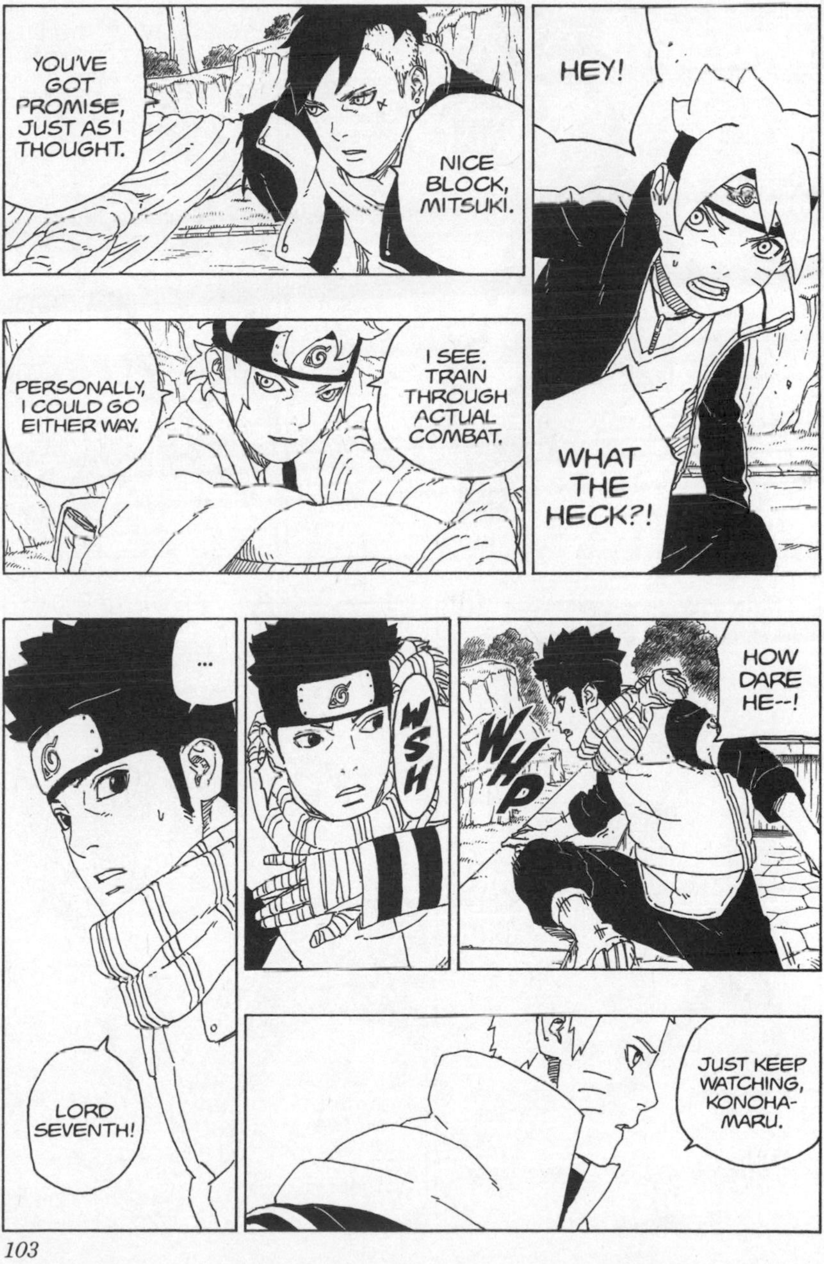
HEY!
WHAT THE HECK?!
NICE BLOCK, MITSUKI.
YOU'VE GOT PROMISE, JUST AS I THOUGHT.
I SEE. TRAIN THROUGH ACTUAL COMBAT.
PERSONALLY, I COULD GO EITHER WAY.
HOW DARE HE--!
WHP
WSH
JUST KEEP WATCHING, KONOHA-MARU.
...
LORD SEVENTH!

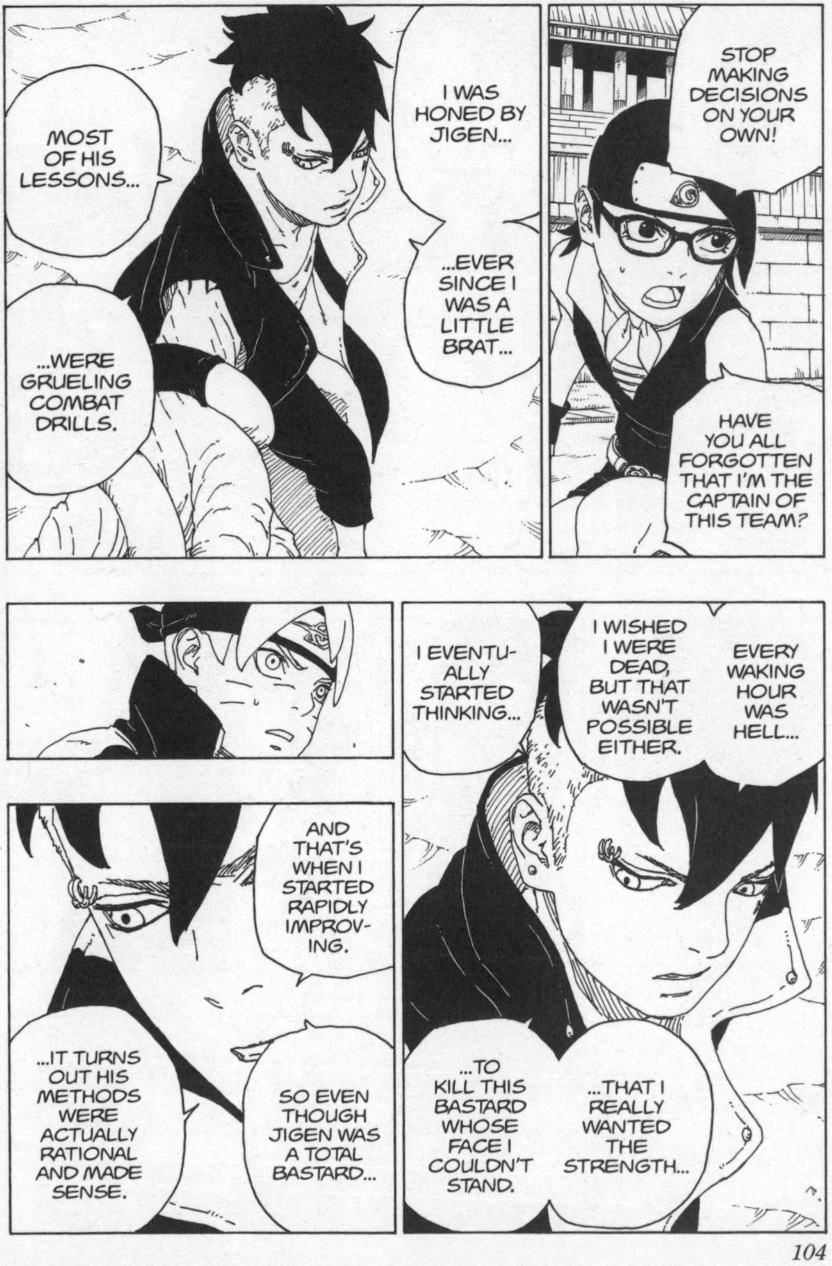

STOP MAKING DECISIONS ON YOUR OWN!
HAVE YOU ALL FORGOTTEN THAT I'M THE CAPTAIN OF THIS TEAM?
I WAS HONED BY JIGEN...
...EVER SINCE I WAS A LITTLE BRAT...
MOST OF HIS LESSONS...
...WERE GRUELING COMBAT DRILLS.
EVERY WAKING HOUR WAS HELL...
I WISHED I WERE DEAD, BUT THAT WASN'T POSSIBLE EITHER.
I EVENTUALLY STARTED THINKING...
...THAT I REALLY WANTED THE STRENGTH...
...TO KILL THIS BASTARD WHOSE FACE I COULDN'T STAND.
AND THAT'S WHEN I STARTED RAPIDLY IMPROVING.
SO EVEN THOUGH JIGEN WAS A TOTAL BASTARD...
...IT TURNS OUT HIS METHODS WERE ACTUALLY RATIONAL AND MADE SENSE.

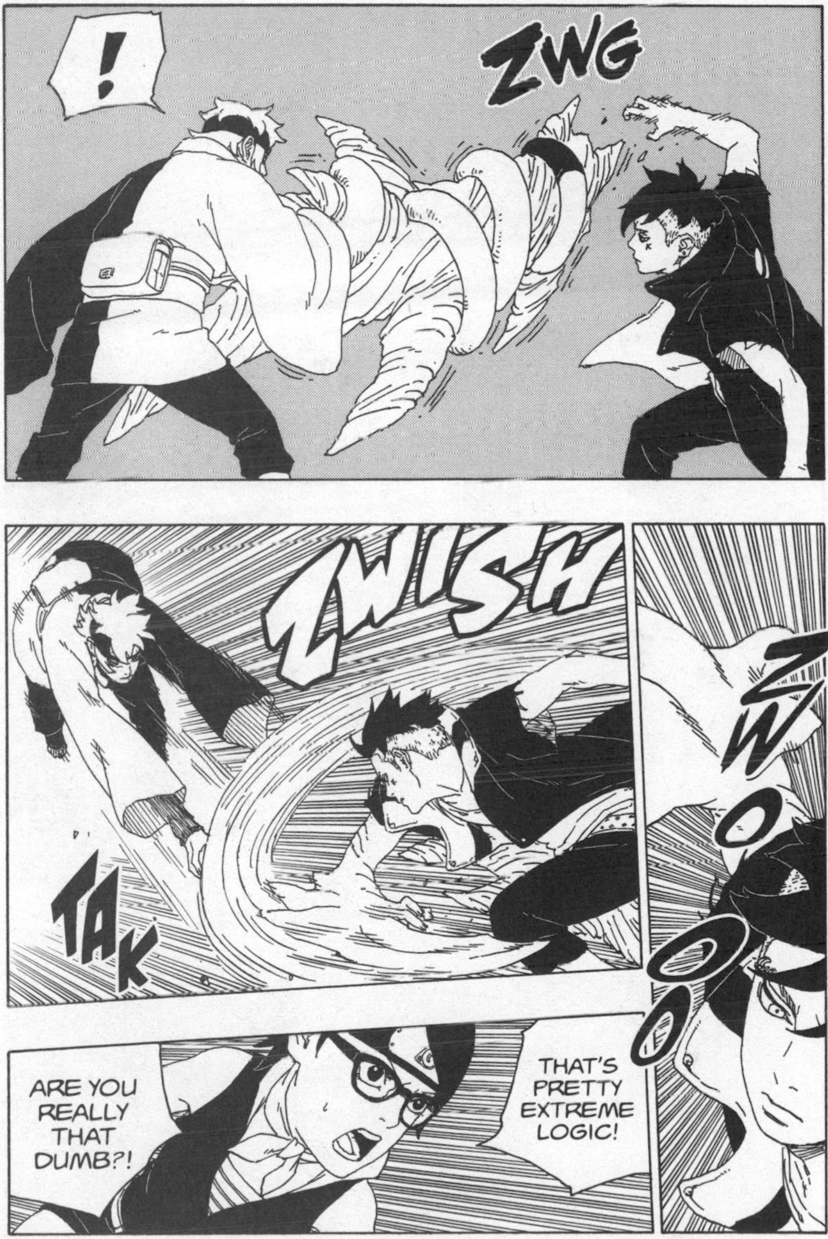
ZWG
!
ZWOOOOO
ZWISH
TAK
THAT'S PRETTY EXTREME LOGIC!
ARE YOU REALLY THAT DUMB?!

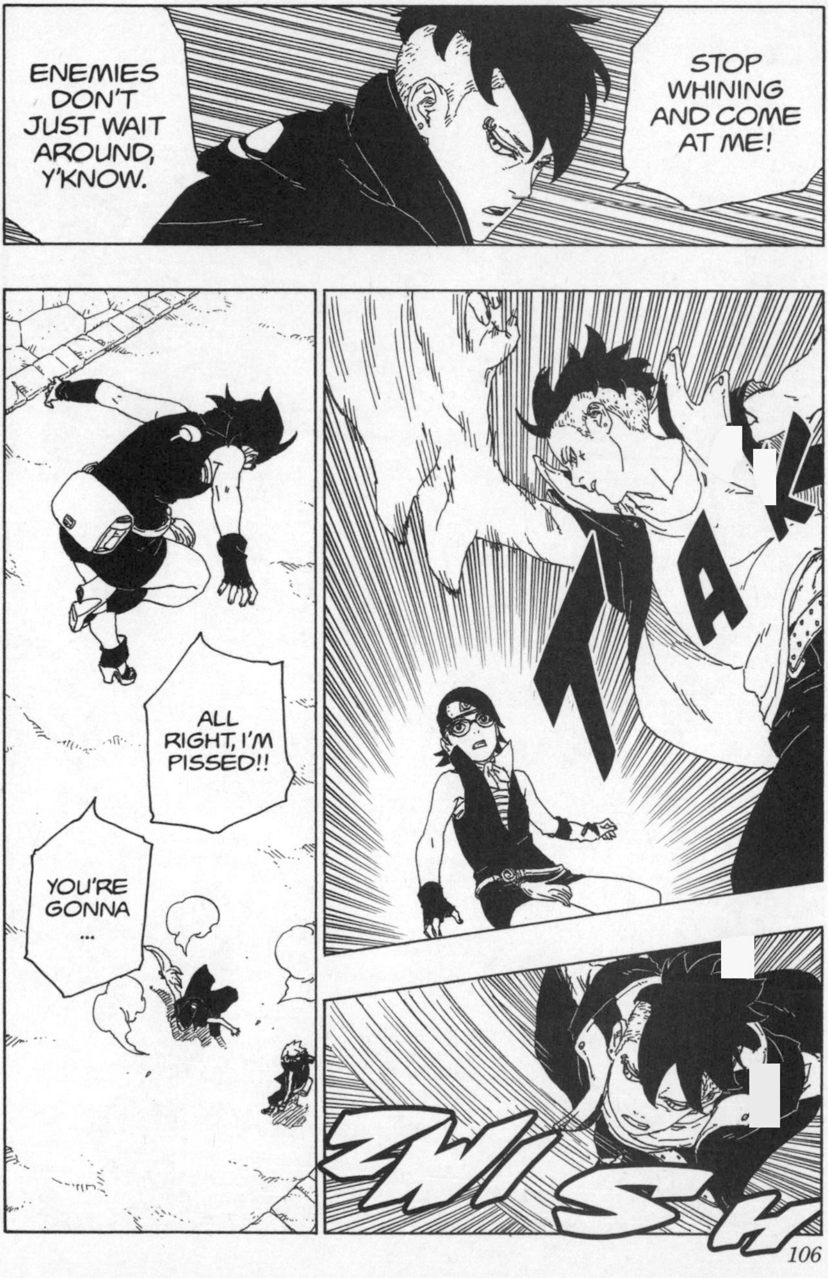
STOP WHINING AND COME AT ME!
ENEMIES DON'T JUST WAIT AROUND, Y'KNOW.
TAK
ZWISH
ALL RIGHT, I'M PISSED!!
YOU'RE GONNA ...

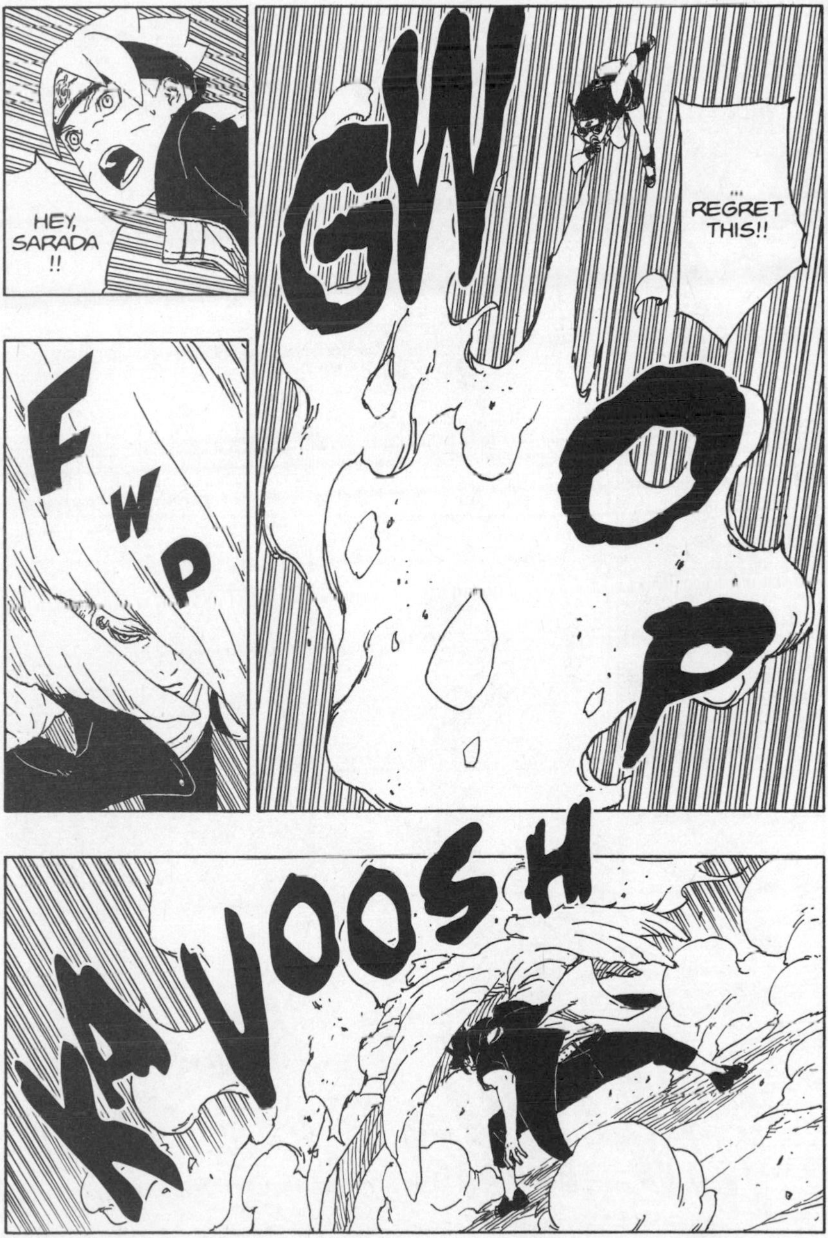
...REGRET THIS!!
GWOOP
HEY, SARADA !!
FWP
KAVOOSH

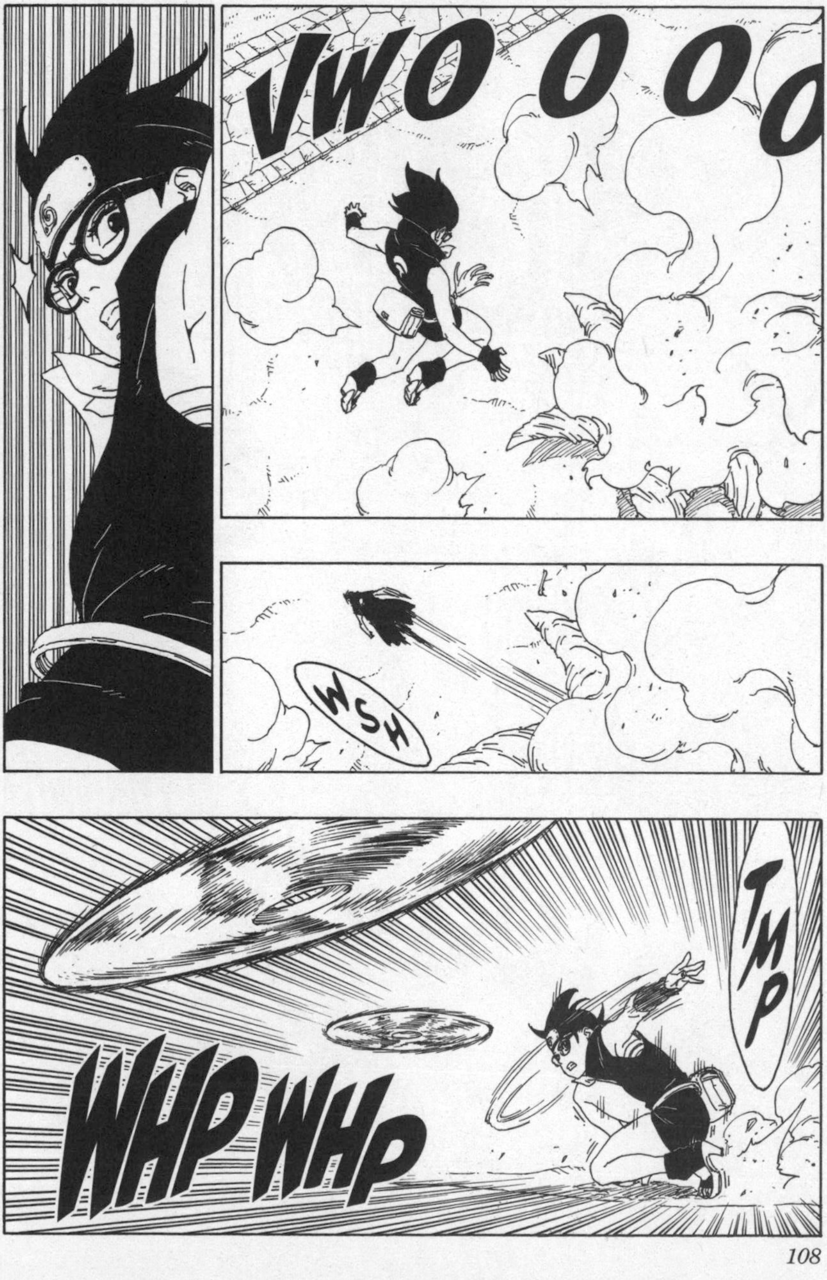
VWO O O O
WSH
TMP
WHP WHP

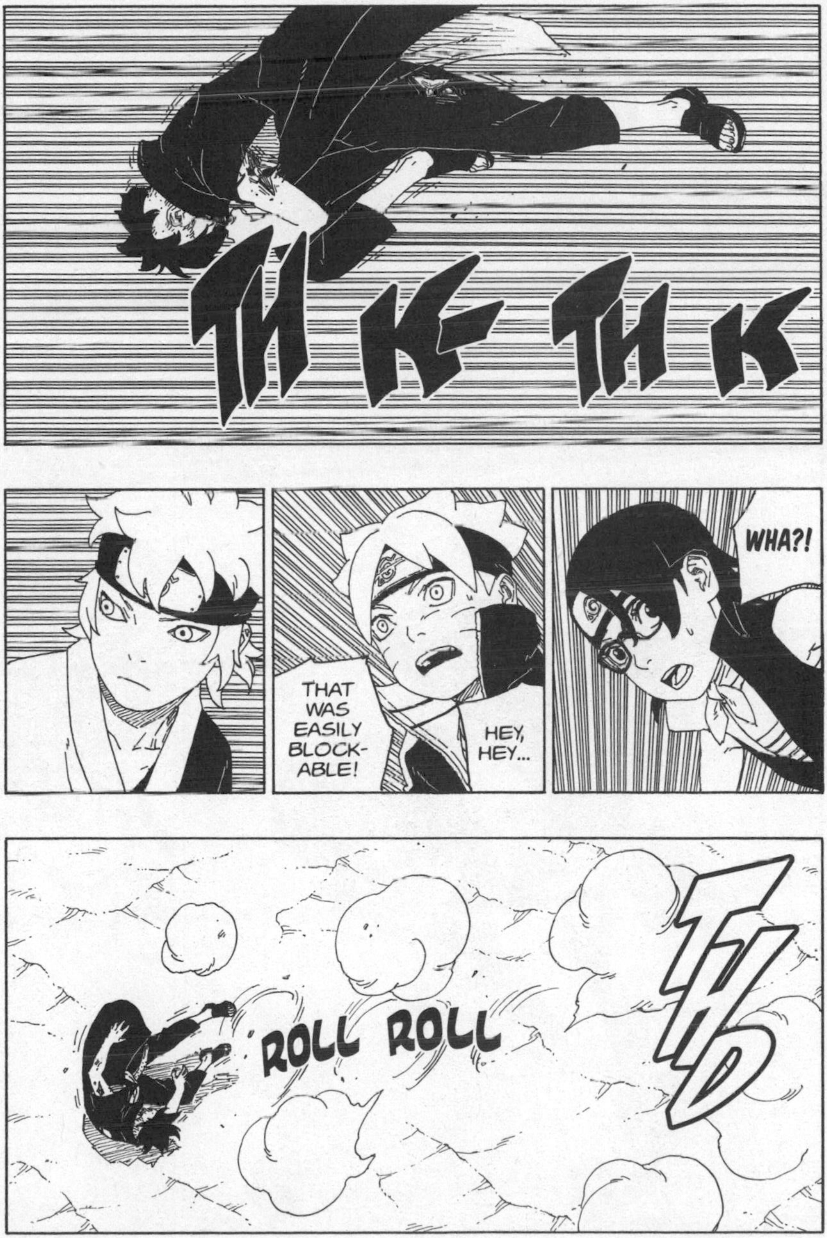
TH K- TH K
WHA?!
HEY, HEY...
THAT WAS EASILY BLOCKABLE!
THD
ROLL ROLL

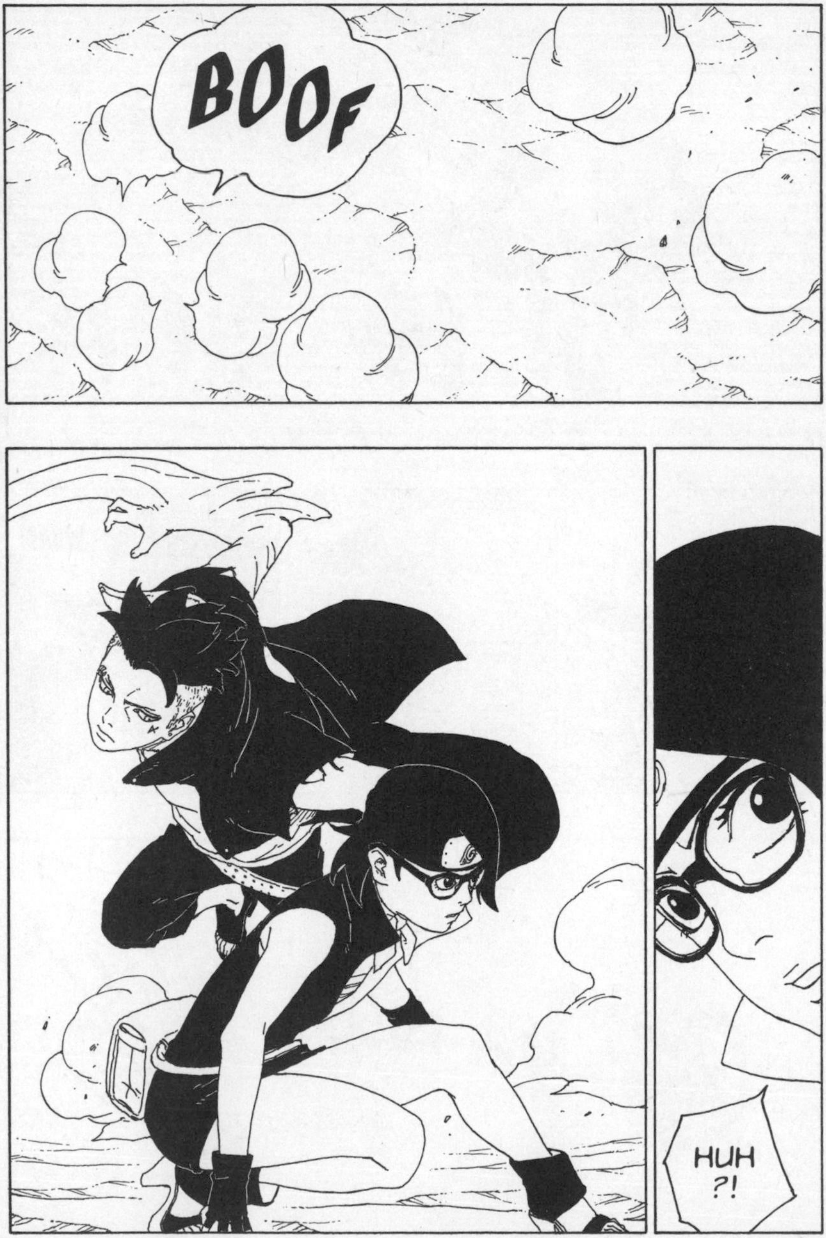
BOOF
HUH ?!

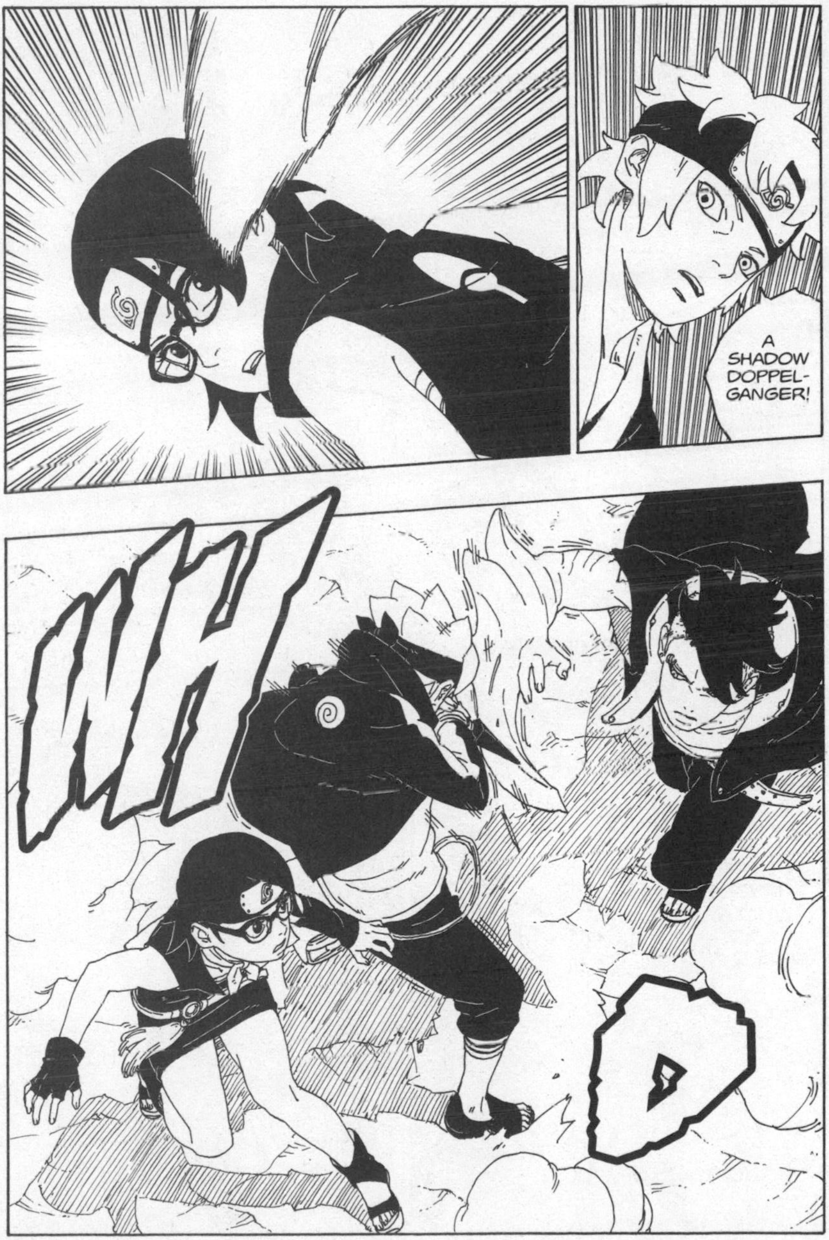
A SHADOW DOPPEL-GANGER!

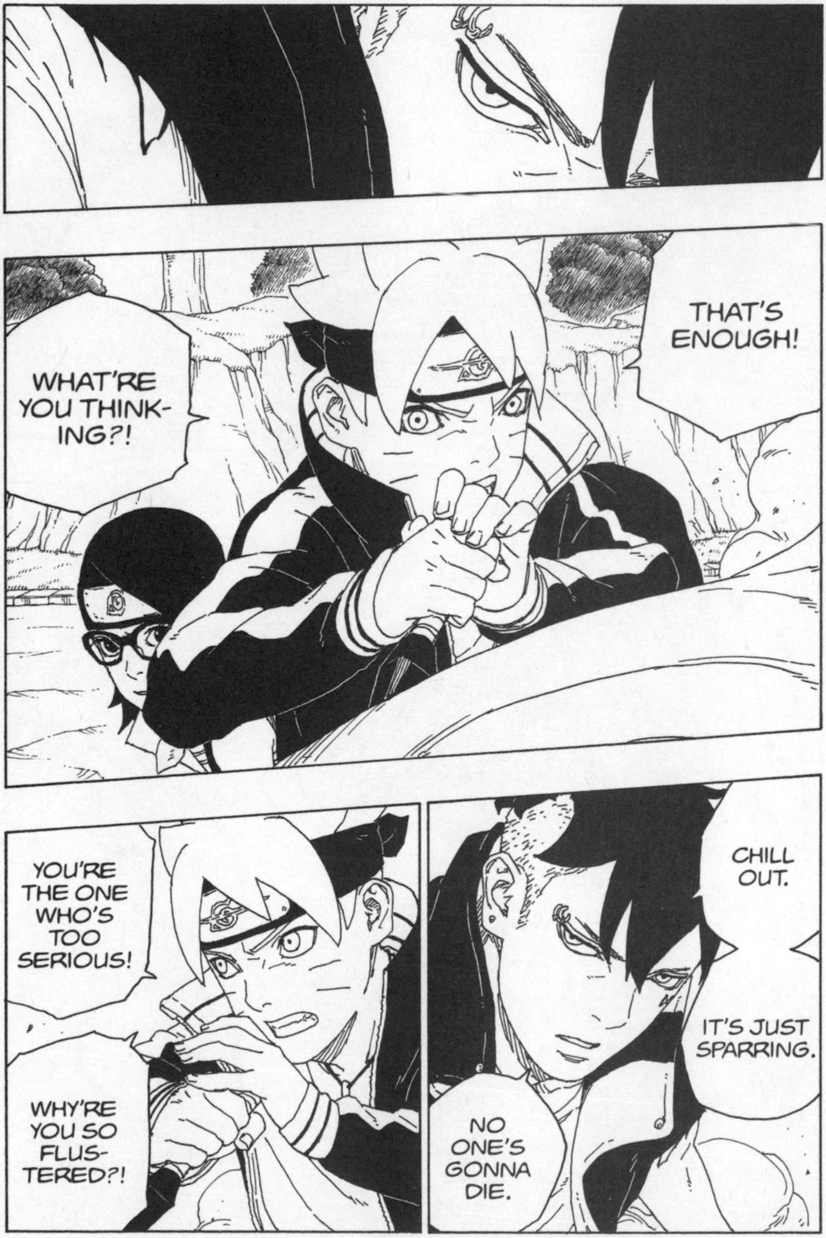
THAT'S ENOUGH!
WHAT'RE YOU THINKING?!
CHILL OUT.
IT'S JUST SPARRING.
NO ONE'S GONNA DIE.
YOU'RE THE ONE WHO'S TOO SERIOUS!
WHY'RE YOU SO FLUSTERED?!

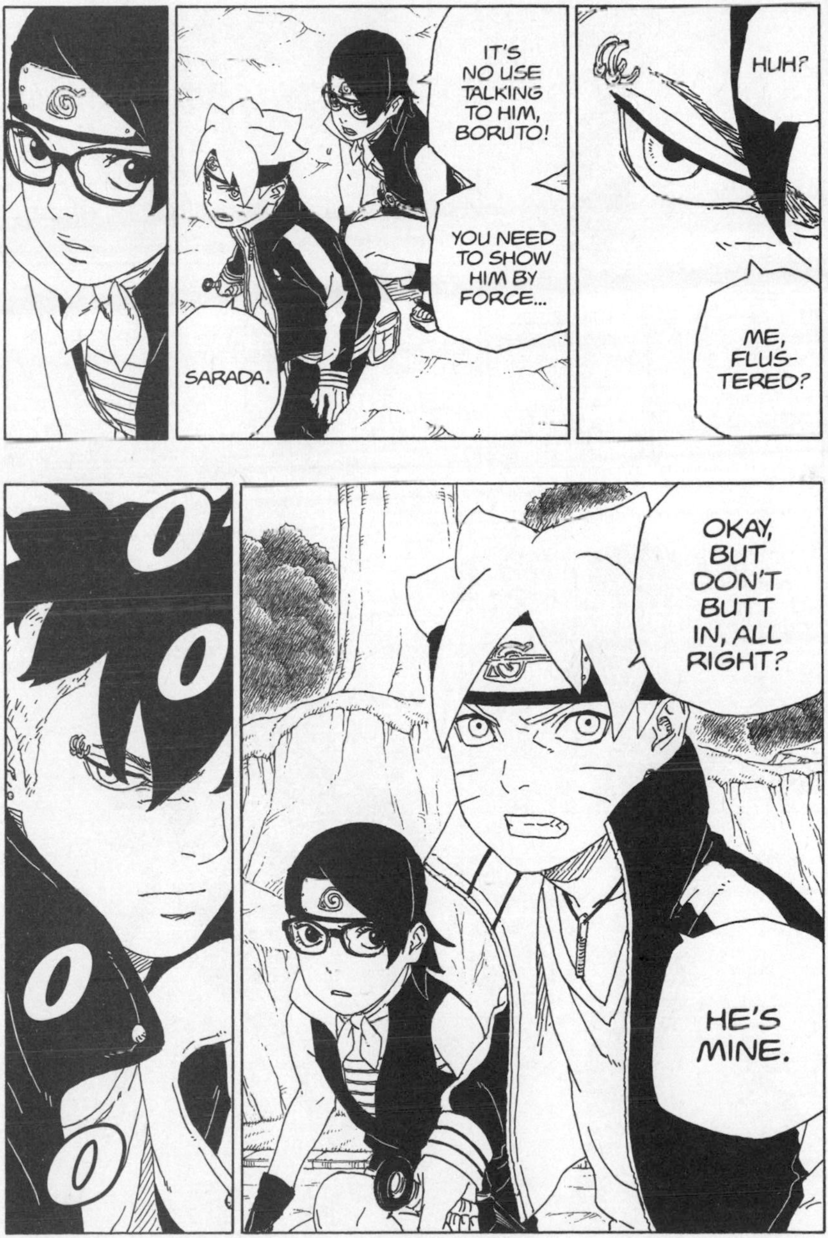
HUH?
ME, FLUSTERED?
IT'S NO USE TALKING TO HIM, BORUTO!
YOU NEED TO SHOW HIM BY FORCE...
SARADA.
OKAY, BUT DON'T BUTT IN, ALL RIGHT?
HE'S MINE.

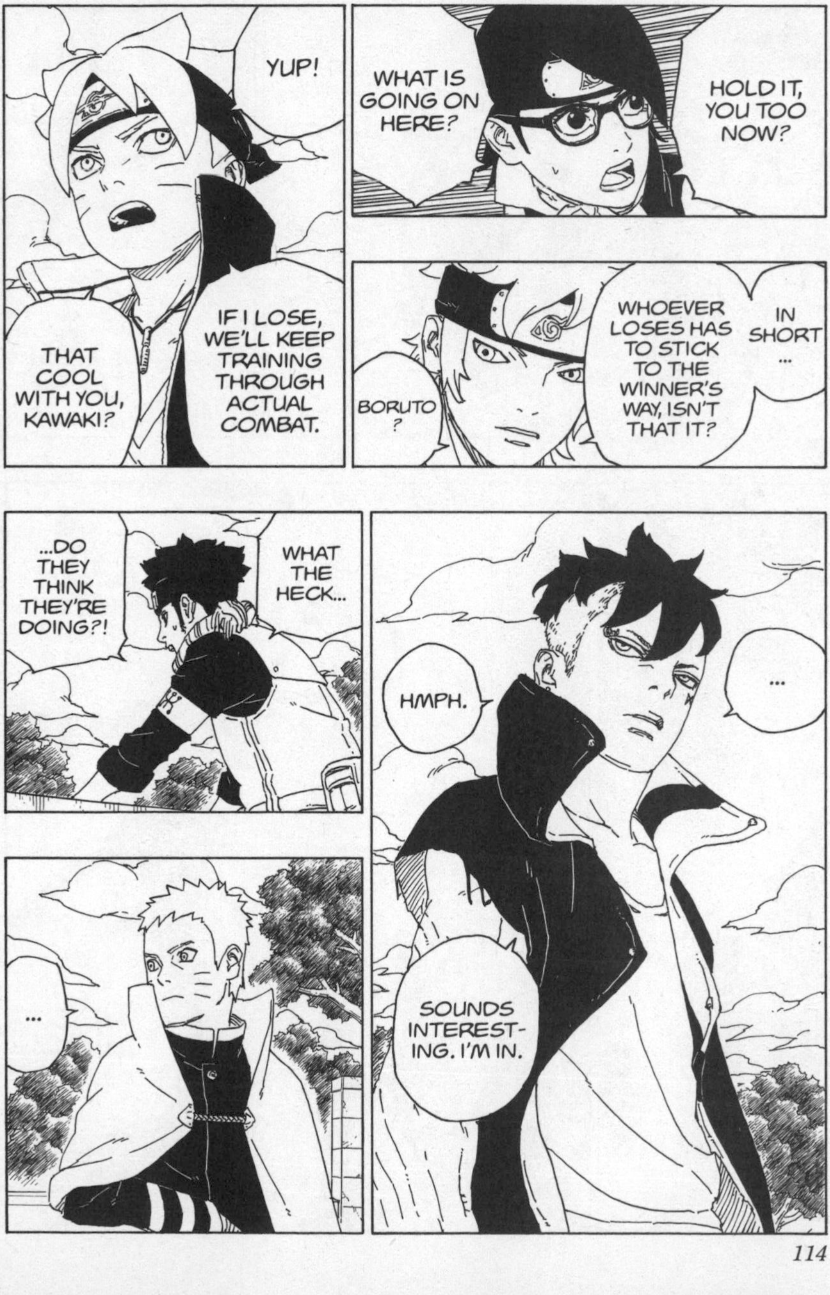
HOLD IT, YOU TOO NOW?
WHAT IS GOING ON HERE?
IN SHORT ...
WHOEVER LOSES HAS TO STICK TO THE WINNER'S WAY, ISN'T THAT IT?
BORUTO ?
YUP!
IF I LOSE, WE'LL KEEP TRAINING THROUGH ACTUAL COMBAT.
THAT COOL WITH YOU, KAWAKI?
...
HMPH.
SOUNDS INTEREST-ING. I'M IN.
WHAT THE HECK...
...DO THEY THINK THEY'RE DOING?!
...

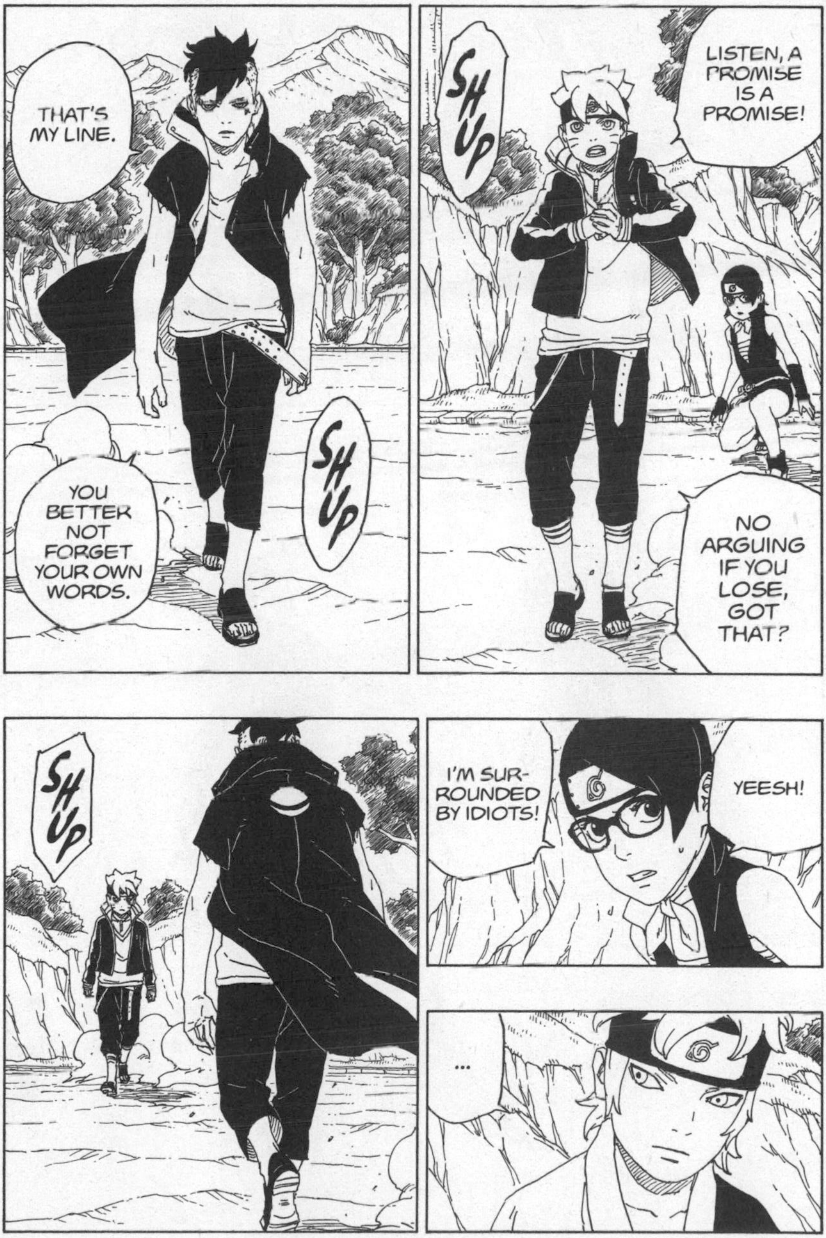
LISTEN, A PROMISE IS A PROMISE!
SHUP
NO ARGUING IF YOU LOSE, GOT THAT?
THAT'S MY LINE.
SHUP
YOU BETTER NOT FORGET YOUR OWN WORDS.
YEESH!
I'M SURROUNDED BY IDIOTS!
...
SHUP

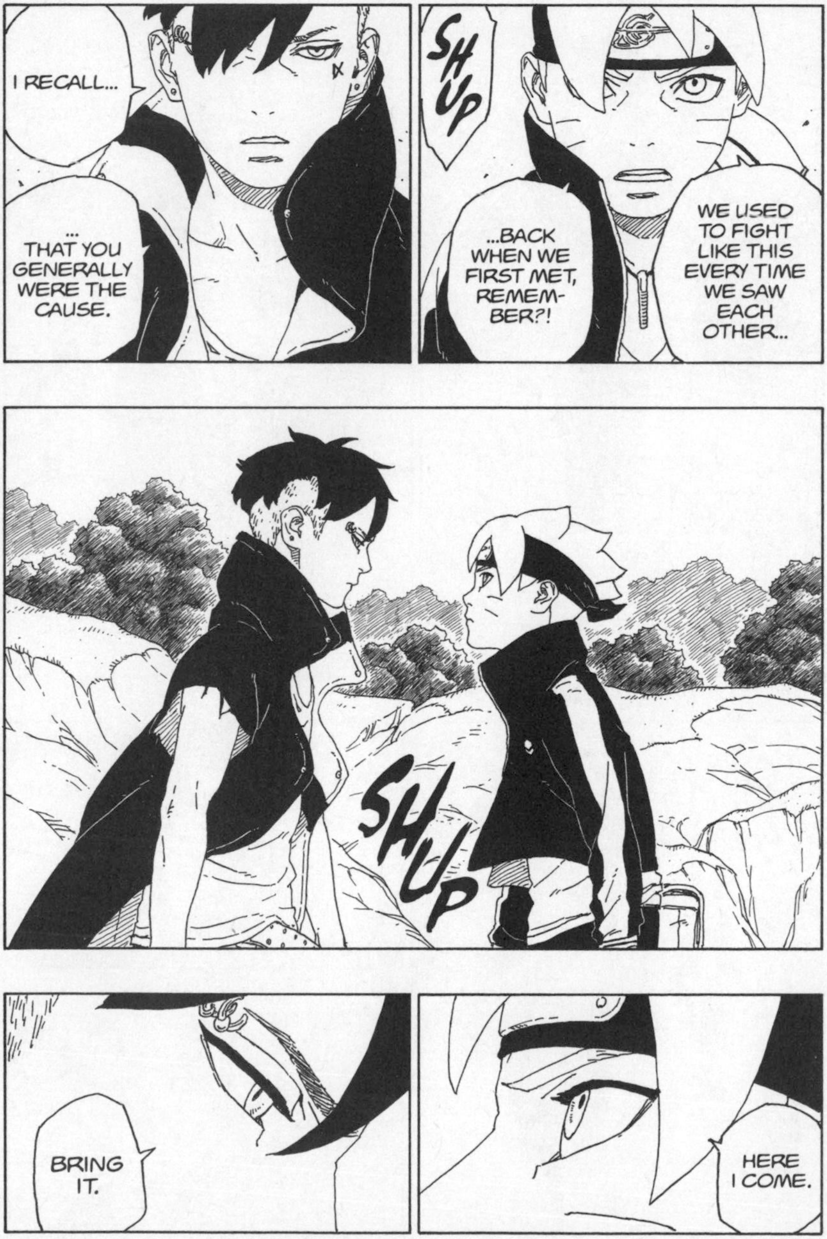
SHUP
WE USED TO FIGHT LIKE THIS EVERY TIME WE SAW EACH OTHER...
...BACK WHEN WE FIRST MET, REMEMBER?!
I RECALL...
...THAT YOU GENERALLY WERE THE CAUSE.
SHUP
HERE I COME.
BRING IT.

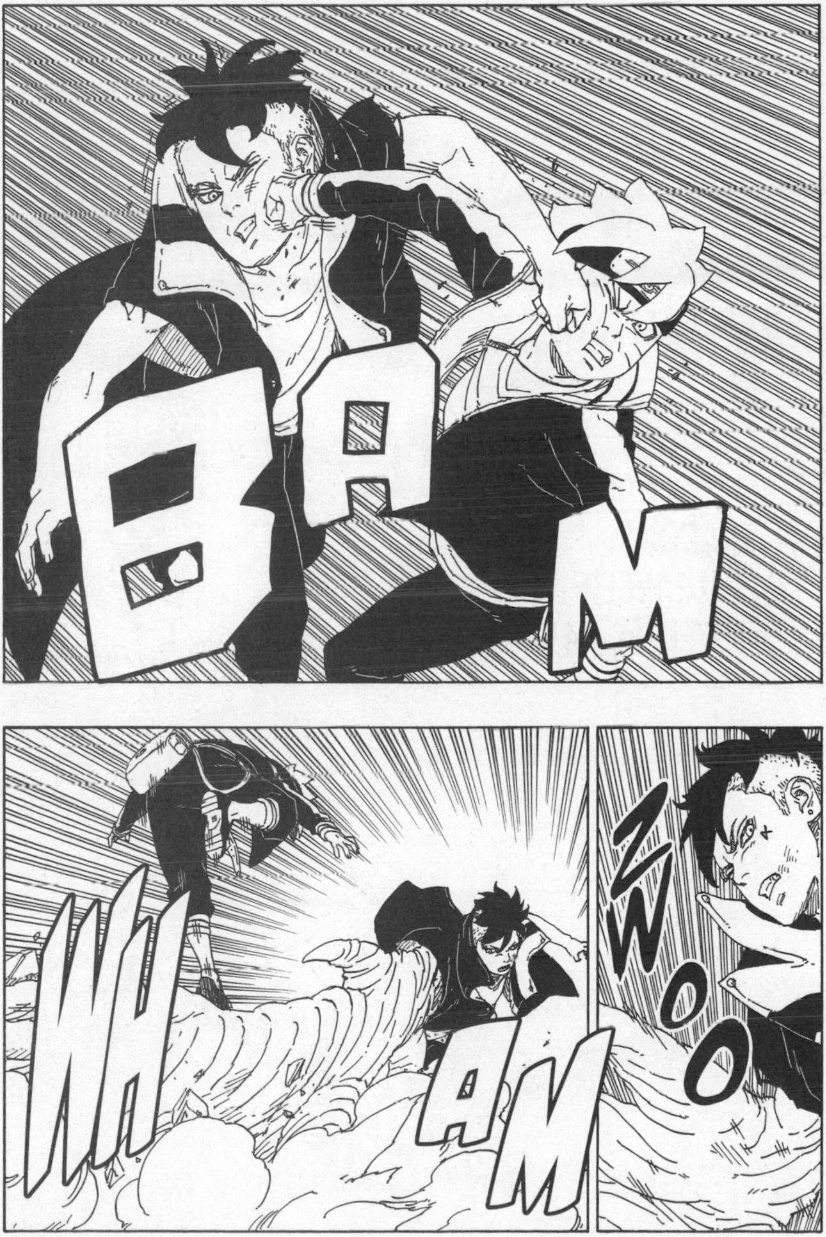
BAM
ZWOOO
WHAM

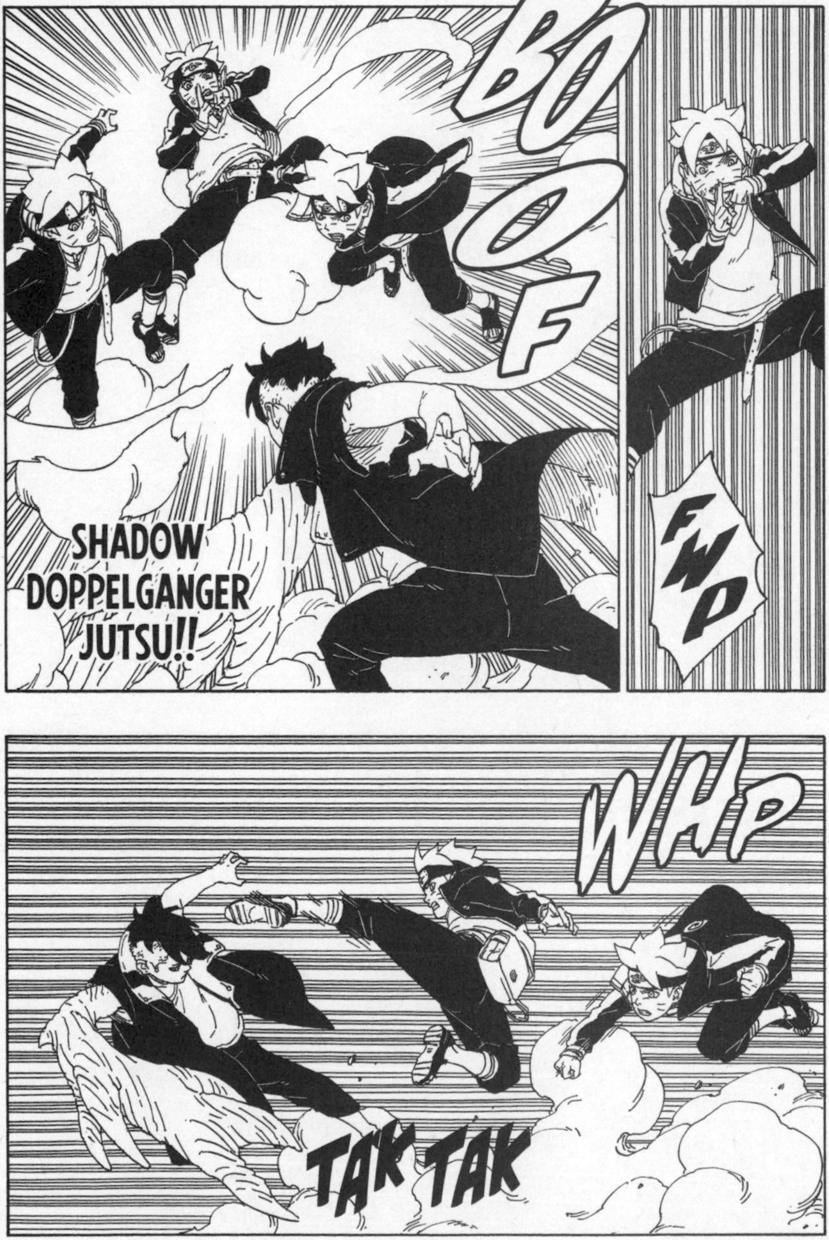
FWP
BOOF
SHADOW DOPPELGANGER JUTSU!!
WHP
TAK TAK

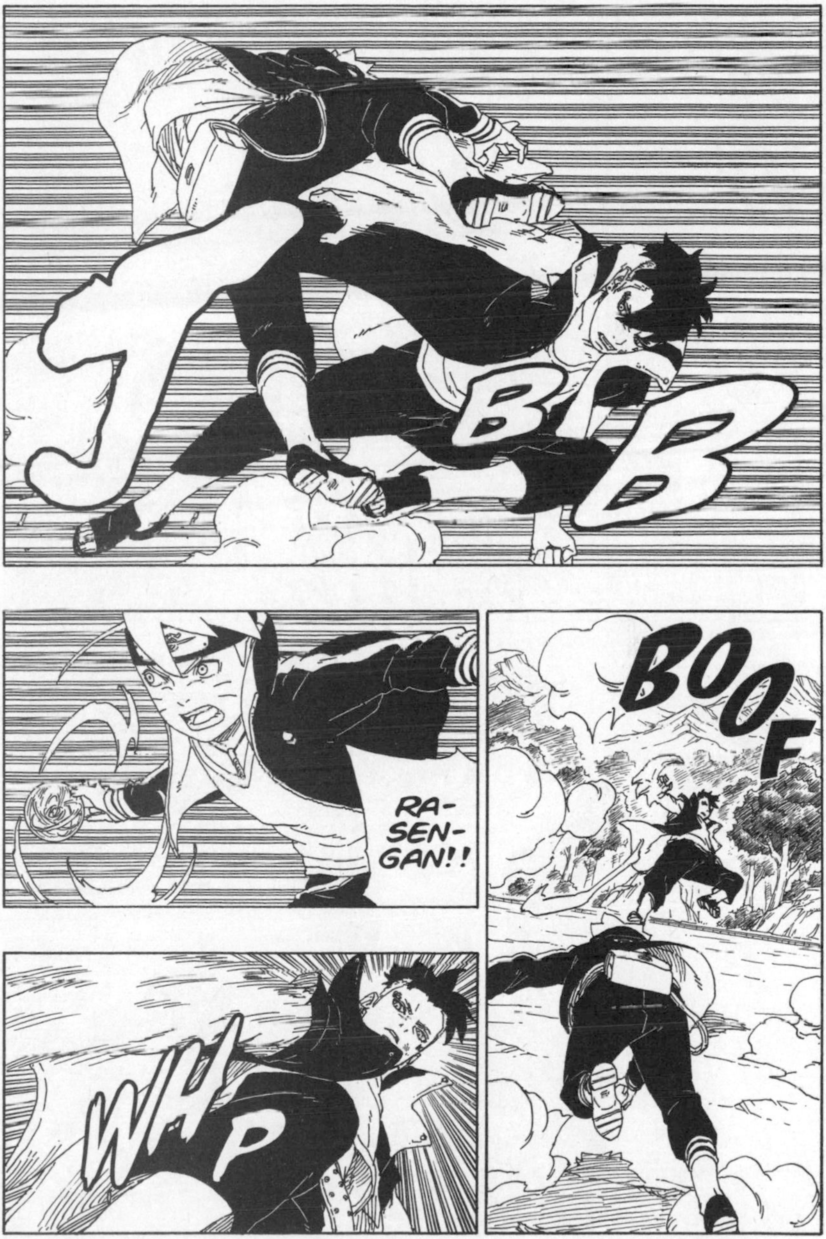
BBB
BOOF
RA-SEN-GAN!!
WHP

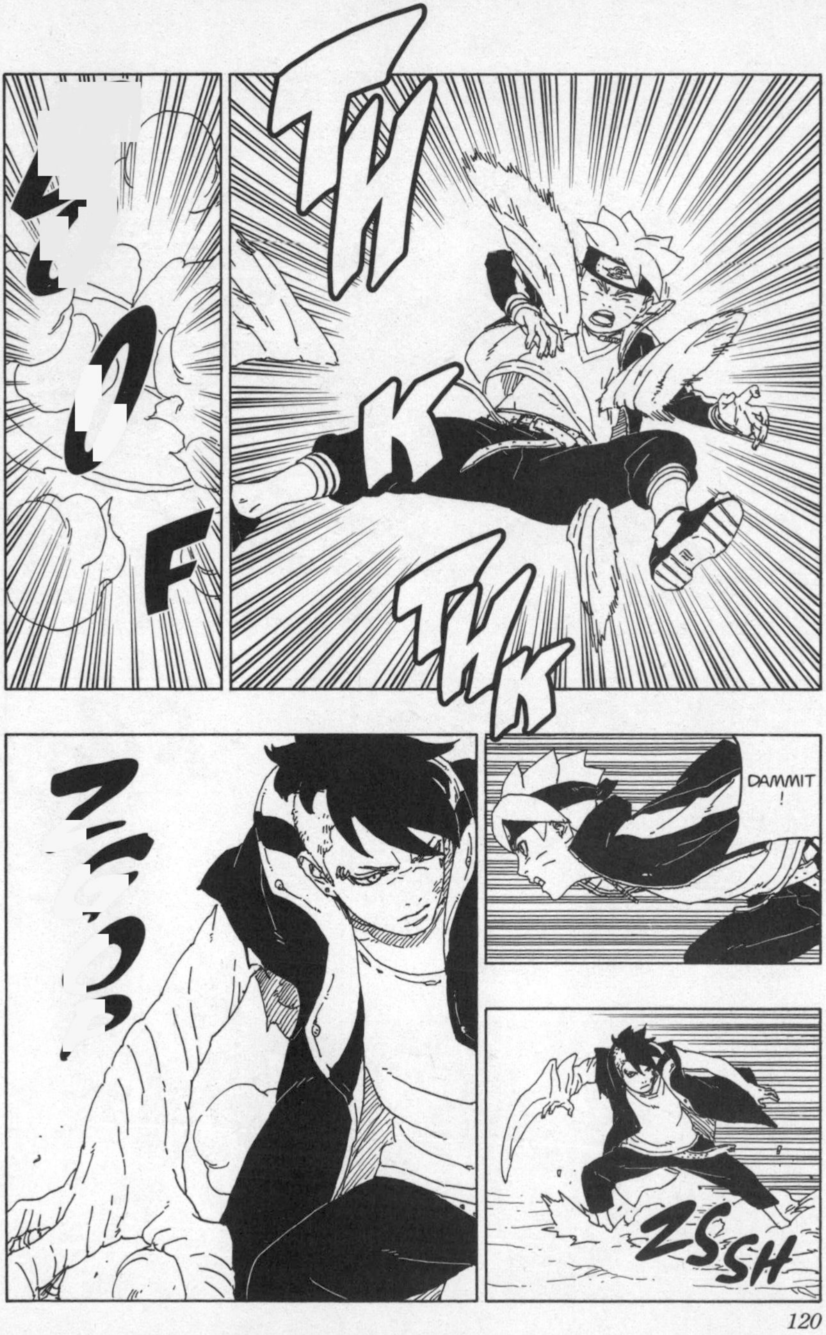
TH
K
THK
F
DAMMIT!
ZSSH

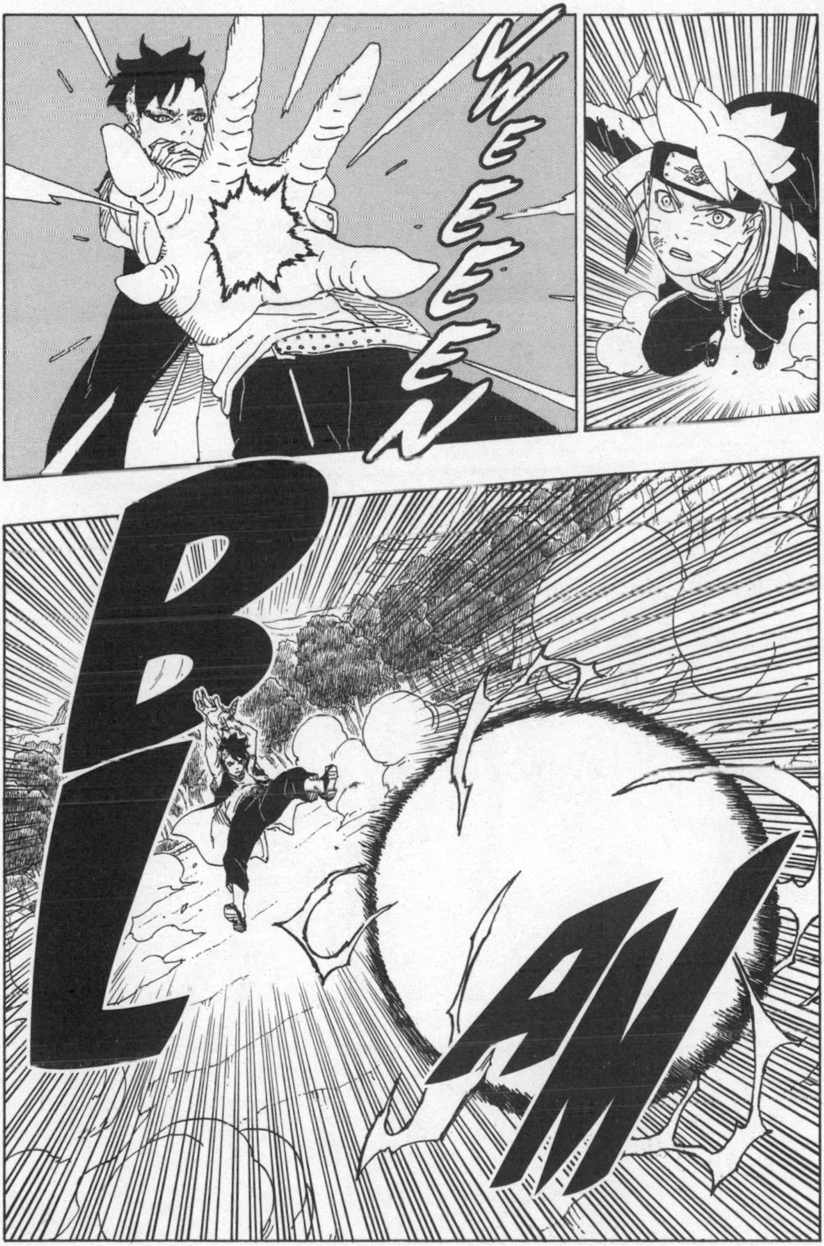
VWEEEEN
BLAM

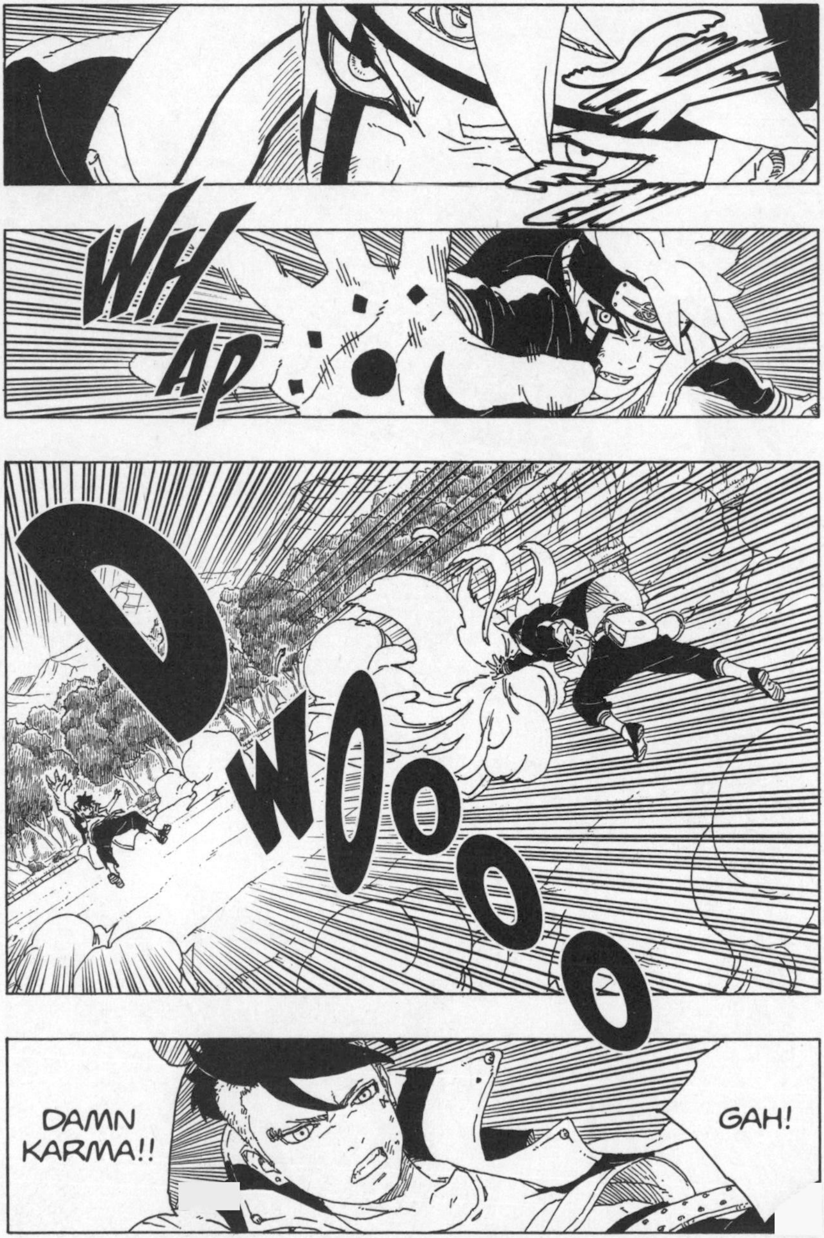
WHAP
DWOOOO
GAH!
DAMN KARMA!!

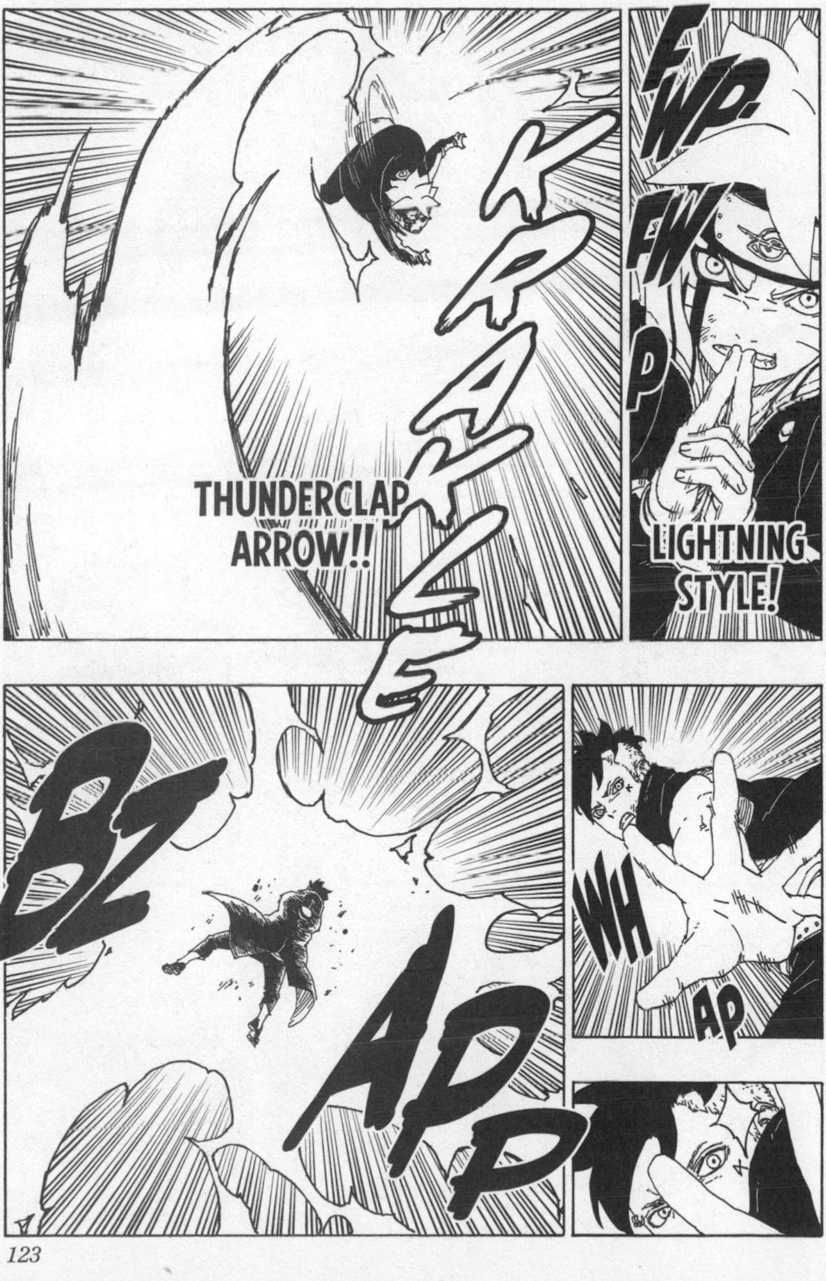
FWP. FWP
LIGHTNING STYLE!
THUNDERCLAP ARROW!!
WHAP
BZAPP

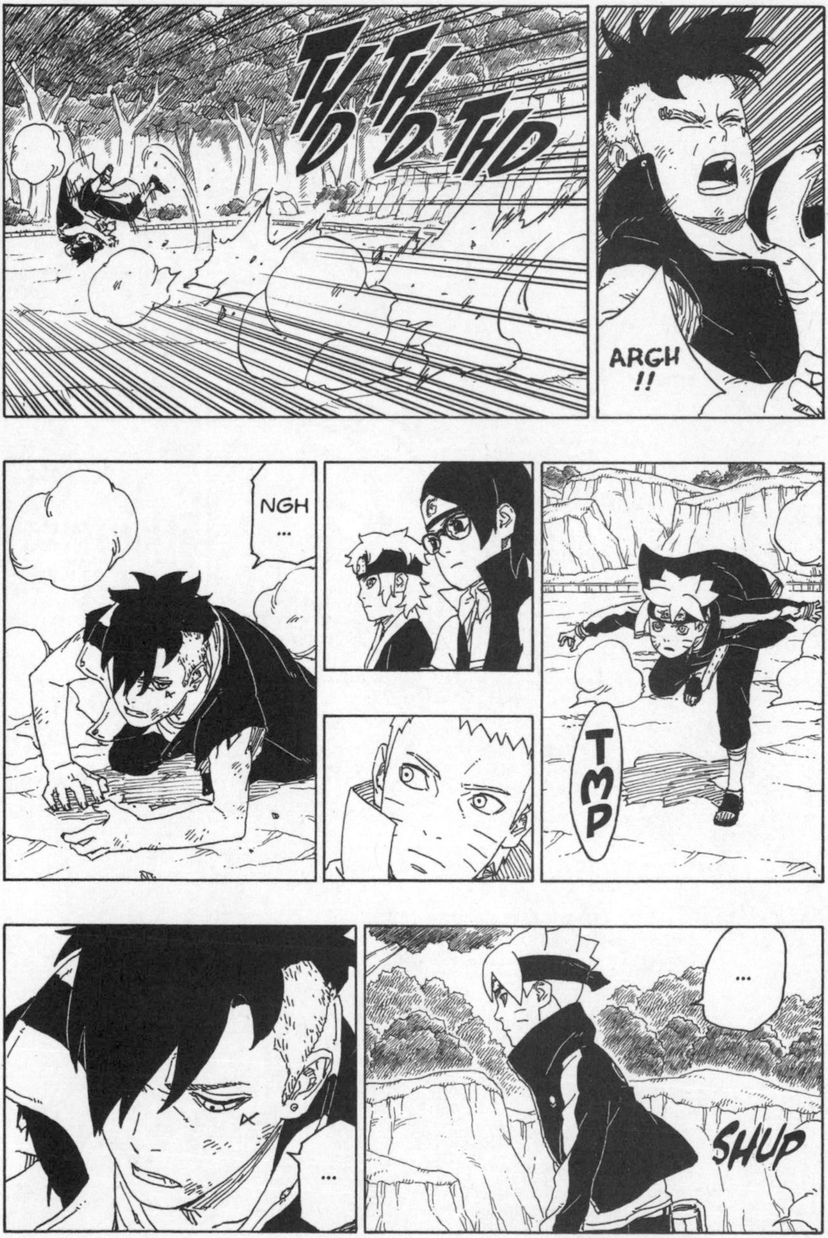
ARGH !!
THD THD THD
TMP
NGH ...
...
SHUP
...

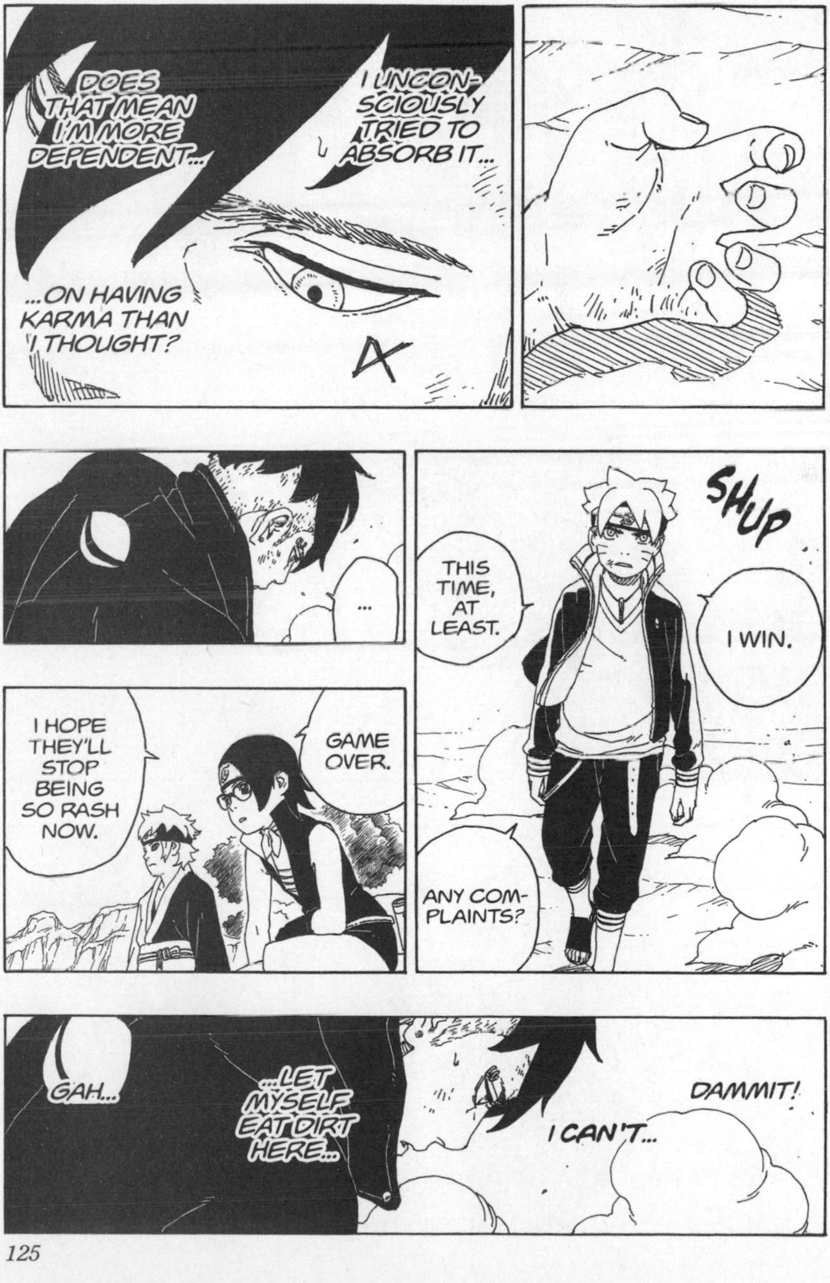
I UNCON-SCIOUSLY TRIED TO ABSORB IT...
DOES THAT MEAN I'M MORE DEPENDENT...
...ON HAVING KARMA THAN I THOUGHT?
SHUP
I WIN.
THIS TIME, AT LEAST.
ANY COM-PLAINTS?
...
GAME OVER.
I HOPE THEY'LL STOP BEING SO RASH NOW.
DAMMIT!
I CAN'T...
...LET MYSELF EAT DIRT HERE...
GAH...

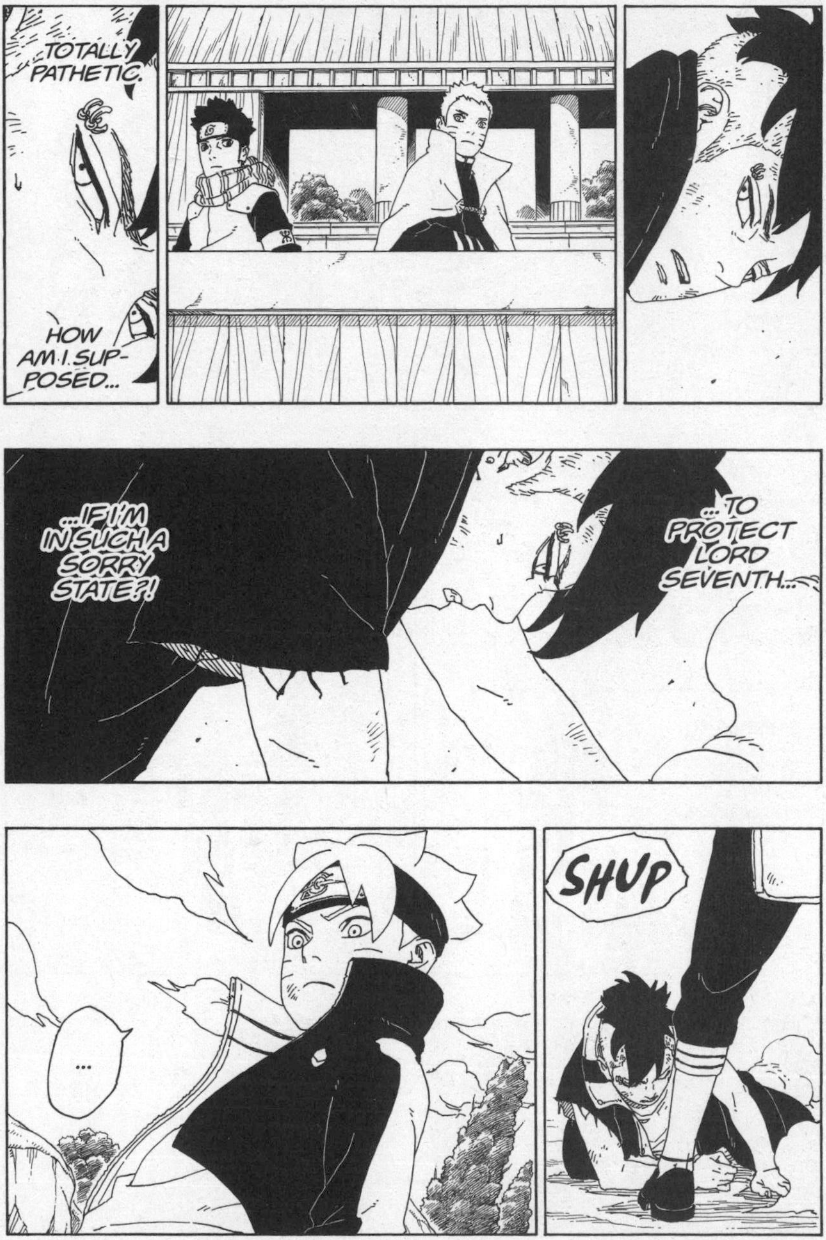
TOTALLY PATHETIC.
HOW AM I SUP-POSED...
...TO PROTECT LORD SEVENTH...
...IF I'M IN SUCH A SORRY STATE?!
SHUP
...

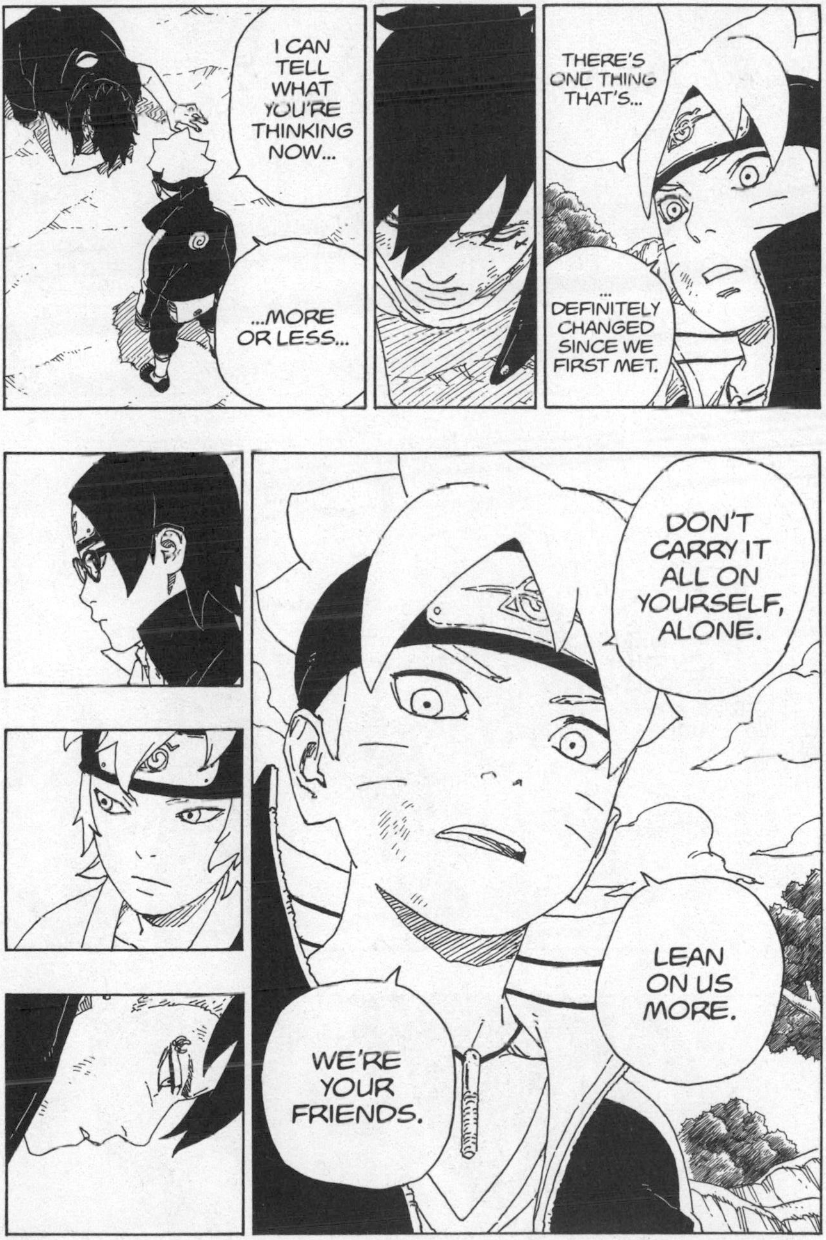
THERE'S ONE THING THAT'S...
... DEFINITELY CHANGED SINCE WE FIRST MET.
I CAN TELL WHAT YOU'RE THINKING NOW...
...MORE OR LESS...
DON'T CARRY IT ALL ON YOURSELF, ALONE.
LEAN ON US MORE.
WE'RE YOUR FRIENDS.

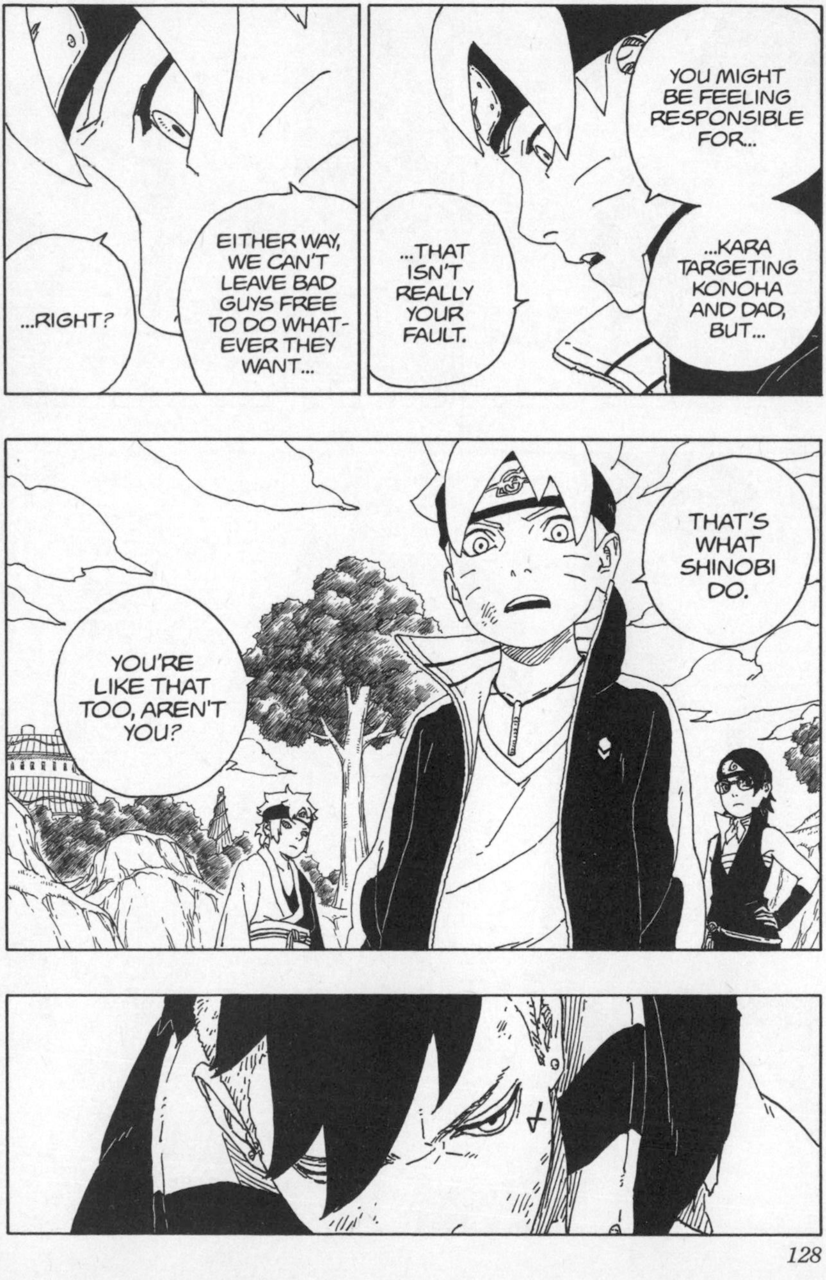
YOU MIGHT BE FEELING RESPONSIBLE FOR...
...KARA TARGETING KONOHA AND DAD, BUT...
...THAT ISN'T REALLY YOUR FAULT.
EITHER WAY, WE CAN'T LEAVE BAD GUYS FREE TO DO WHAT-EVER THEY WANT...
...RIGHT?
THAT'S WHAT SHINOBI DO.
YOU'RE LIKE THAT TOO, AREN'T YOU?

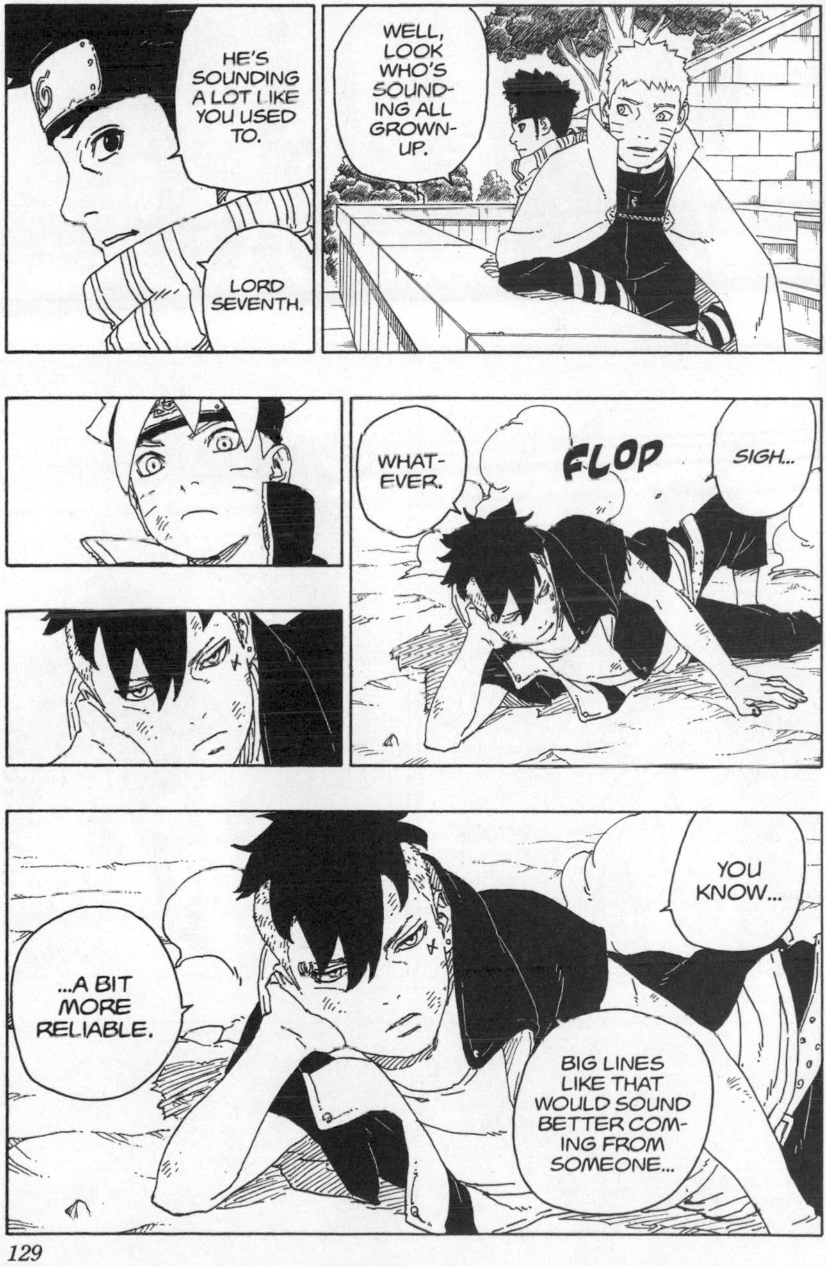
WELL, LOOK WHO'S SOUND-ING ALL GROWN-UP.
HE'S SOUNDING A LOT LIKE YOU USED TO.
LORD SEVENTH.
SIGH...
FLOP
WHAT-EVER.
YOU KNOW...
BIG LINES LIKE THAT WOULD SOUND BETTER COM-ING FROM SOMEONE...
...A BIT MORE RELIABLE.

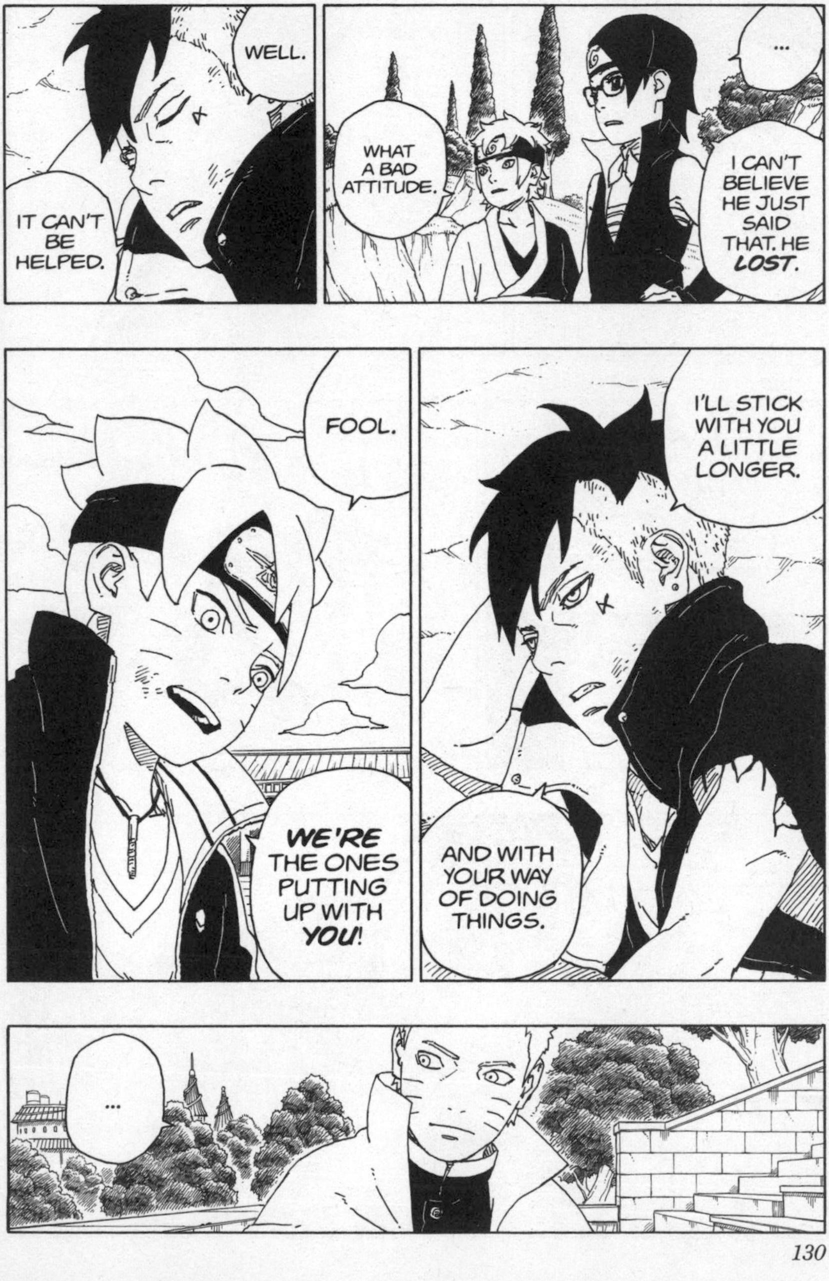
...
I CAN'T BELIEVE HE JUST SAID THAT. HE ***LOST.***
WHAT A BAD ATTITUDE.
WELL.
IT CAN'T BE HELPED.
I'LL STICK WITH YOU A LITTLE LONGER.
AND WITH YOUR WAY OF DOING THINGS.
FOOL.
WE'RE THE ONES PUTTING UP WITH ***YOU***!
...

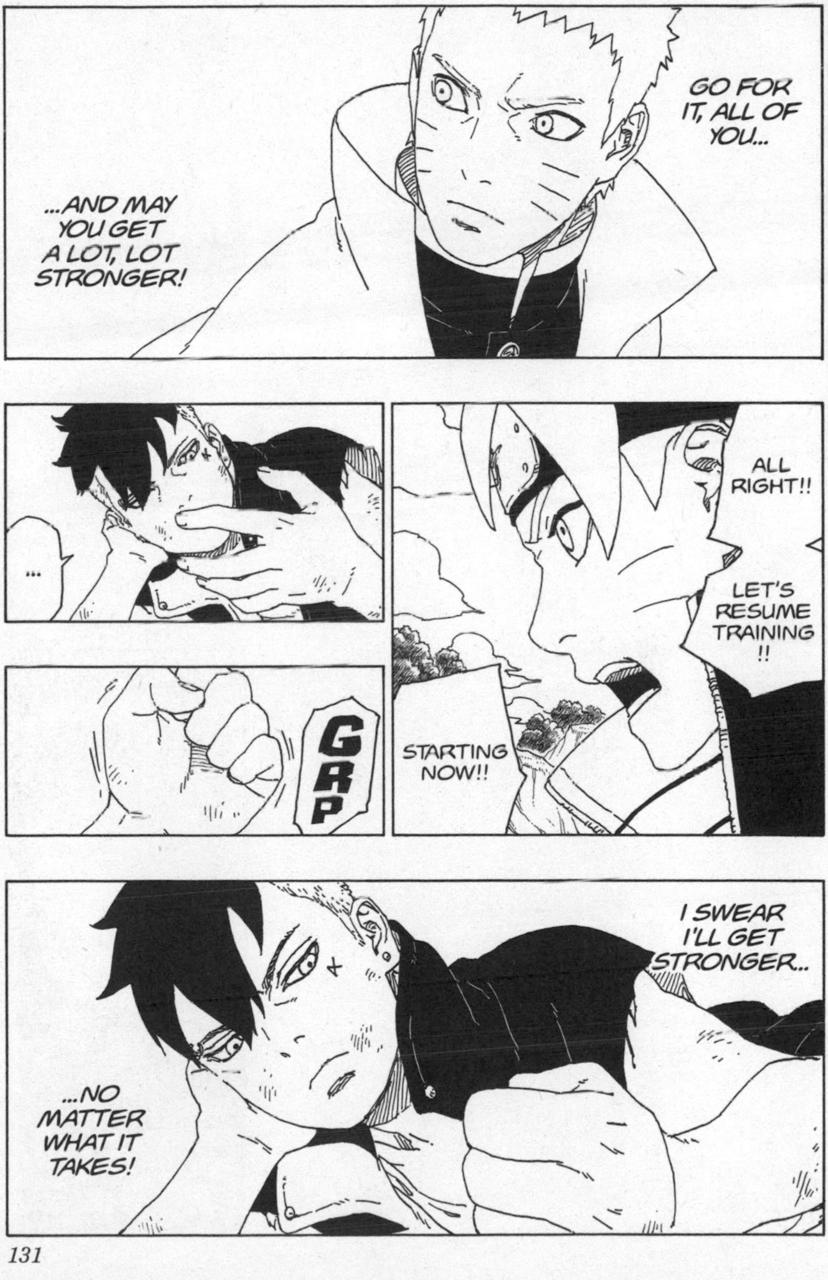
GO FOR IT, ALL OF YOU...
...AND MAY YOU GET A LOT, LOT STRONGER!
ALL RIGHT!!
LET'S RESUME TRAINING !!
STARTING NOW!!
...
GRP
I SWEAR I'LL GET STRONGER...
...NO MATTER WHAT IT TAKES!

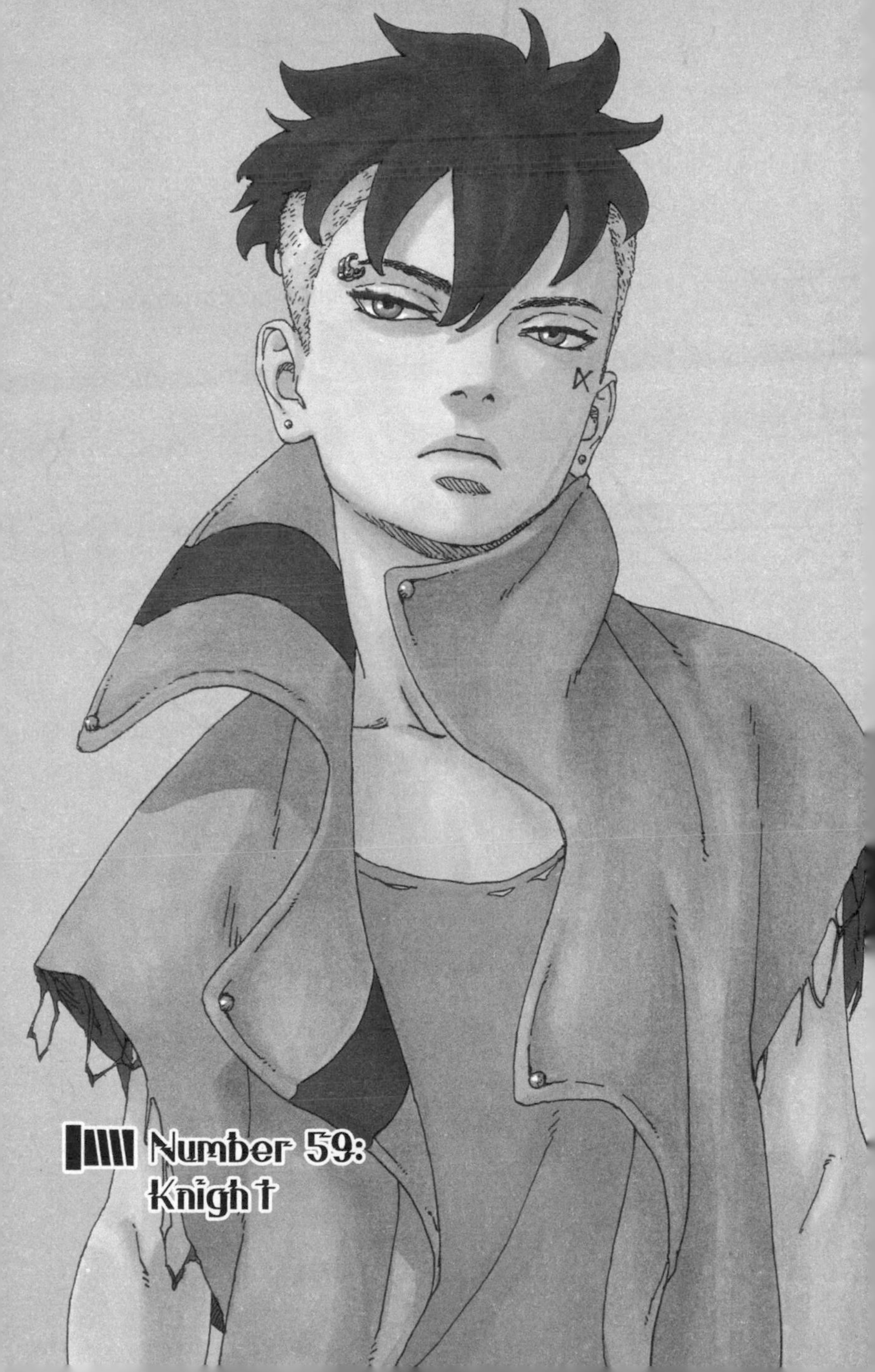

Number 59: Knight

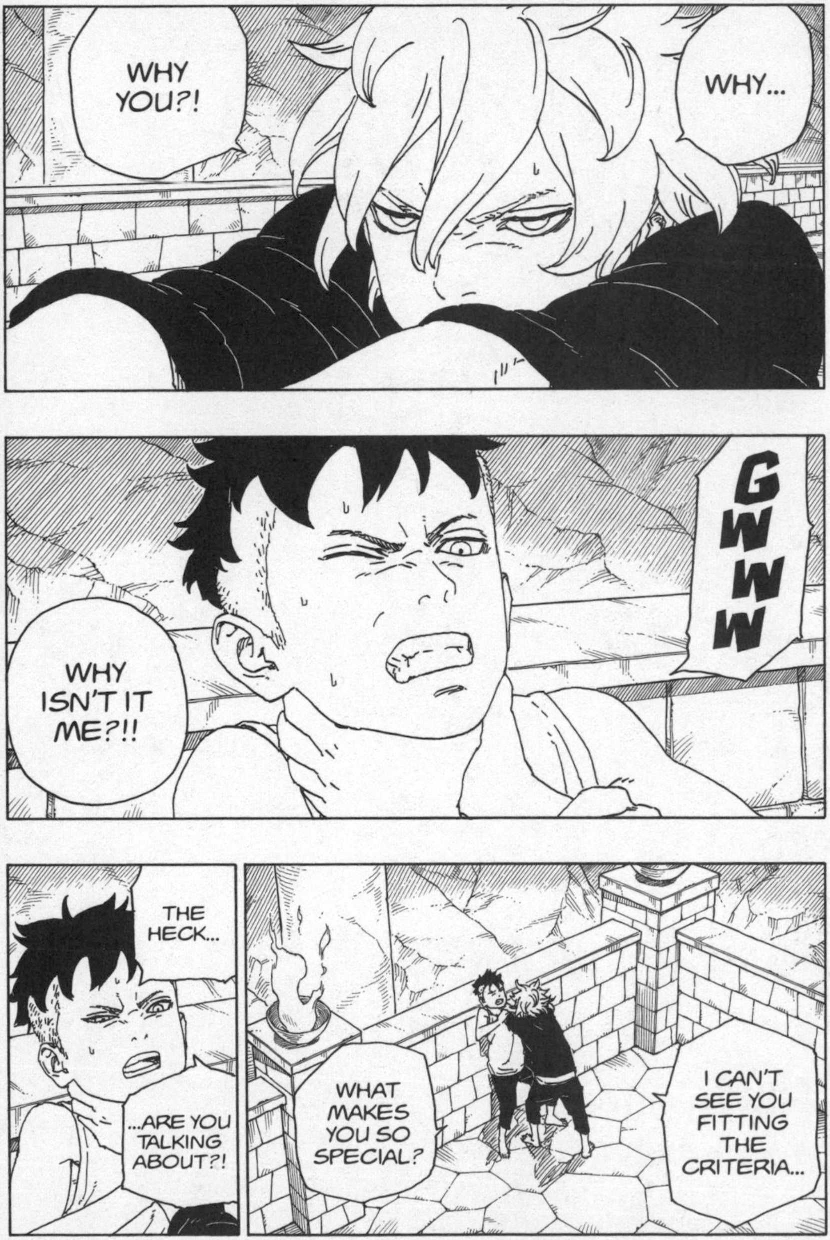
WHY...
WHY YOU?!
GWWW
WHY ISN'T IT ME?!!
I CAN'T SEE YOU FITTING THE CRITERIA...
WHAT MAKES YOU SO SPECIAL?
THE HECK...
...ARE YOU TALKING ABOUT?!

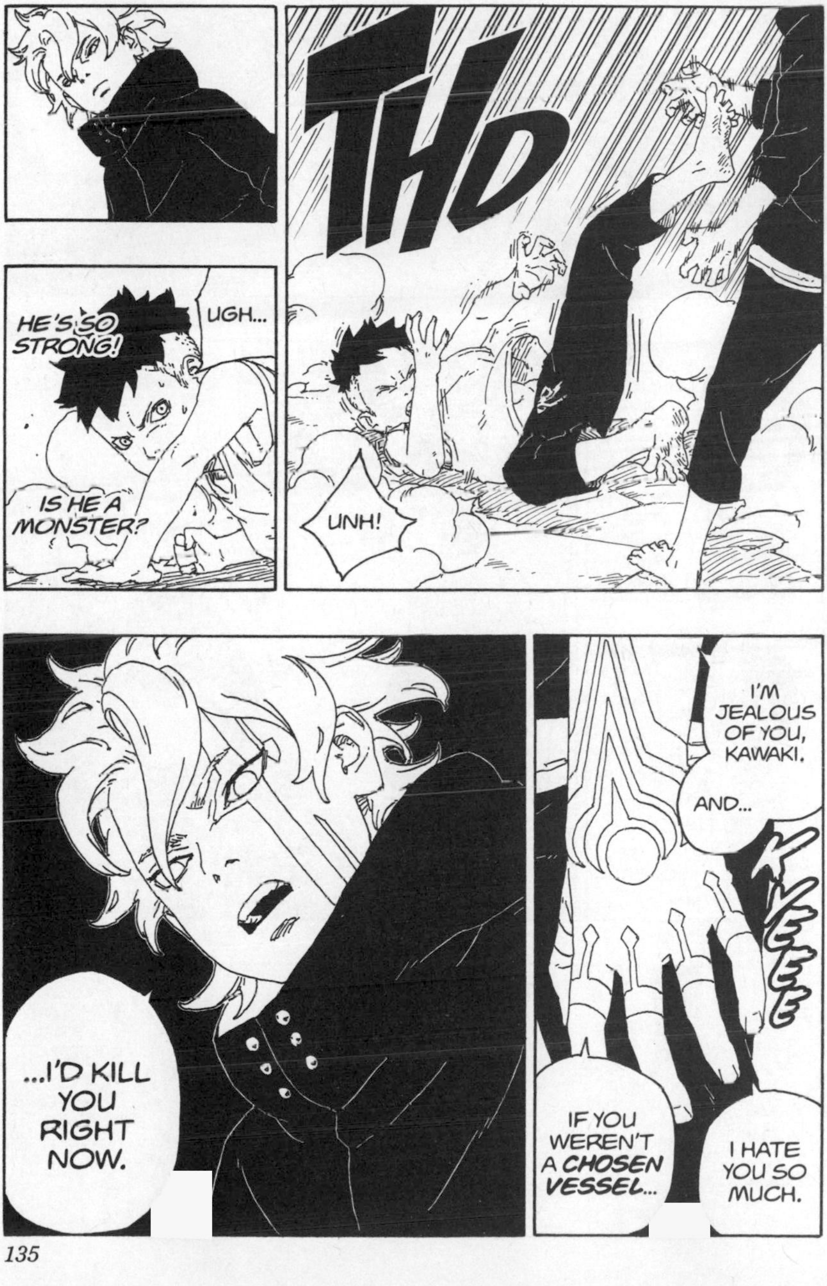
THD
UNH!
UGH...
HE'S SO STRONG!
IS HE A MONSTER?
I'M JEALOUS OF YOU, KAWAKI.
AND...
KVEEEE
I HATE YOU SO MUCH.
IF YOU WEREN'T A CHOSEN VESSEL...
...I'D KILL YOU RIGHT NOW.

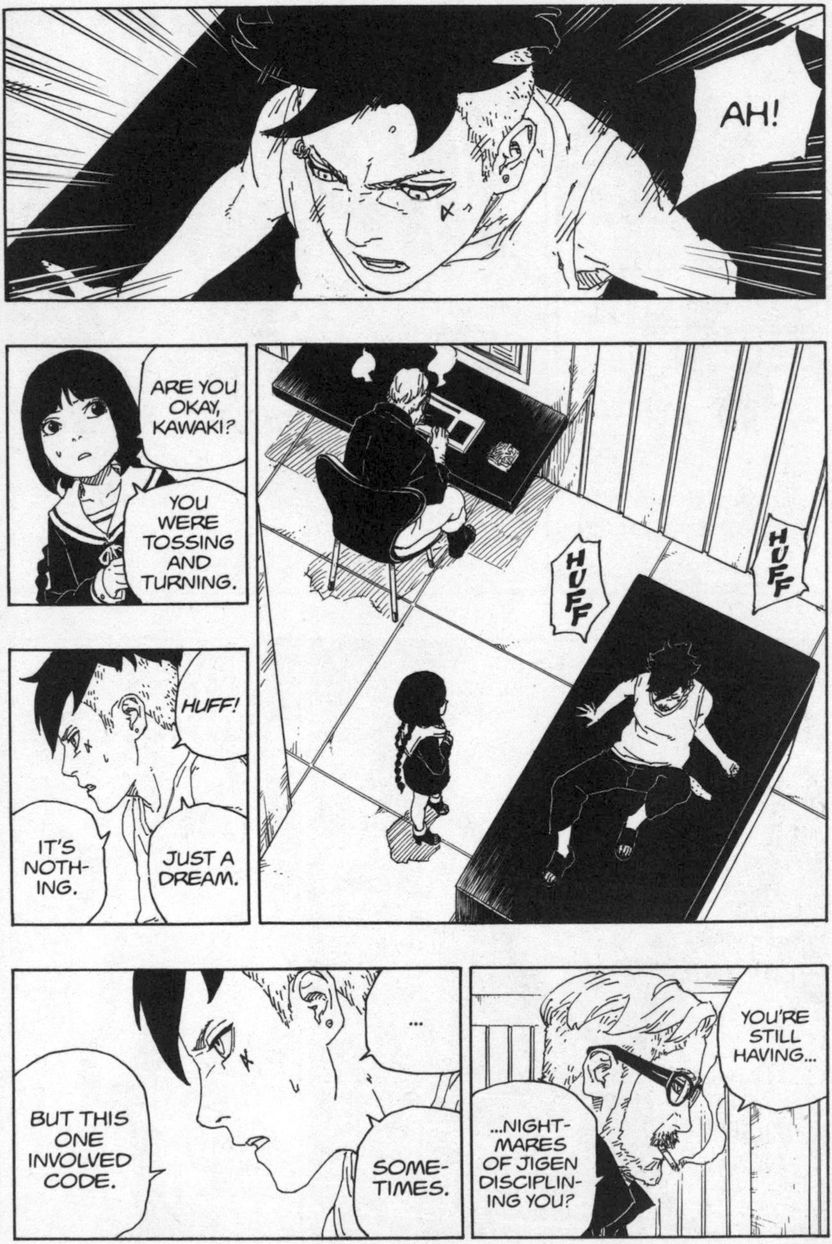
AH!
HUFF
HUFF
ARE YOU OKAY, KAWAKI?
YOU WERE TOSSING AND TURNING.
HUFF!
JUST A DREAM.
IT'S NOTHING.
YOU'RE STILL HAVING...
...NIGHTMARES OF JIGEN DISCIPLINING YOU?
...
SOMETIMES.
BUT THIS ONE INVOLVED CODE.

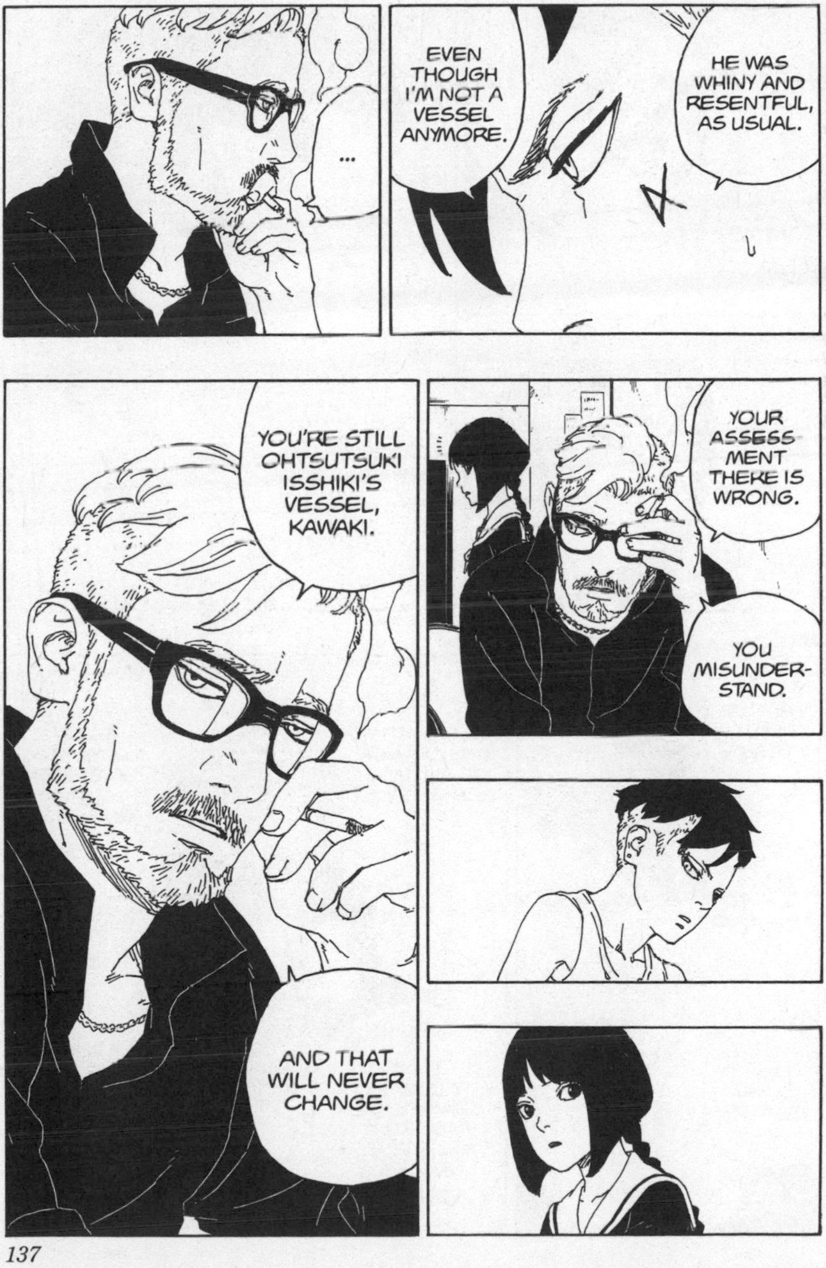

HE WAS WHINY AND RESENTFUL, AS USUAL.
EVEN THOUGH I'M NOT A VESSEL ANYMORE.
...
YOUR ASSESS-MENT THERE IS WRONG.
YOU MISUNDER-STAND.
YOU'RE STILL OHTSUTSUKI ISSHIKI'S VESSEL, KAWAKI.
AND THAT WILL NEVER CHANGE.

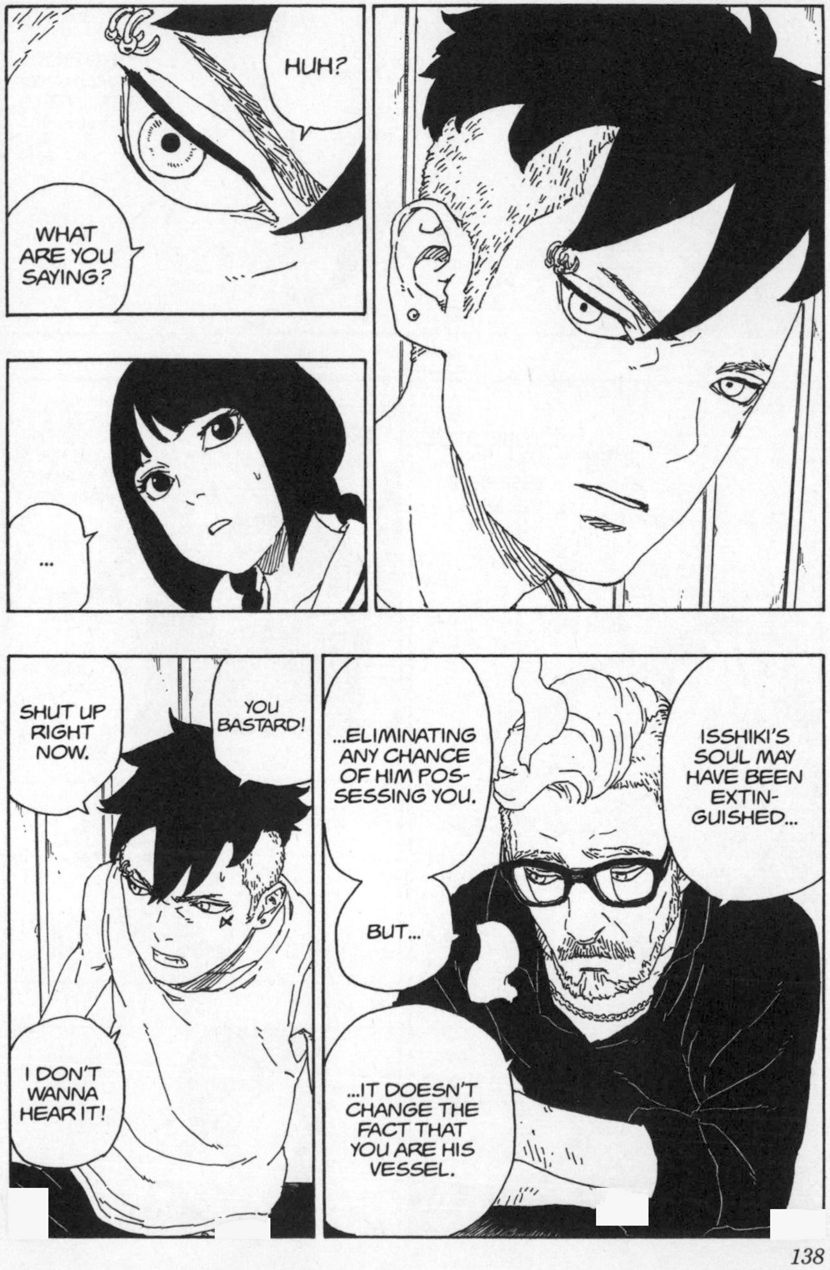
HUH?
WHAT ARE YOU SAYING?
...
ISSHIKI'S SOUL MAY HAVE BEEN EXTINGUISHED...
...ELIMINATING ANY CHANCE OF HIM POSSESSING YOU.
BUT...
...IT DOESN'T CHANGE THE FACT THAT YOU ARE HIS VESSEL.
YOU BASTARD!
SHUT UP RIGHT NOW.
I DON'T WANNA HEAR IT!

YOUR BODY REMAINING OHTSUTSUKI-FIED IS PROOF OF THAT.
THAT'S YOUR REALITY.
YOU NEED TO ACCEPT IT.
BA
!
CTNK
KAWAKI!!!
ARE YOU DEAF, YOU GEEZER?!
I TOLD YOU TO STUFF IT!
I'M FED UP WITH YOU!

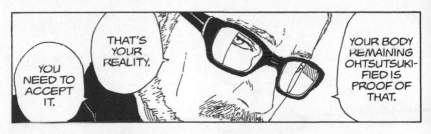

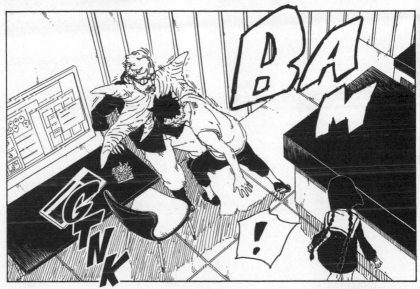

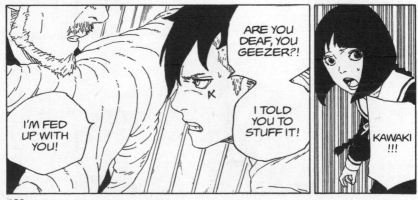

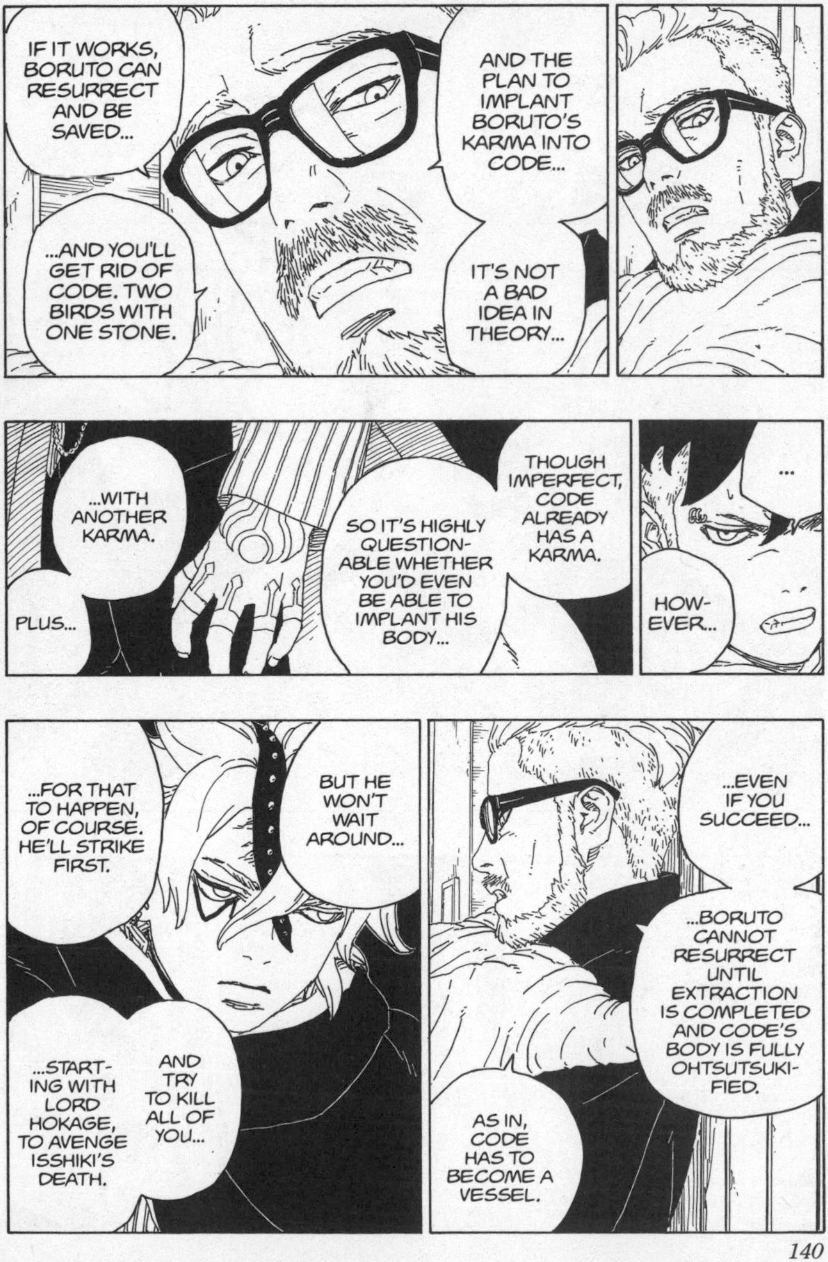
AND THE PLAN TO IMPLANT BORUTO'S KARMA INTO CODE...
IF IT WORKS, BORUTO CAN RESURRECT AND BE SAVED...
...AND YOU'LL GET RID OF CODE. TWO BIRDS WITH ONE STONE.
IT'S NOT A BAD IDEA IN THEORY...
...
HOW-EVER...
THOUGH IMPERFECT, CODE ALREADY HAS A KARMA.
SO IT'S HIGHLY QUESTION-ABLE WHETHER YOU'D EVEN BE ABLE TO IMPLANT HIS BODY...
...WITH ANOTHER KARMA.
PLUS...
...EVEN IF YOU SUCCEED...
...BORUTO CANNOT RESURRECT UNTIL EXTRACTION IS COMPLETED AND CODE'S BODY IS FULLY OHTSUTSUKI-FIED.
AS IN, CODE HAS TO BECOME A VESSEL.
BUT HE WON'T WAIT AROUND...
...FOR THAT TO HAPPEN, OF COURSE. HE'LL STRIKE FIRST.
AND TRY TO KILL ALL OF YOU...
...START-ING WITH LORD HOKAGE, TO AVENGE ISSHIKI'S DEATH.

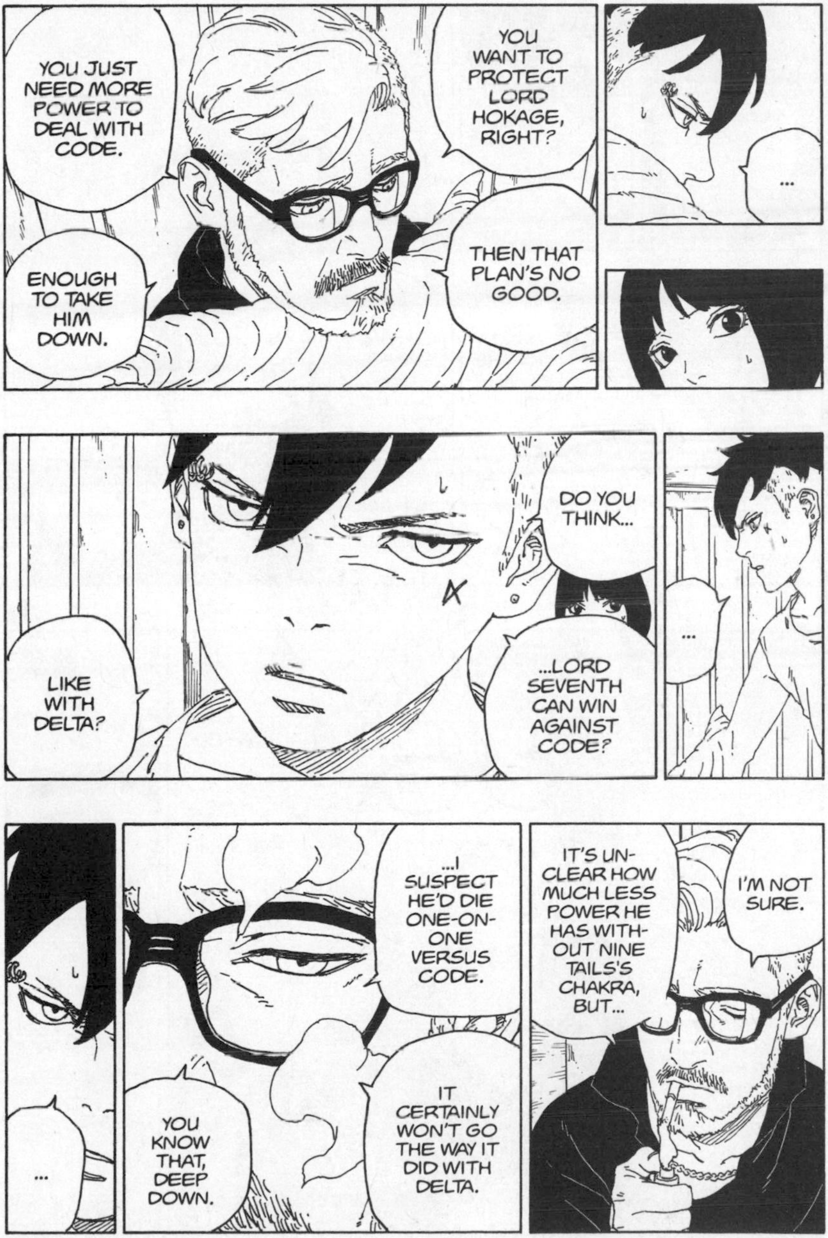
...
YOU WANT TO PROTECT LORD HOKAGE, RIGHT?
THEN THAT PLAN'S NO GOOD.
YOU JUST NEED MORE POWER TO DEAL WITH CODE.
ENOUGH TO TAKE HIM DOWN.
...
DO YOU THINK...
...LORD SEVENTH CAN WIN AGAINST CODE?
LIKE WITH DELTA?
I'M NOT SURE.
IT'S UN-CLEAR HOW MUCH LESS POWER HE HAS WITH-OUT NINE TAILS'S CHAKRA, BUT...
...I SUSPECT HE'D DIE ONE-ON-ONE VERSUS CODE.
IT CERTAINLY WON'T GO THE WAY IT DID WITH DELTA.
YOU KNOW THAT, DEEP DOWN.
...

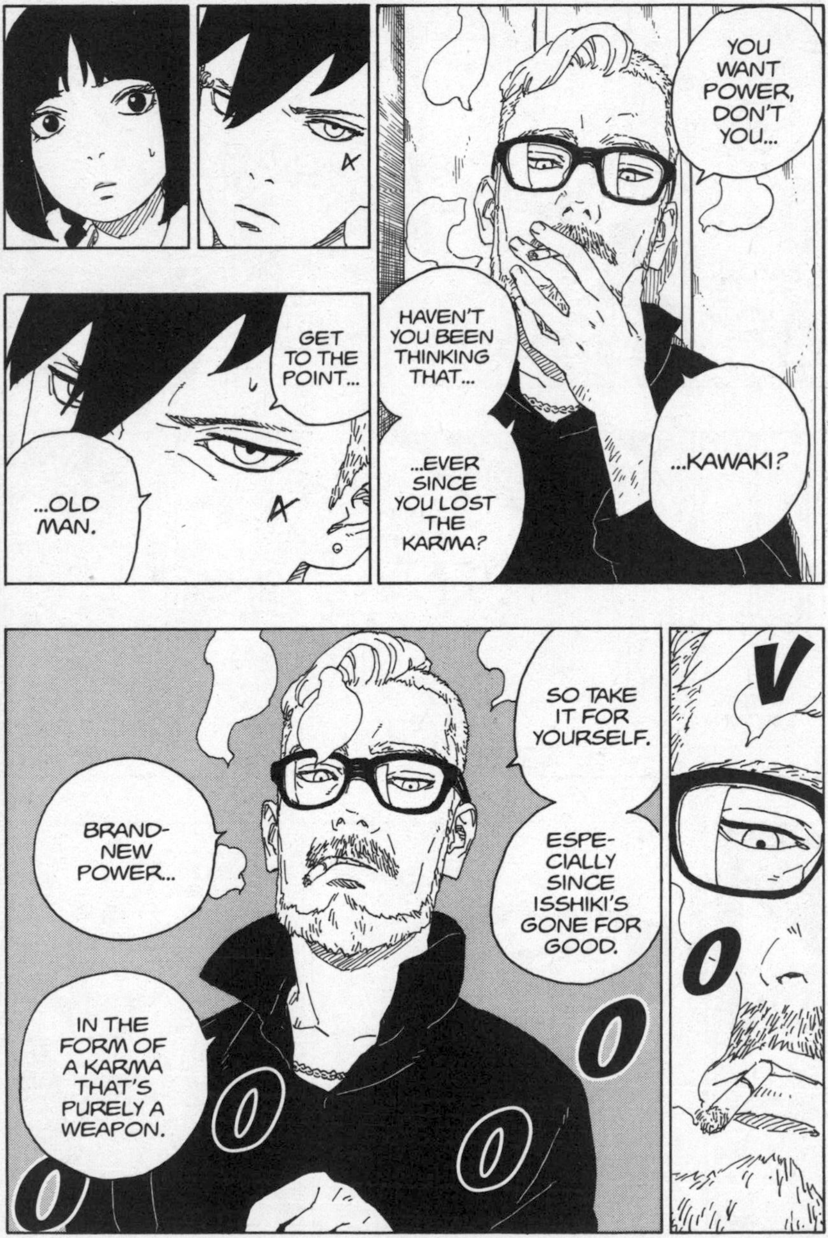
YOU WANT POWER, DON'T YOU...
...KAWAKI?
HAVEN'T YOU BEEN THINKING THAT...
...EVER SINCE YOU LOST THE KARMA?
GET TO THE POINT...
...OLD MAN.
V
O
SO TAKE IT FOR YOURSELF.
ESPE-CIALLY SINCE ISSHIKI'S GONE FOR GOOD.
BRAND-NEW POWER...
IN THE FORM OF A KARMA THAT'S PURELY A WEAPON.
O
O
O
O

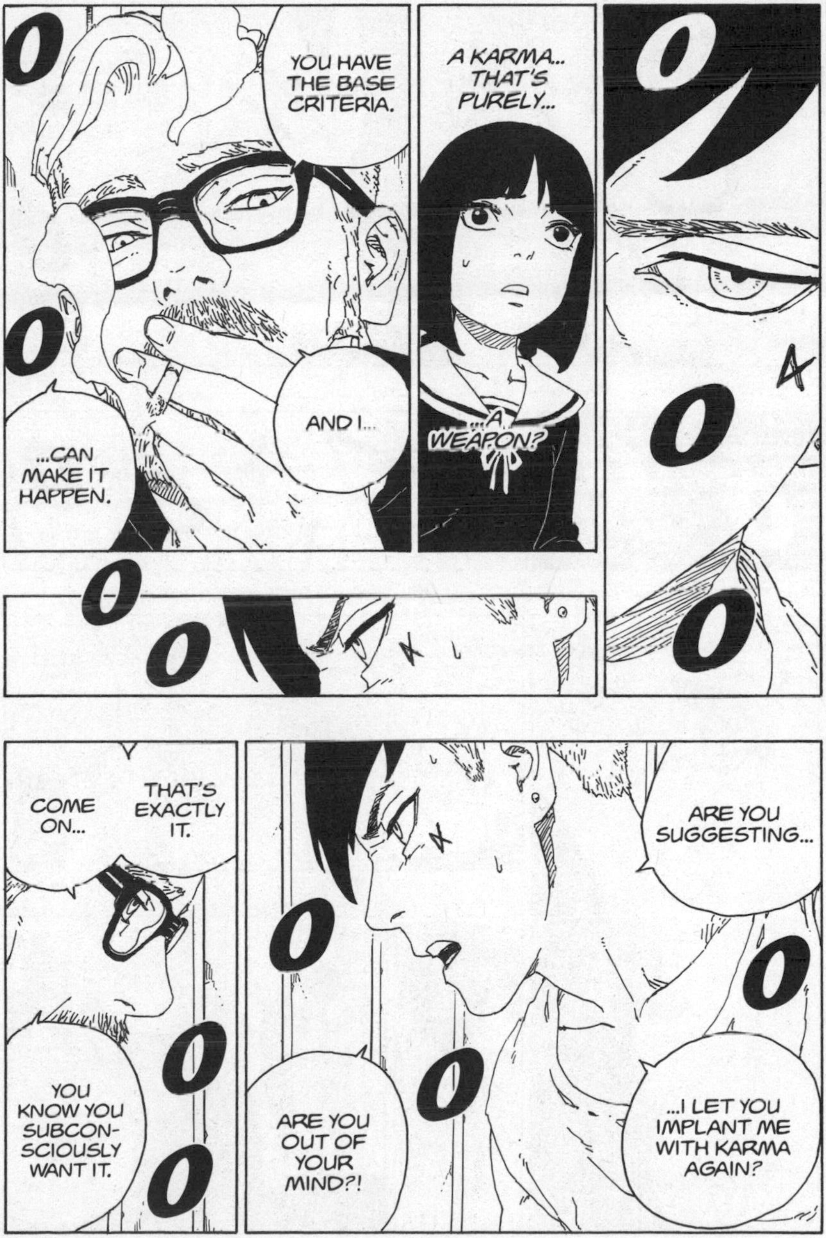
A KARMA... THAT'S PURELY...
...A WEAPON?
YOU HAVE THE BASE CRITERIA.
AND I...
...CAN MAKE IT HAPPEN.
ARE YOU SUGGESTING...
...I LET YOU IMPLANT ME WITH KARMA AGAIN?
ARE YOU OUT OF YOUR MIND?!
THAT'S EXACTLY IT.
COME ON...
YOU KNOW YOU SUBCONSCIOUSLY WANT IT.

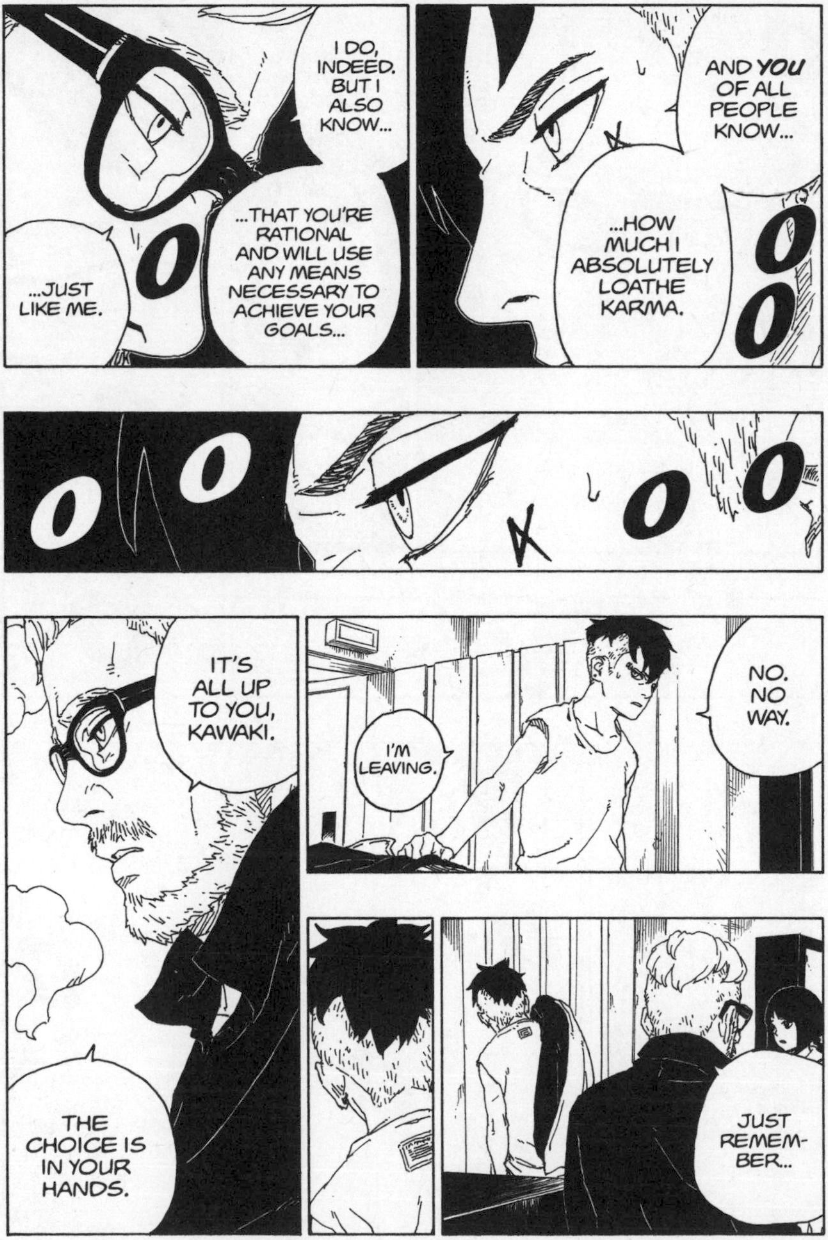
AND ***YOU*** OF ALL PEOPLE KNOW...
...HOW MUCH I ABSOLUTELY LOATHE THE KARMA.
I DO, INDEED. BUT I ALSO KNOW...
...THAT YOU'RE RATIONAL AND WILL USE ANY MEANS NECESSARY TO ACHIEVE YOUR GOALS...
...JUST LIKE ME.
NO. NO WAY.
I'M LEAVING.
JUST REMEMBER...
IT'S ALL UP TO YOU, KAWAKI.
THE CHOICE IS IN YOUR HANDS.

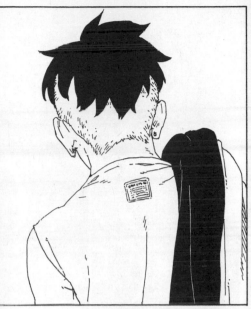

SHUP

VWOOOO.

KAWAKI...

...

...

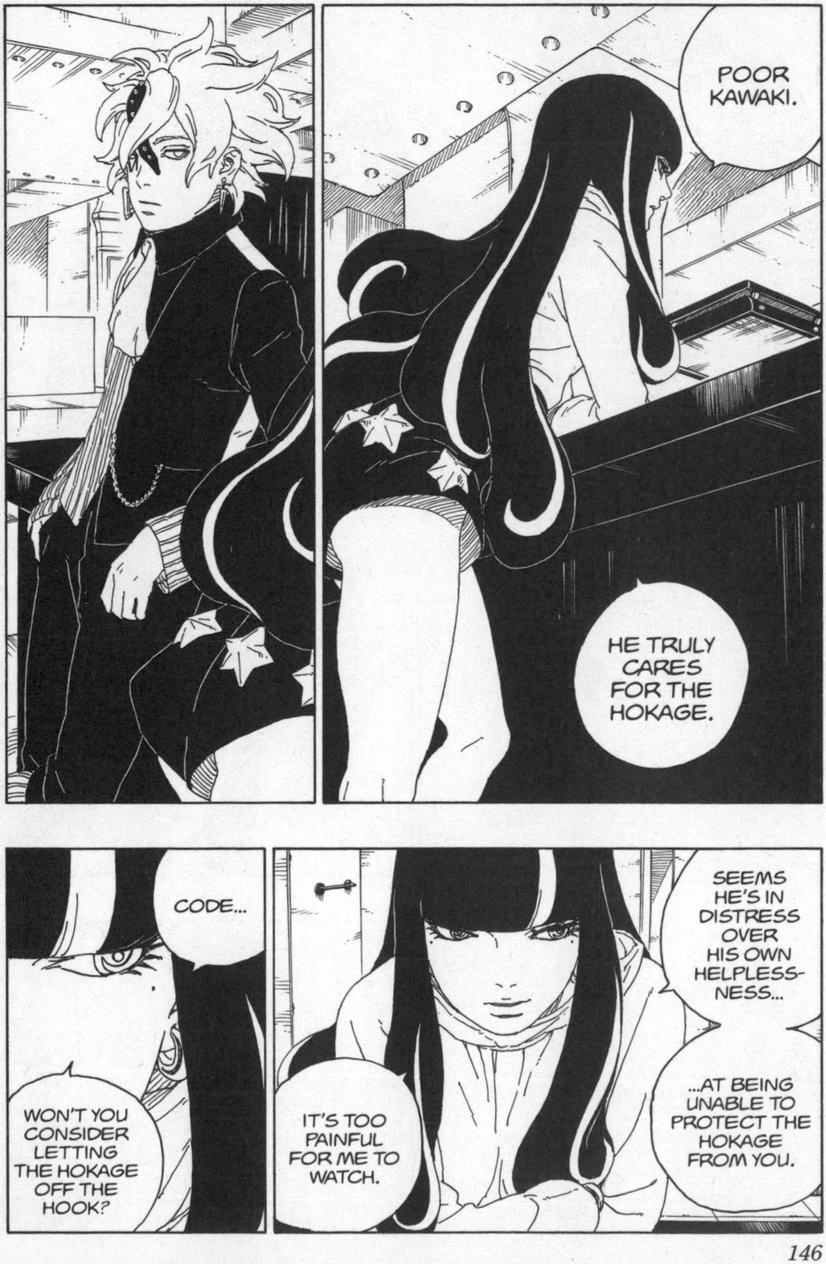
POOR KAWAKI.
HE TRULY CARES FOR THE HOKAGE.
SEEMS HE'S IN DISTRESS OVER HIS OWN HELPLESS-NESS...
...AT BEING UNABLE TO PROTECT THE HOKAGE FROM YOU.
IT'S TOO PAINFUL FOR ME TO WATCH.
CODE...
WON'T YOU CONSIDER LETTING THE HOKAGE OFF THE HOOK?

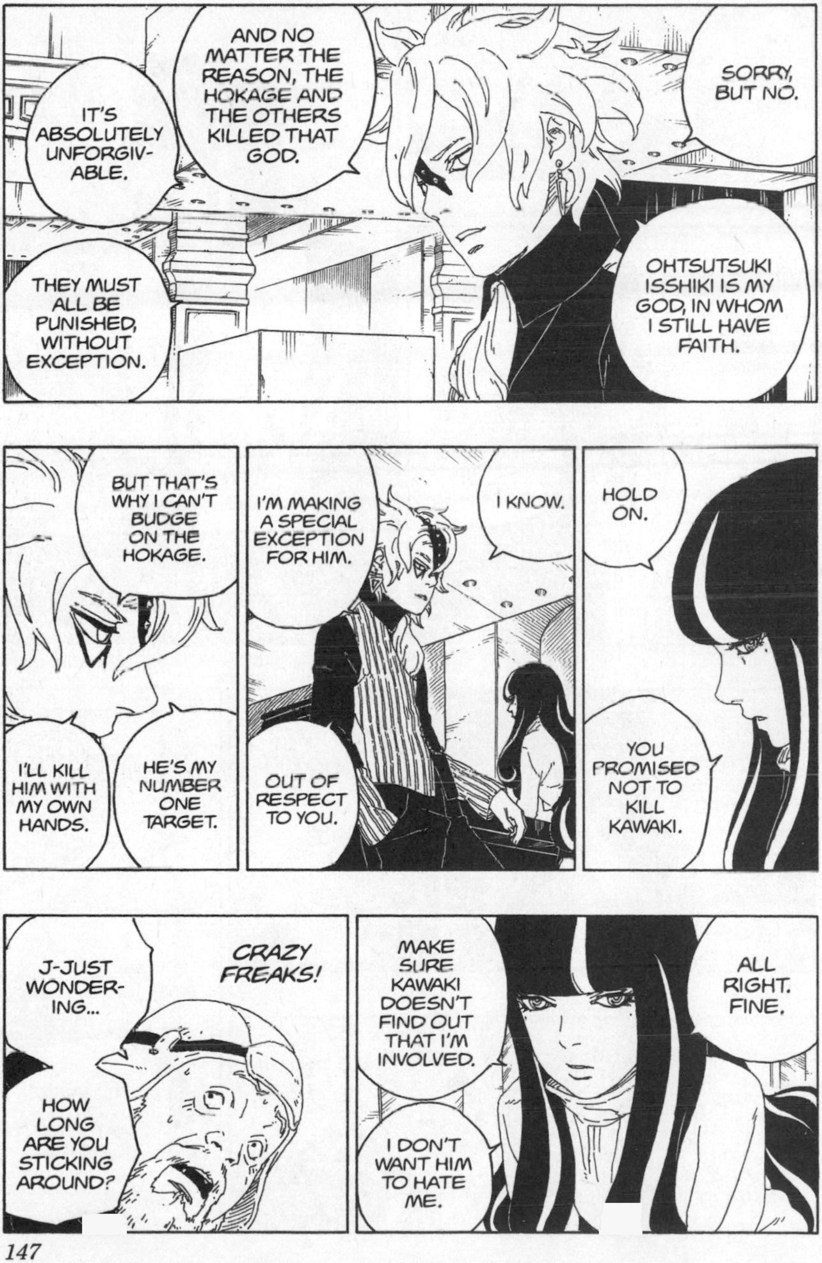

SORRY, BUT NO.
OHTSUTSUKI ISSHIKI IS MY GOD, IN WHOM I STILL HAVE FAITH.
AND NO MATTER THE REASON, THE HOKAGE AND THE OTHERS KILLED THAT GOD.
IT'S ABSOLUTELY UNFORGIVABLE.
THEY MUST ALL BE PUNISHED, WITHOUT EXCEPTION.
HOLD ON.
YOU PROMISED NOT TO KILL KAWAKI.
I KNOW.
I'M MAKING A SPECIAL EXCEPTION FOR HIM.
OUT OF RESPECT TO YOU.
BUT THAT'S WHY I CAN'T BUDGE ON THE HOKAGE.
HE'S MY NUMBER ONE TARGET.
I'LL KILL HIM WITH MY OWN HANDS.
ALL RIGHT. FINE.
MAKE SURE KAWAKI DOESN'T FIND OUT THAT I'M INVOLVED.
I DON'T WANT HIM TO HATE ME.
CRAZY FREAKS!
J-JUST WONDERING...
HOW LONG ARE YOU STICKING AROUND?

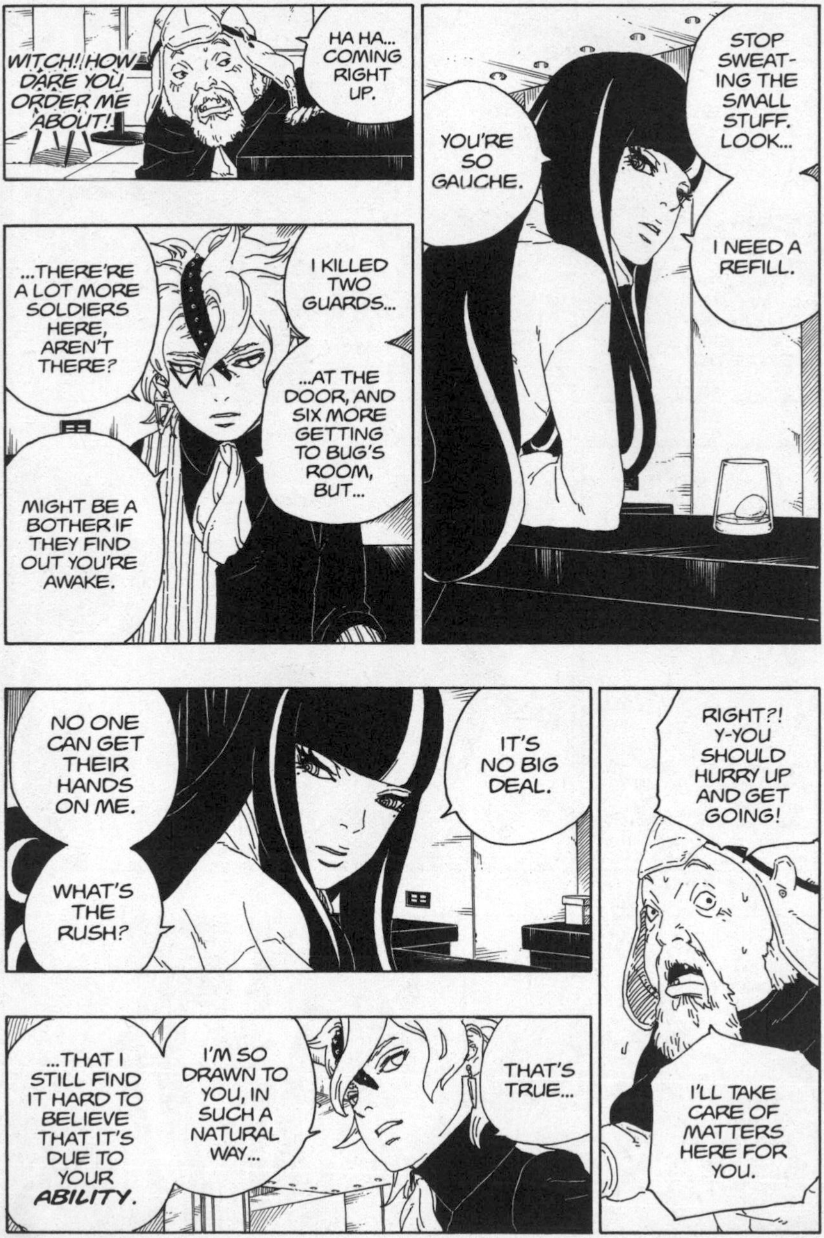
STOP SWEATING THE SMALL STUFF. LOOK...
YOU'RE SO GAUCHE.
I NEED A REFILL.
HA HA... COMING RIGHT UP.
WITCH! HOW DARE YOU ORDER ME ABOUT!
I KILLED TWO GUARDS...
...AT THE DOOR, AND SIX MORE GETTING TO BUG'S ROOM, BUT...
...THERE'RE A LOT MORE SOLDIERS HERE, AREN'T THERE?
MIGHT BE A BOTHER IF THEY FIND OUT YOU'RE AWAKE.
RIGHT?! Y-YOU SHOULD HURRY UP AND GET GOING!
I'LL TAKE CARE OF MATTERS HERE FOR YOU.
IT'S NO BIG DEAL.
NO ONE CAN GET THEIR HANDS ON ME.
WHAT'S THE RUSH?
THAT'S TRUE...
I'M SO DRAWN TO YOU, IN SUCH A NATURAL WAY...
...THAT I STILL FIND IT HARD TO BELIEVE THAT IT'S DUE TO YOUR **ABILITY**.

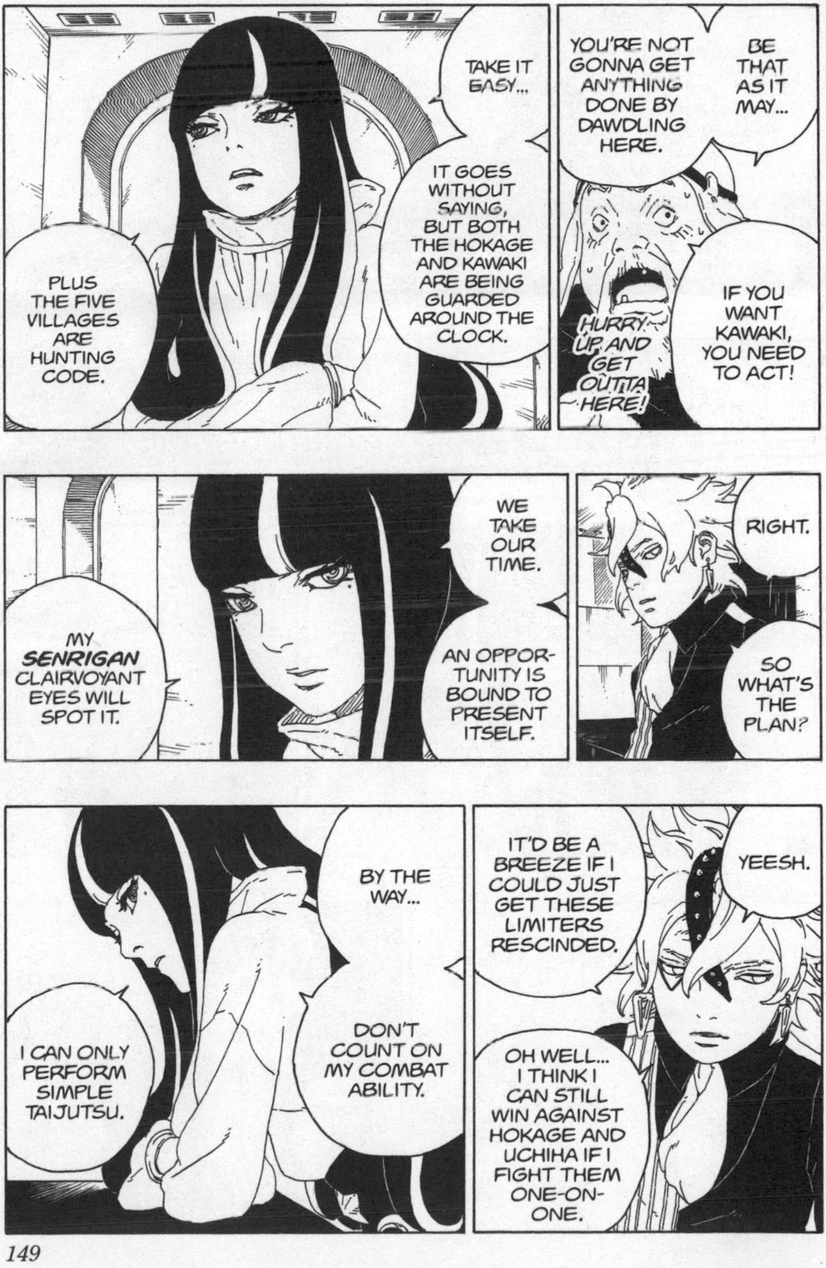
BE THAT AS IT MAY...
YOU'RE NOT GONNA GET ANYTHING DONE BY DAWDLING HERE.
HURRY UP AND GET OUTTA HERE!
IF YOU WANT KAWAKI, YOU NEED TO ACT!
TAKE IT EASY...
IT GOES WITHOUT SAYING, BUT BOTH THE HOKAGE AND KAWAKI ARE BEING GUARDED AROUND THE CLOCK.
PLUS THE FIVE VILLAGES ARE HUNTING CODE.
RIGHT.
SO WHAT'S THE PLAN?
WE TAKE OUR TIME.
AN OPPORTUNITY IS BOUND TO PRESENT ITSELF.
MY ***SENRIGAN*** CLAIRVOYANT EYES WILL SPOT IT.
YEESH.
IT'D BE A BREEZE IF I COULD JUST GET THESE LIMITERS RESCINDED.
OH WELL... I THINK I CAN STILL WIN AGAINST HOKAGE AND UCHIHA IF I FIGHT THEM ONE-ON-ONE.
BY THE WAY...
DON'T COUNT ON MY COMBAT ABILITY.
I CAN ONLY PERFORM SIMPLE TAIJUTSU.

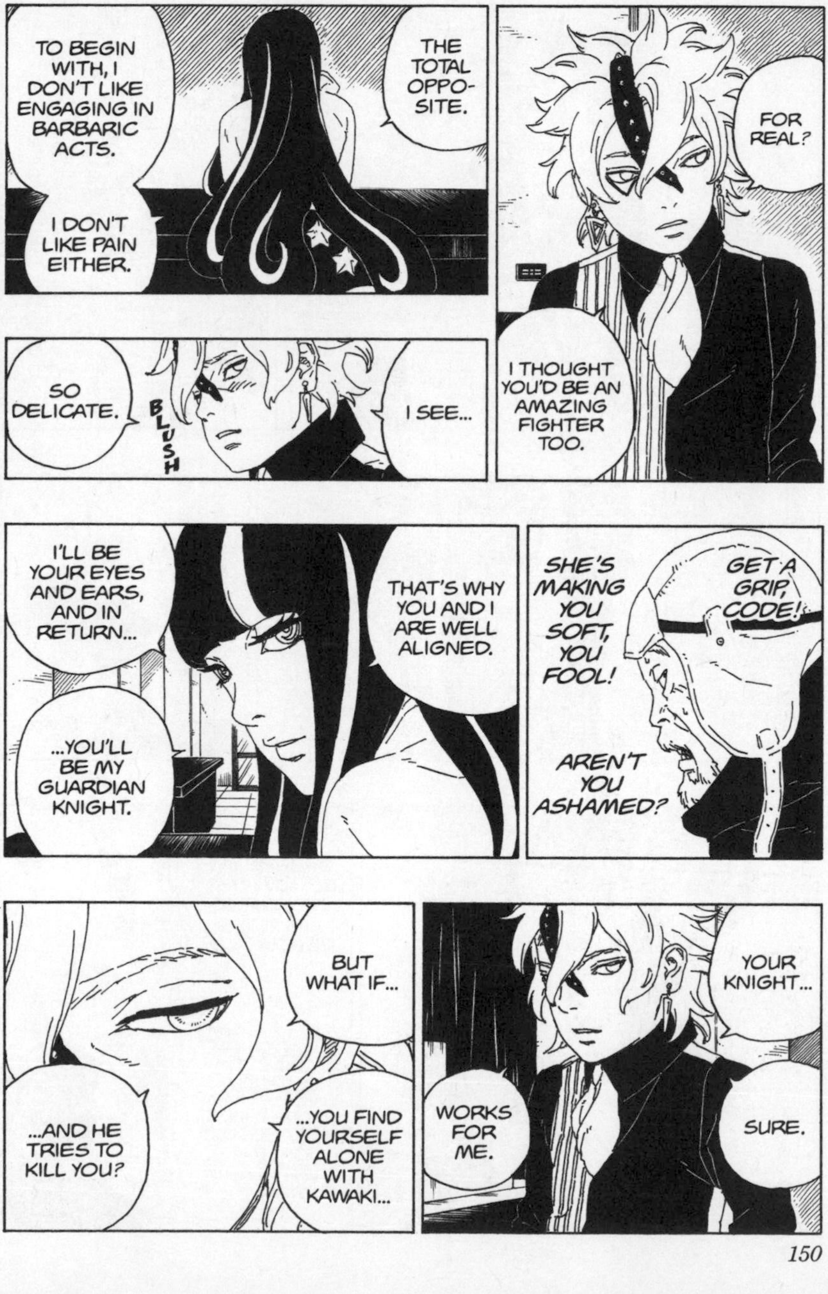
FOR REAL?
I THOUGHT YOU'D BE AN AMAZING FIGHTER TOO.
THE TOTAL OPPO-SITE.
TO BEGIN WITH, I DON'T LIKE ENGAGING IN BARBARIC ACTS.
I DON'T LIKE PAIN EITHER.
I SEE...
BLUSH
SO DELICATE.
GET A GRIP, CODE!
SHE'S MAKING YOU SOFT, YOU FOOL!
AREN'T YOU ASHAMED?
THAT'S WHY YOU AND I ARE WELL ALIGNED.
I'LL BE YOUR EYES AND EARS, AND IN RETURN...
...YOU'LL BE MY GUARDIAN KNIGHT.
YOUR KNIGHT...
SURE.
WORKS FOR ME.
BUT WHAT IF...
...YOU FIND YOURSELF ALONE WITH KAWAKI...
...AND HE TRIES TO KILL YOU?

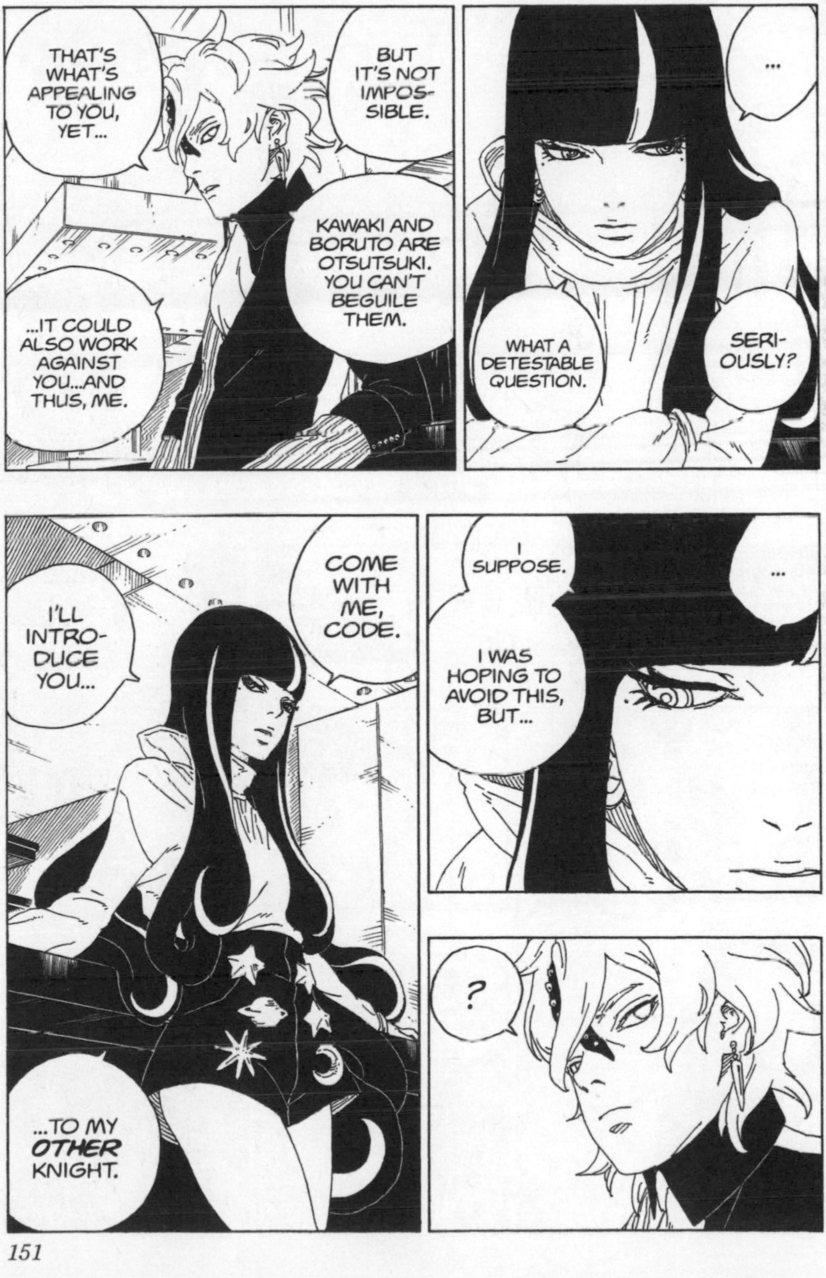
...
SERIOUSLY?
WHAT A DETESTABLE QUESTION.
BUT IT'S NOT IMPOSSIBLE.
THAT'S WHAT'S APPEALING TO YOU, YET...
KAWAKI AND BORUTO ARE OTSUTSUKI. YOU CAN'T BEGUILE THEM.
...IT COULD ALSO WORK AGAINST YOU...AND THUS, ME.
...
I SUPPOSE.
I WAS HOPING TO AVOID THIS, BUT...
?
COME WITH ME, CODE.
I'LL INTRODUCE YOU...
...TO MY *OTHER* KNIGHT.

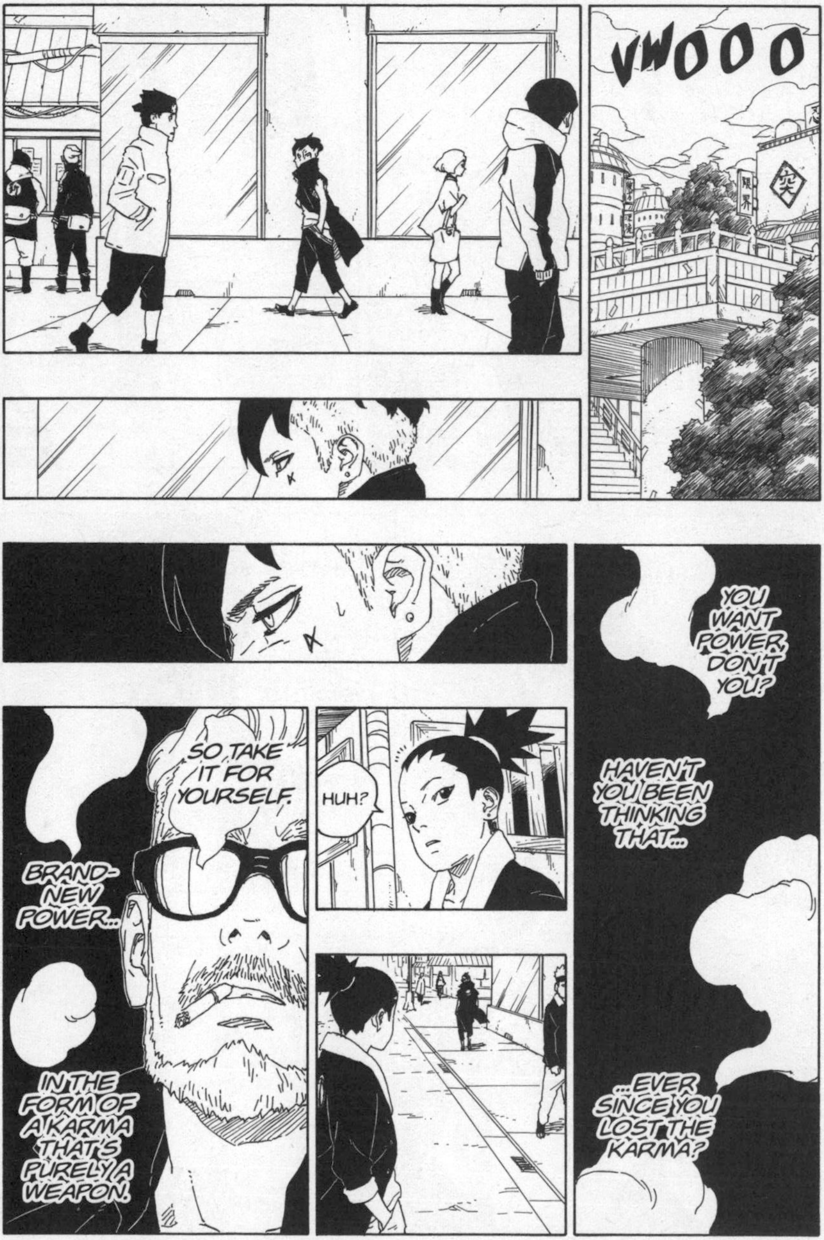
VWOOO
YOU WANT POWER, DON'T YOU?
HAVEN'T YOU BEEN THINKING THAT...
...EVER SINCE YOU LOST THE KARMA?
HUH?
SO TAKE IT FOR YOURSELF.
BRAND-NEW POWER...
IN THE FORM OF A KARMA THAT'S PURELY A WEAPON.

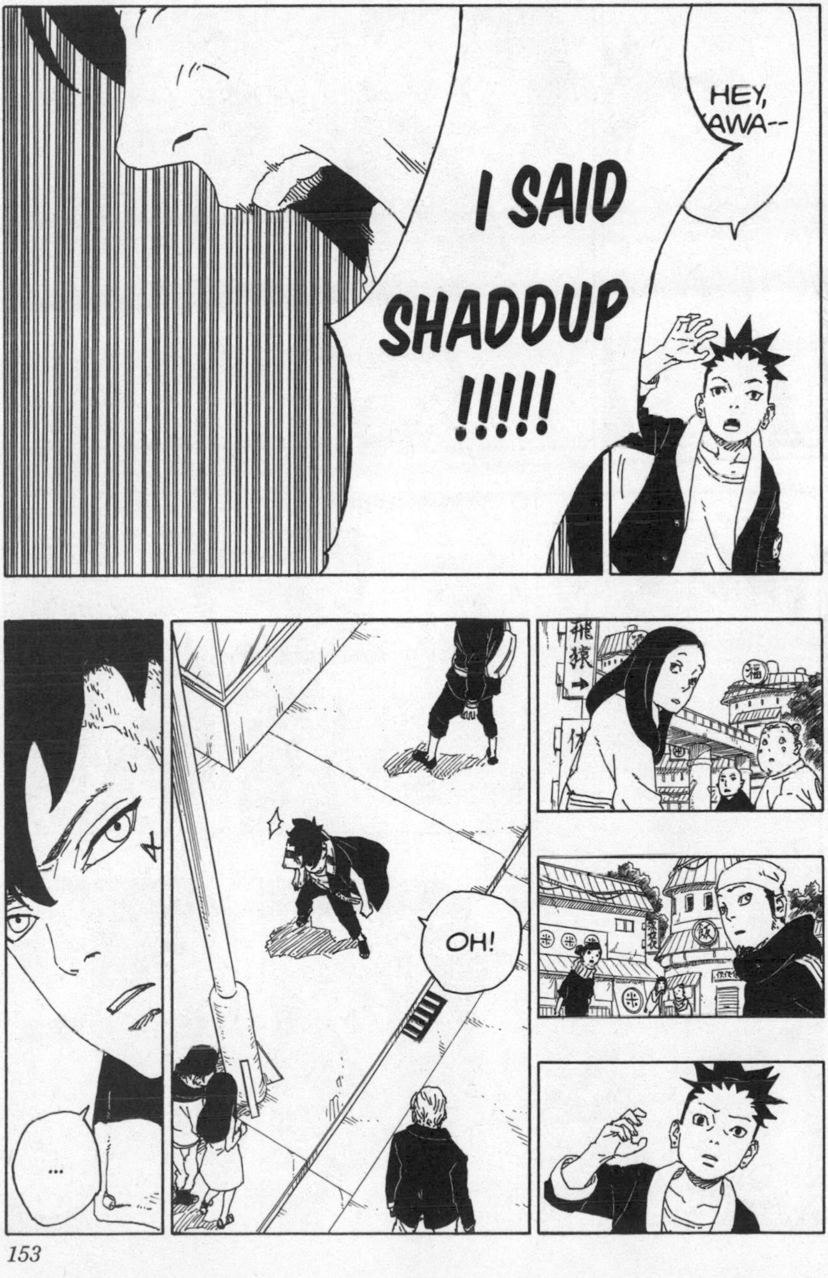
HEY, KAWA--
I SAID SHADDUP !!!!!
OH!
...

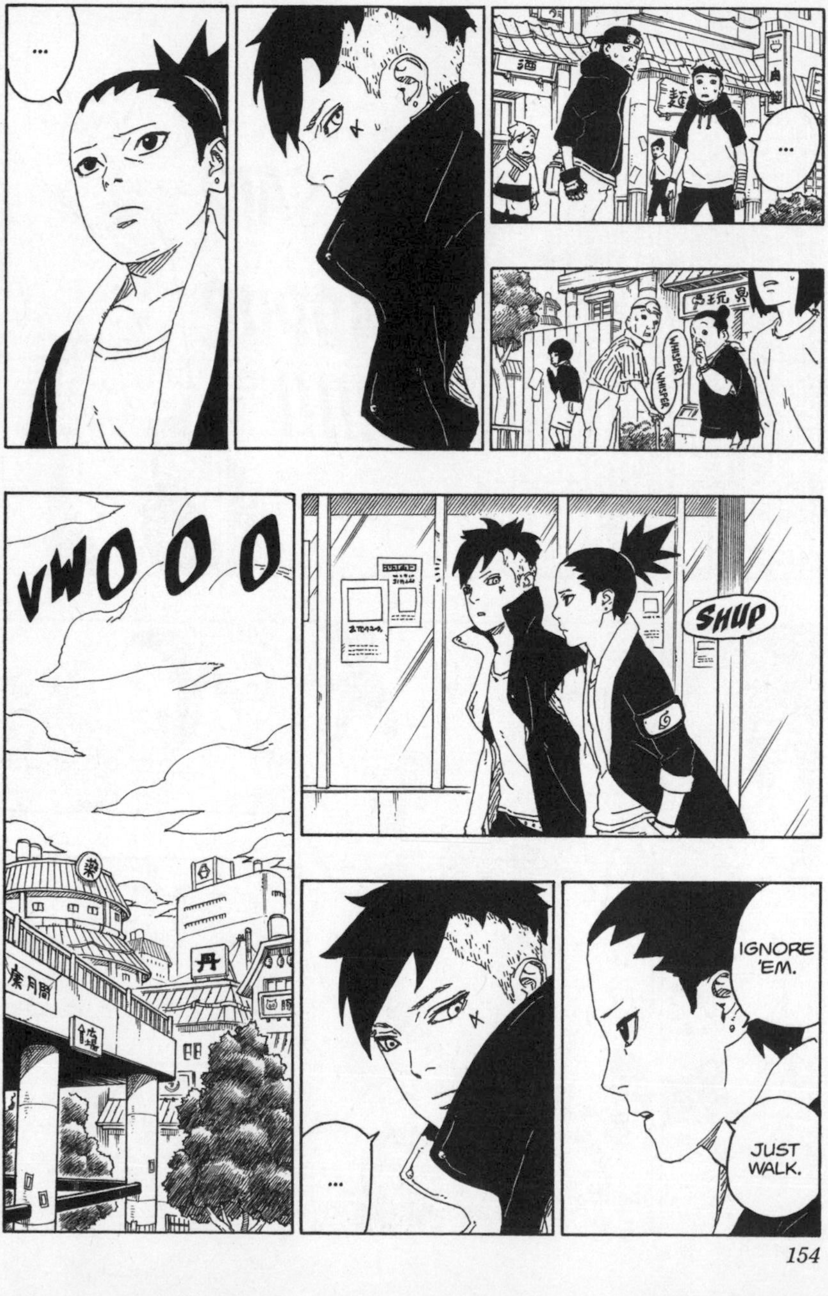
...
WHISPER
WHISPER
...
SHUP
IGNORE 'EM.
JUST WALK.
...
VWOOO

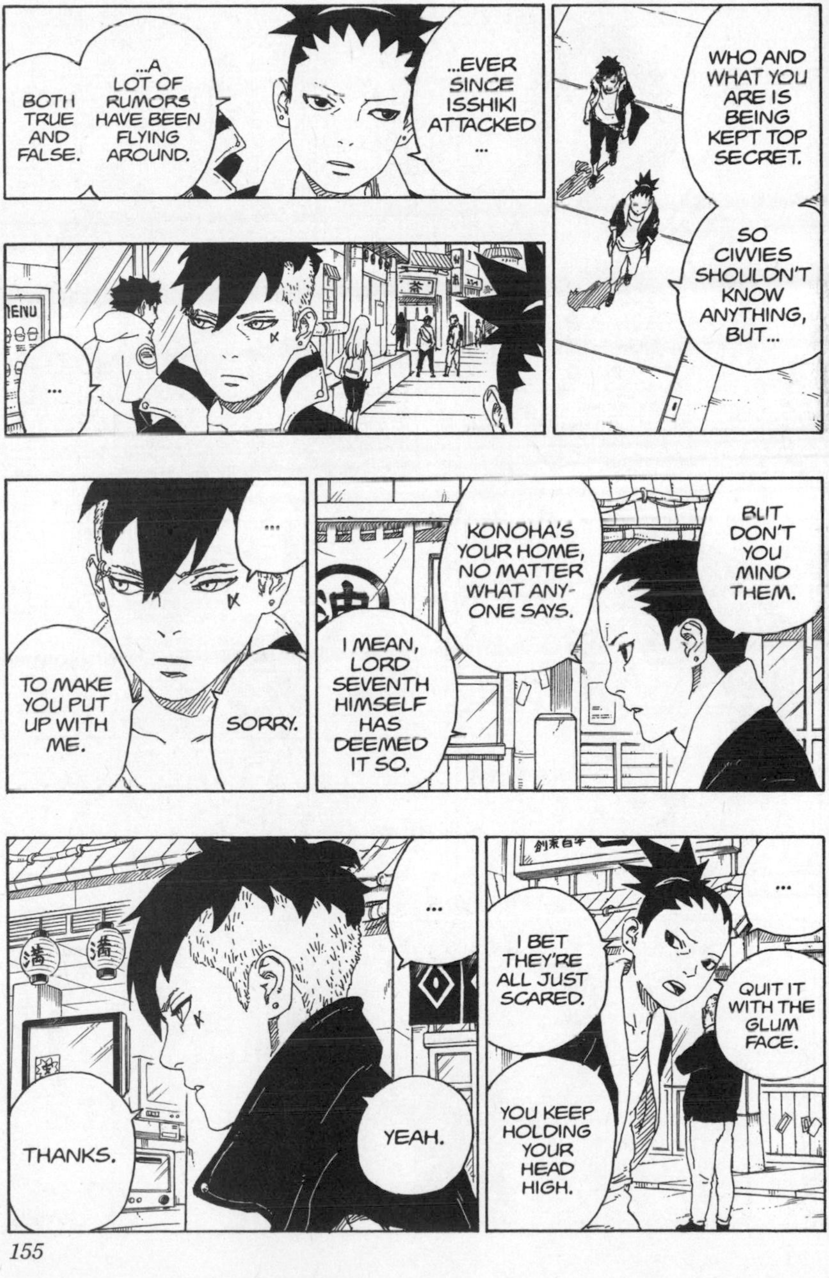
WHO AND WHAT YOU ARE IS BEING KEPT TOP SECRET.
SO CIVVIES SHOULDN'T KNOW ANYTHING, BUT...
...EVER SINCE ISSHIKI ATTACKED ...
...A LOT OF RUMORS HAVE BEEN FLYING AROUND.
BOTH TRUE AND FALSE.
...
BUT DON'T YOU MIND THEM.
KONOHA'S YOUR HOME, NO MATTER WHAT ANY-ONE SAYS.
I MEAN, LORD SEVENTH HIMSELF HAS DEEMED IT SO.
...
SORRY.
TO MAKE YOU PUT UP WITH ME.
...
QUIT IT WITH THE GLUM FACE.
I BET THEY'RE ALL JUST SCARED.
YOU KEEP HOLDING YOUR HEAD HIGH.
...
YEAH.
THANKS.

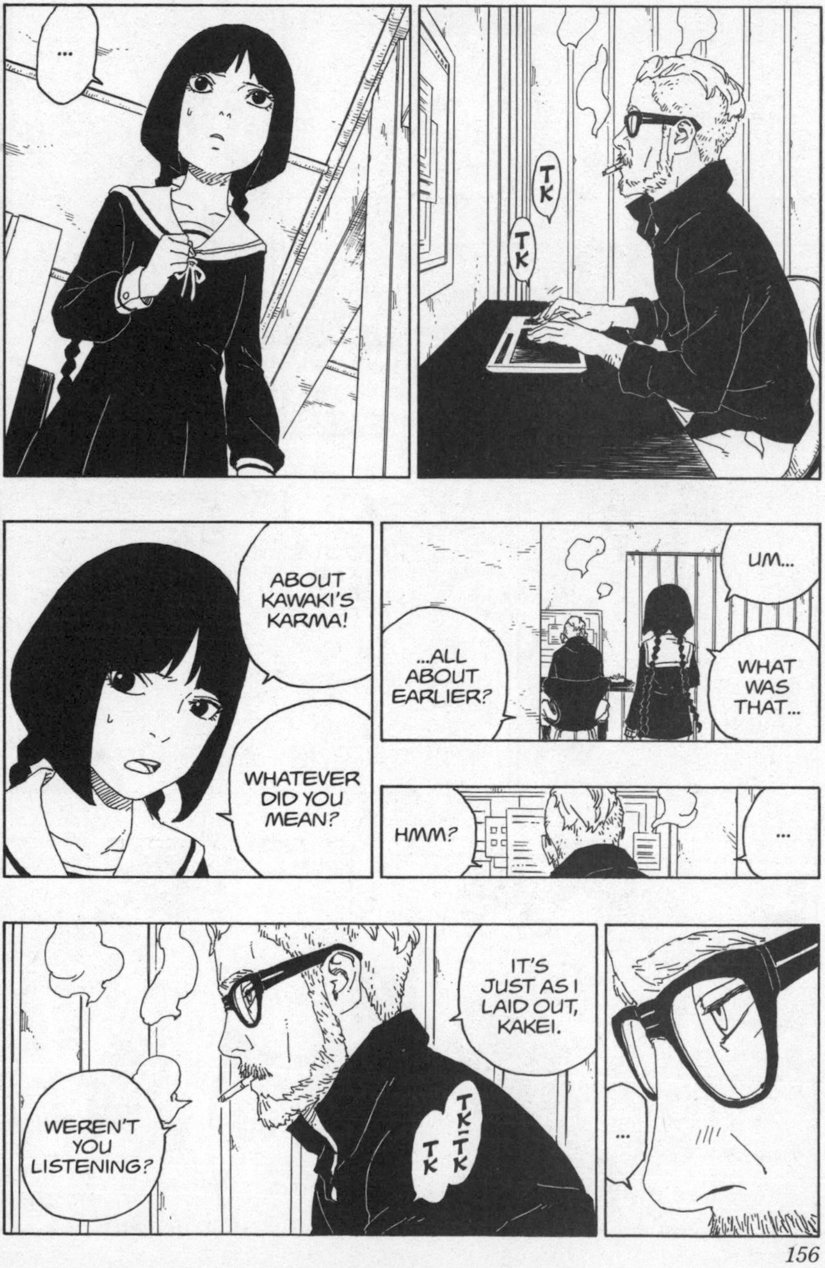
TK
TK
...
UM...
WHAT WAS THAT...
...ALL ABOUT EARLIER?
...
HMM?
ABOUT KAWAKI'S KARMA!
WHATEVER DID YOU MEAN?
...
IT'S JUST AS I LAID OUT, KAKEI.
TK-TK
TK
WEREN'T YOU LISTENING?

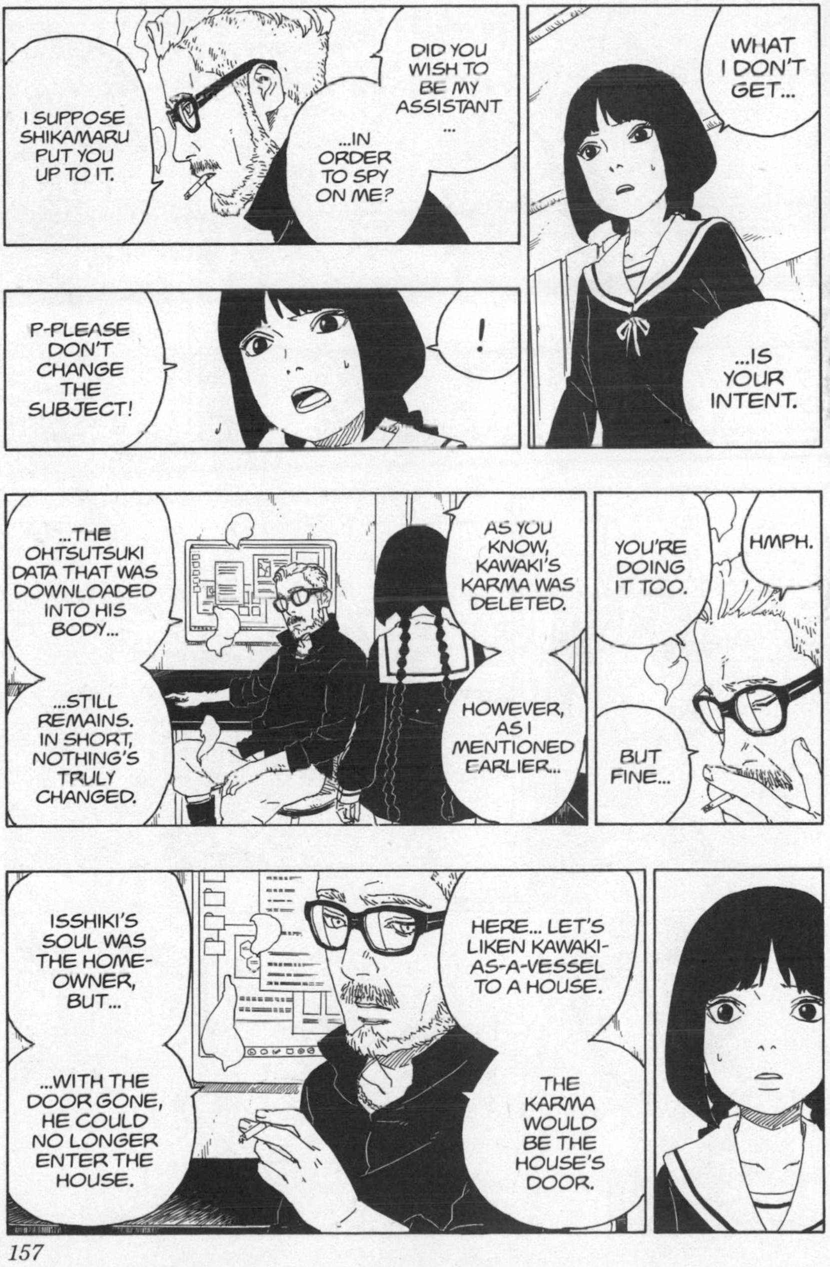
WHAT I DON'T GET...
...IS YOUR INTENT.
DID YOU WISH TO BE MY ASSISTANT ...
...IN ORDER TO SPY ON ME?
I SUPPOSE SHIKAMARU PUT YOU UP TO IT.
!
P-PLEASE DON'T CHANGE THE SUBJECT!
HMPH.
YOU'RE DOING IT TOO.
BUT FINE...
AS YOU KNOW, KAWAKI'S KARMA WAS DELETED.
HOWEVER, AS I MENTIONED EARLIER...
...THE OHTSUTSUKI DATA THAT WAS DOWNLOADED INTO HIS BODY...
...STILL REMAINS. IN SHORT, NOTHING'S TRULY CHANGED.
HERE... LET'S LIKEN KAWAKI-AS-A-VESSEL TO A HOUSE.
THE KARMA WOULD BE THE HOUSE'S DOOR.
ISSHIKI'S SOUL WAS THE HOME-OWNER, BUT...
...WITH THE DOOR GONE, HE COULD NO LONGER ENTER THE HOUSE.

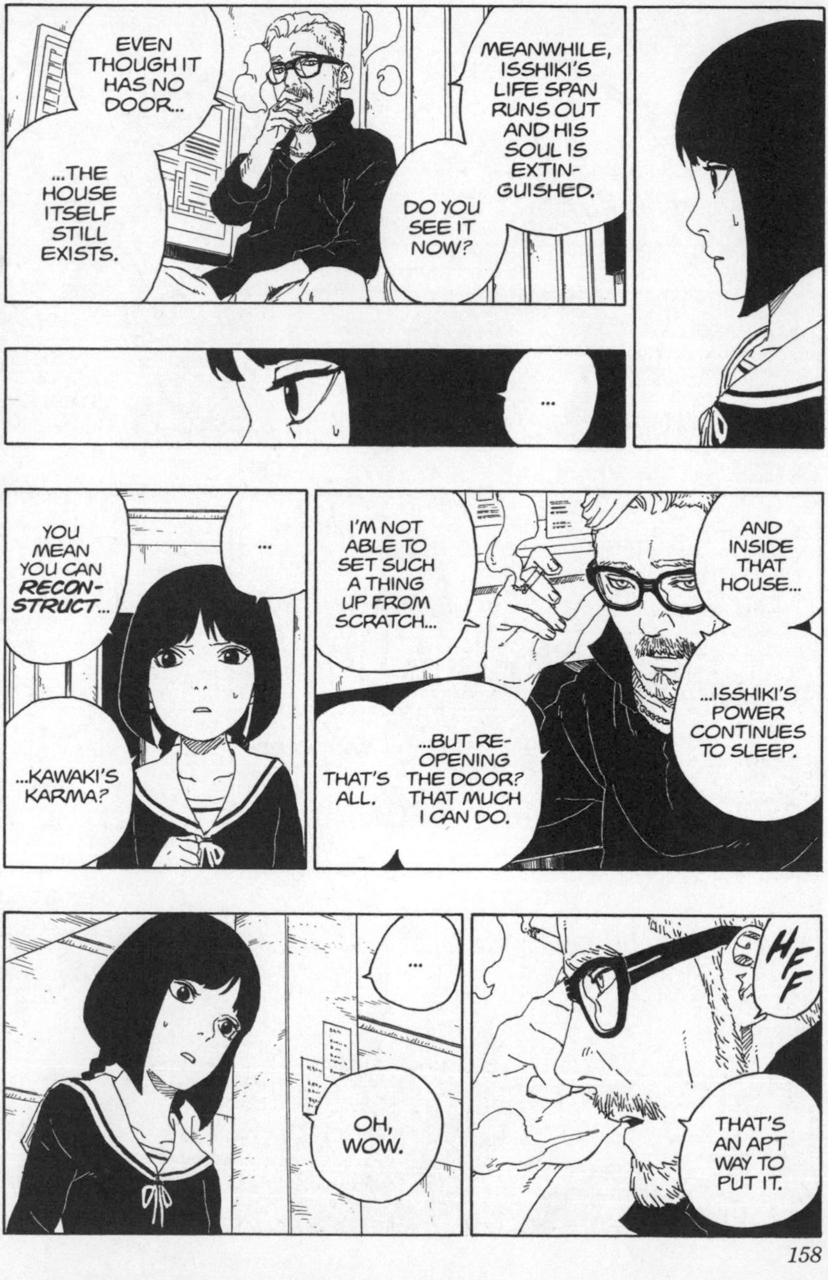
MEANWHILE, ISSHIKI'S LIFE SPAN RUNS OUT AND HIS SOUL IS EXTIN-GUISHED.
DO YOU SEE IT NOW?
EVEN THOUGH IT HAS NO DOOR...
...THE HOUSE ITSELF STILL EXISTS.
...
AND INSIDE THAT HOUSE...
...ISSHIKI'S POWER CONTINUES TO SLEEP.
I'M NOT ABLE TO SET SUCH A THING UP FROM SCRATCH...
...BUT RE-OPENING THE DOOR? THAT MUCH I CAN DO.
THAT'S ALL.
...
YOU MEAN YOU CAN *RECON-STRUCT*...
...KAWAKI'S KARMA?
HFF
THAT'S AN APT WAY TO PUT IT.
...
OH, WOW.

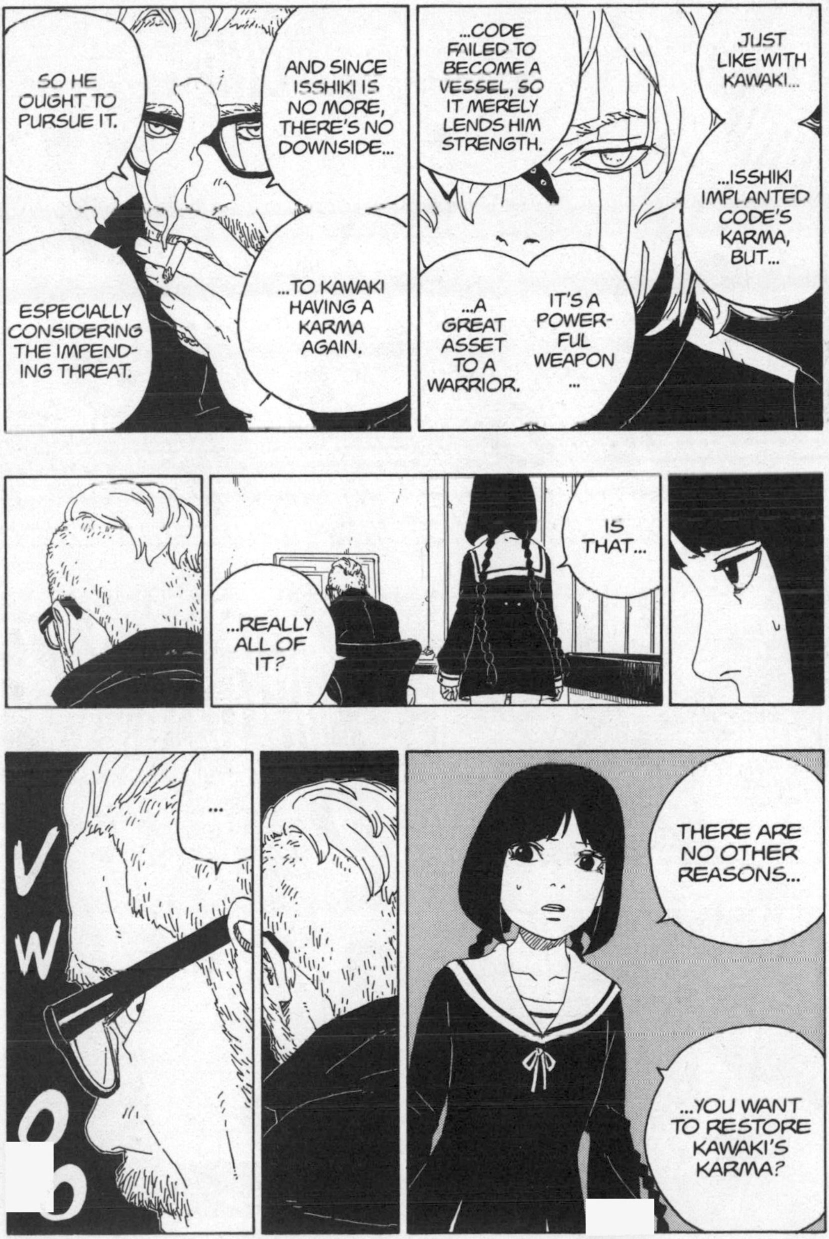
JUST LIKE WITH KAWAKI...
...ISSHIKI IMPLANTED CODE'S KARMA, BUT...
...CODE FAILED TO BECOME A VESSEL, SO IT MERELY LENDS HIM STRENGTH.
IT'S A POWERFUL WEAPON ...
...A GREAT ASSET TO A WARRIOR.
AND SINCE ISSHIKI IS NO MORE, THERE'S NO DOWNSIDE...
...TO KAWAKI HAVING A KARMA AGAIN.
SO HE OUGHT TO PURSUE IT.
ESPECIALLY CONSIDERING THE IMPENDING THREAT.
IS THAT...
...REALLY ALL OF IT?
THERE ARE NO OTHER REASONS...
...YOU WANT TO RESTORE KAWAKI'S KARMA?
...

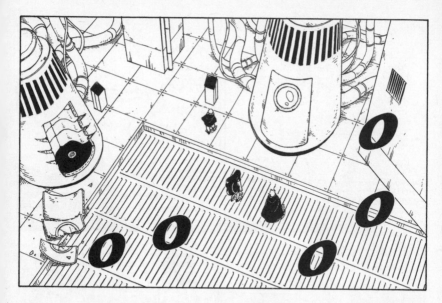

ANOTHER CYBORG THAT BORO STASHED HERE?

WHAT SORT?

WELL...

THE ONLY ONE, OTHER THAN AN OHTSU-TSUKI...

...WHO IS CAPABLE OF KILLING ME.

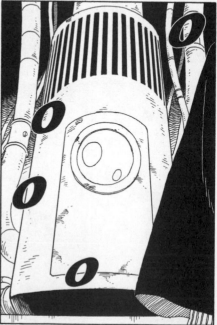

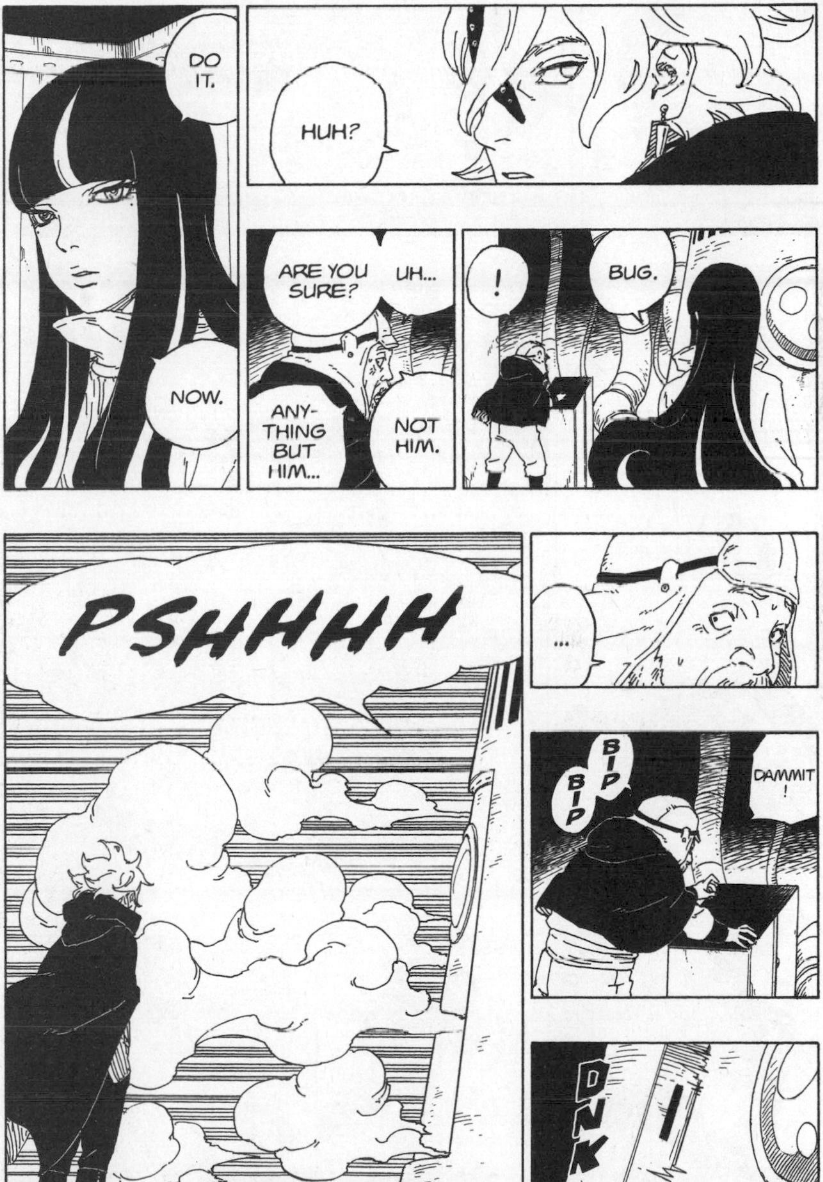
HUH?
BUG.
!
UH...
ARE YOU SURE?
NOT HIM.
ANY-THING BUT HIM...
DO IT.
NOW.
...
DAMMIT!
BIP BIP
DNK
PSHHHH

...

WHEEN

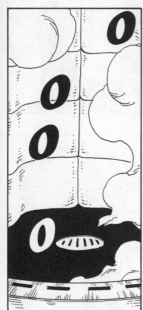

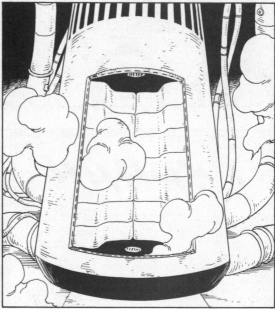

GLANCE

GLANCE

...!

HE'S
DONE
IT
AGAIN.

...

IT'S
EMPTY...

?

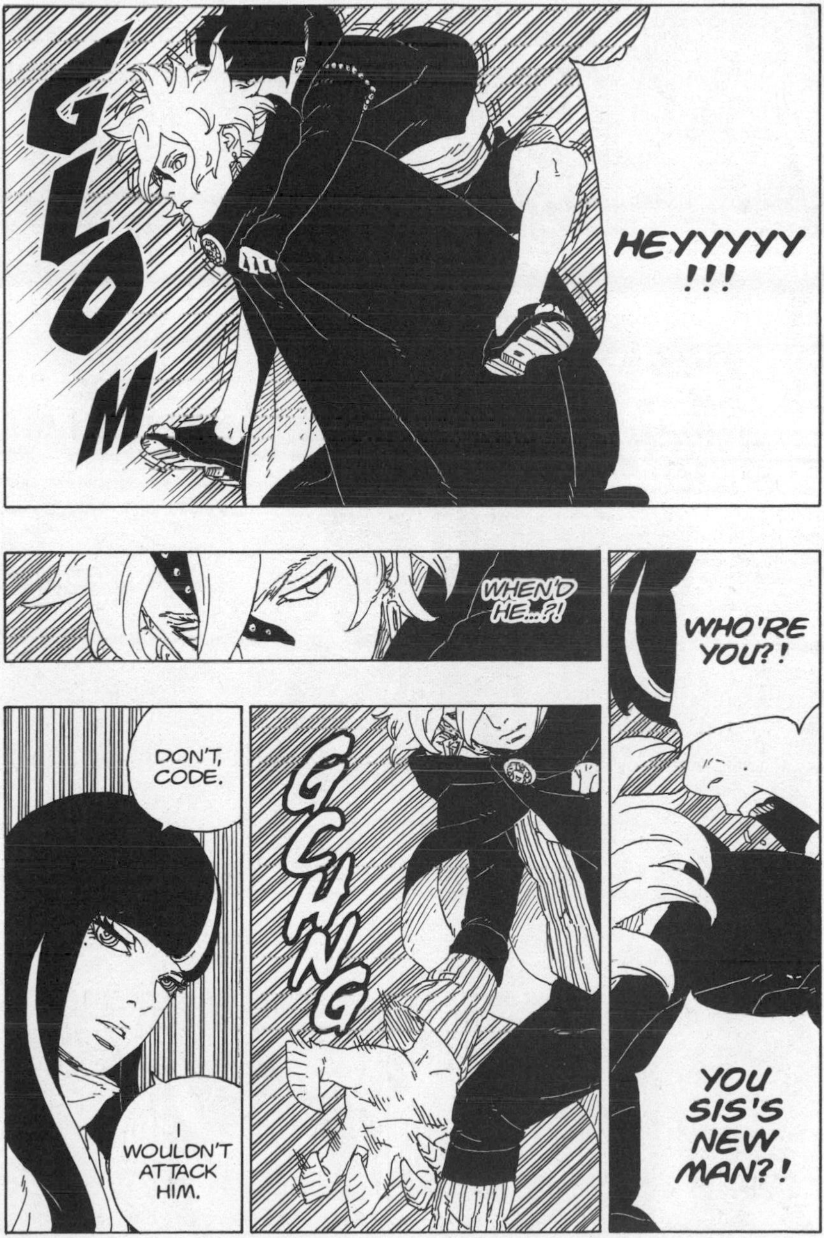
HEYYYYY !!!
GLOM
WHO'RE YOU?!
YOU SIS'S NEW MAN?!
WHEN'D HE...?!
GCHNG
DON'T, CODE.
I WOULDN'T ATTACK HIM.

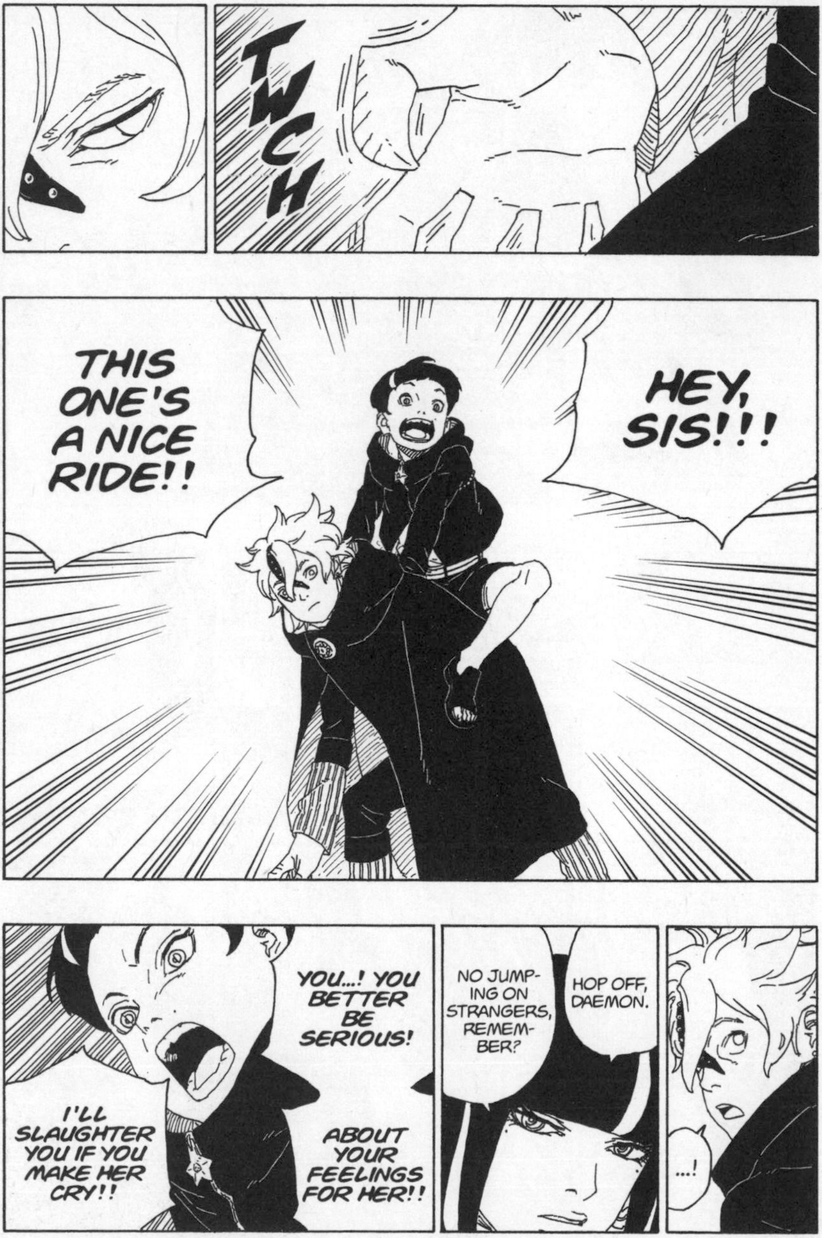
TWCH
HEY, SIS!!!
THIS ONE'S A NICE RIDE!!
...!
HOP OFF, DAEMON.
NO JUMPING ON STRANGERS, REMEMBER?
YOU...! YOU BETTER BE SERIOUS!
ABOUT YOUR FEELINGS FOR HER!!
I'LL SLAUGHTER YOU IF YOU MAKE HER CRY!!

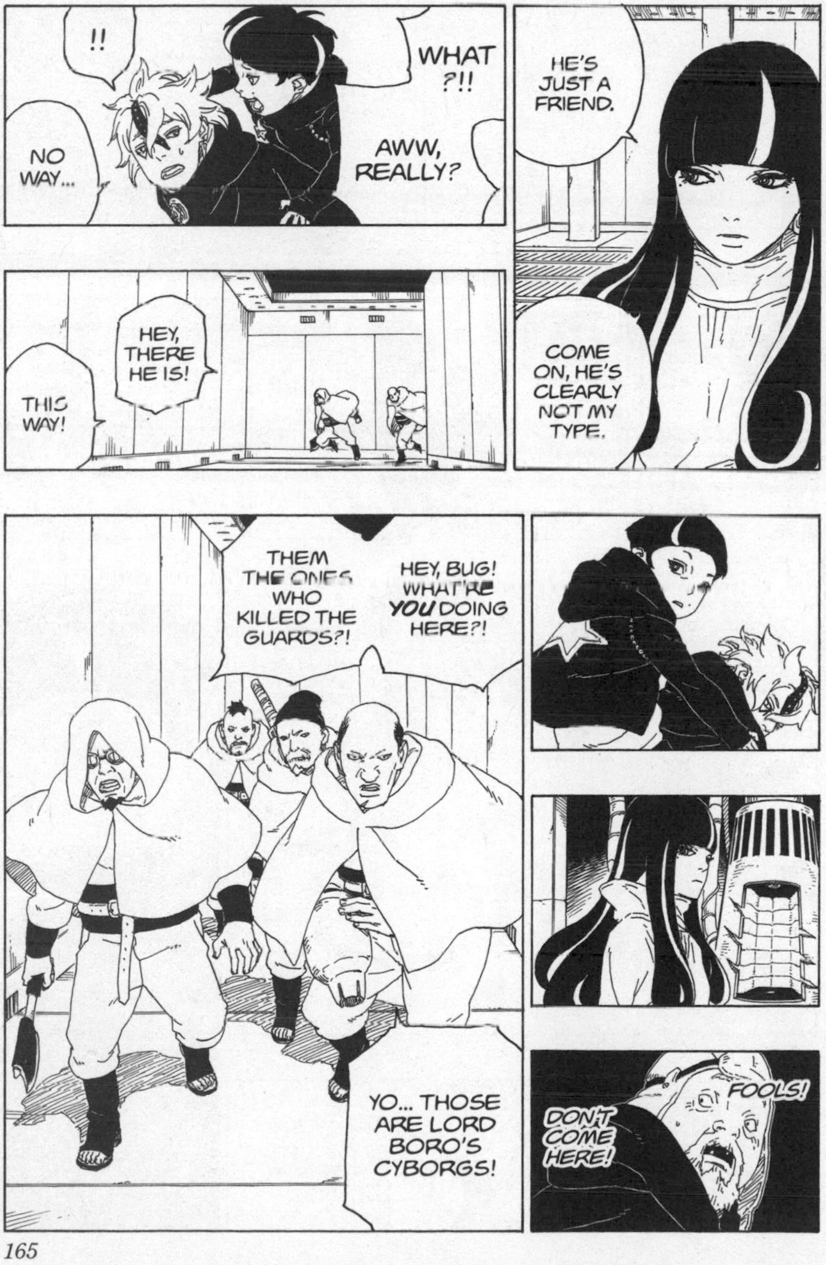
HE'S JUST A FRIEND.
COME ON, HE'S CLEARLY NOT MY TYPE.
WHAT ?!!
!!
AWW, REALLY?
NO WAY...
HEY, THERE HE IS!
THIS WAY!
FOOLS!
DON'T COME HERE!
HEY, BUG! WHAT'RE *YOU* DOING HERE?!
THEM THE ONES WHO KILLED THE GUARDS?!
YO... THOSE ARE LORD BORO'S CYBORGS!

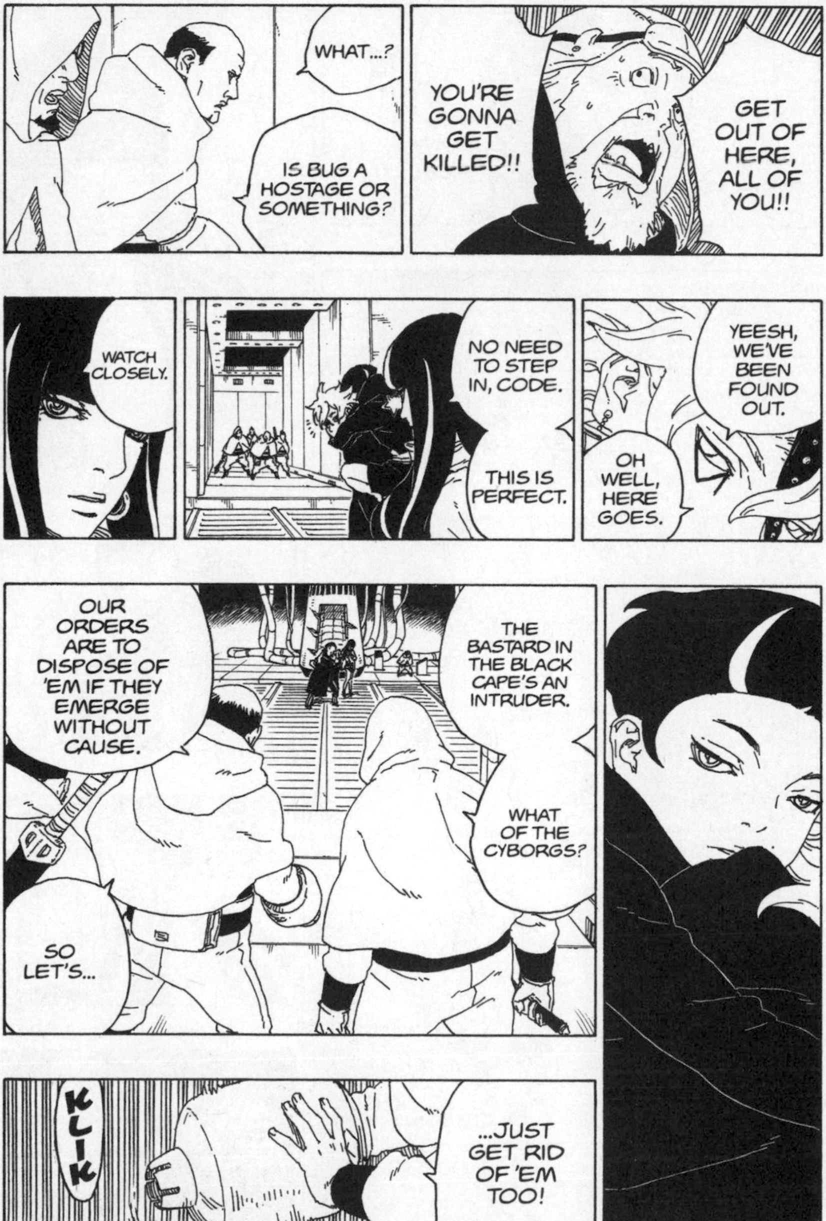
GET OUT OF HERE, ALL OF YOU!!
YOU'RE GONNA GET KILLED!!
WHAT...?
IS BUG A HOSTAGE OR SOMETHING?
YEESH, WE'VE BEEN FOUND OUT.
OH WELL, HERE GOES.
NO NEED TO STEP IN, CODE.
THIS IS PERFECT.
WATCH CLOSELY.
THE BASTARD IN THE BLACK CAPE'S AN INTRUDER.
OUR ORDERS ARE TO DISPOSE OF 'EM IF THEY EMERGE WITHOUT CAUSE.
WHAT OF THE CYBORGS?
SO LET'S...
...JUST GET RID OF 'EM TOO!
KLIK

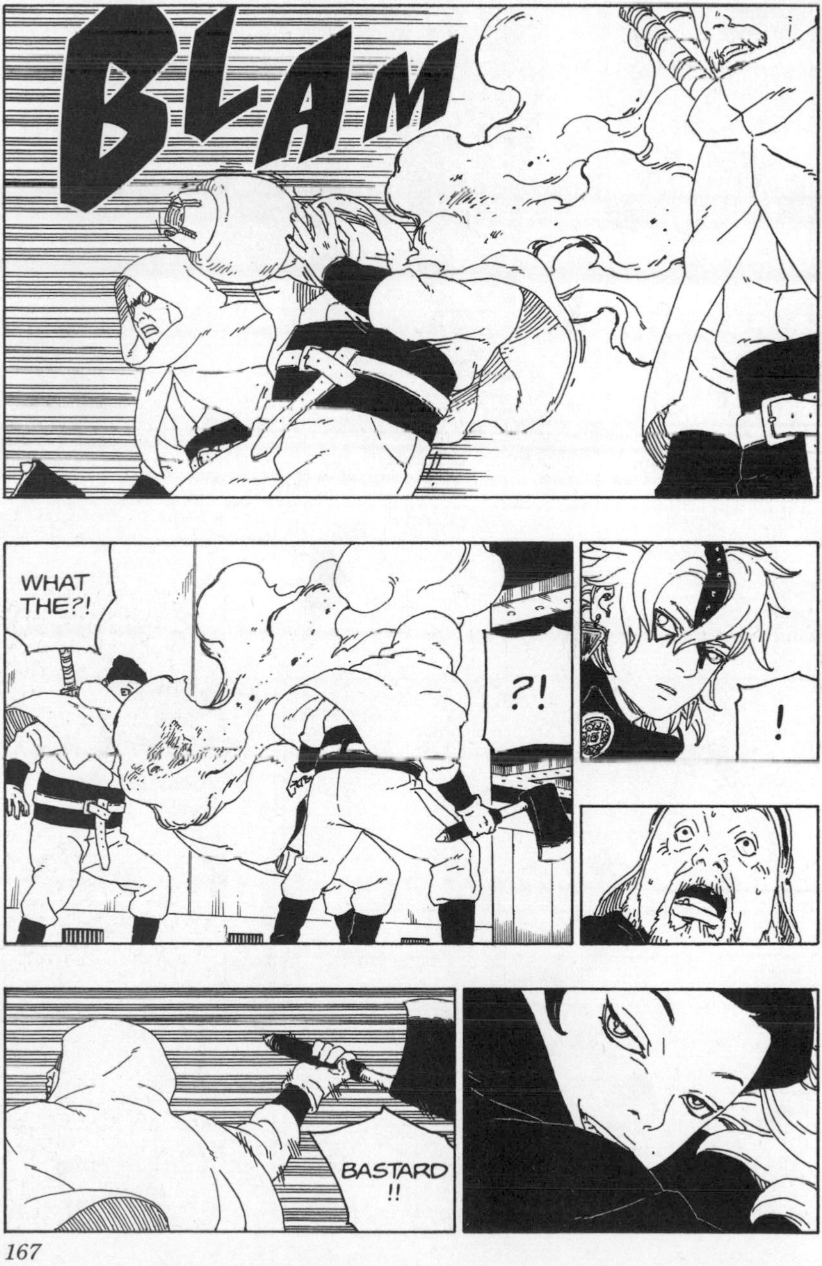
BLAM
!
?!
WHAT THE?!
BASTARD !!

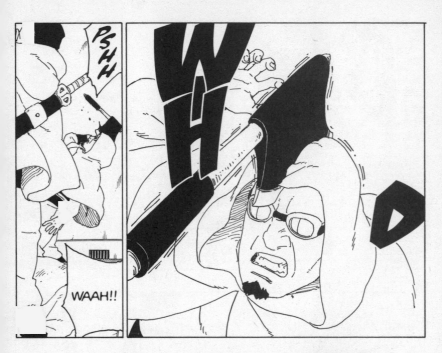

PSHH

WAAH!!

W

H

WAAH!!

W-WHAT THE HECK?!

WSH

TEE HEE!

STUUU-PID!

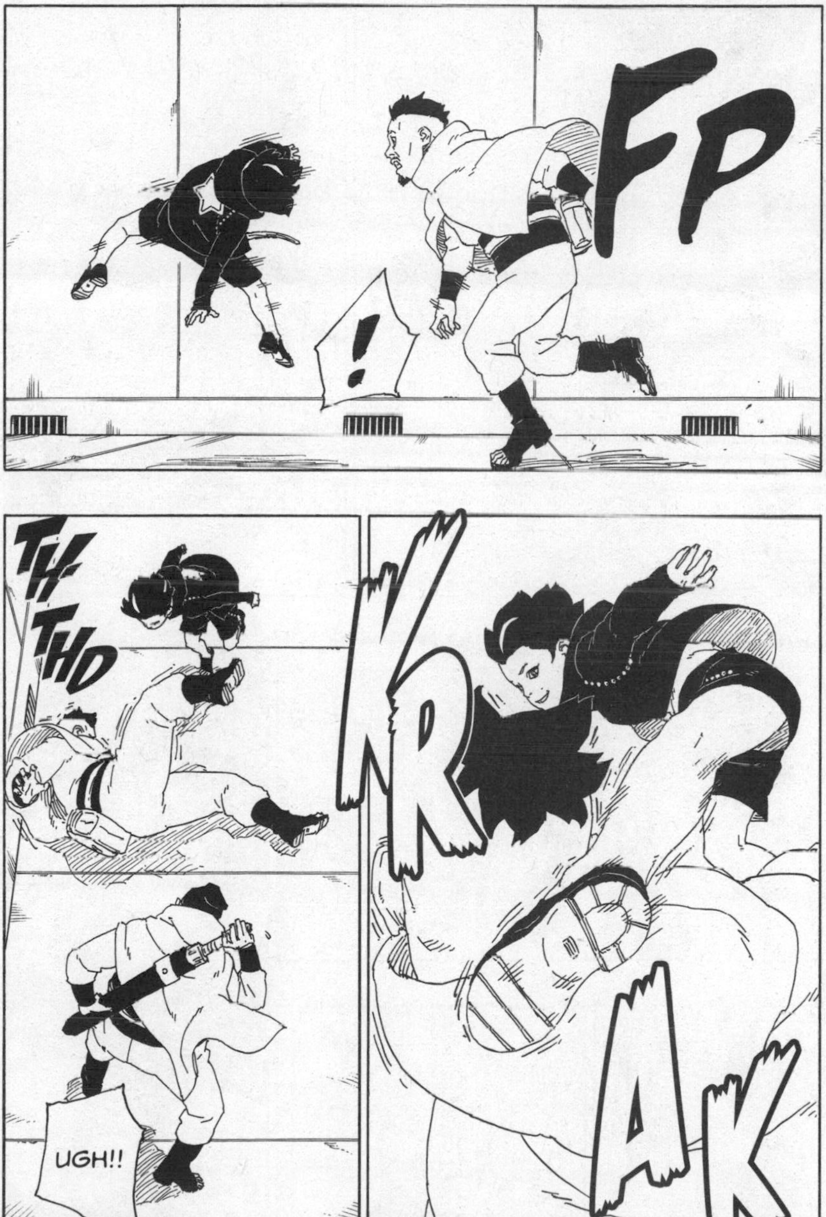
FP
!
KRAK
TH-THD
UGH!!

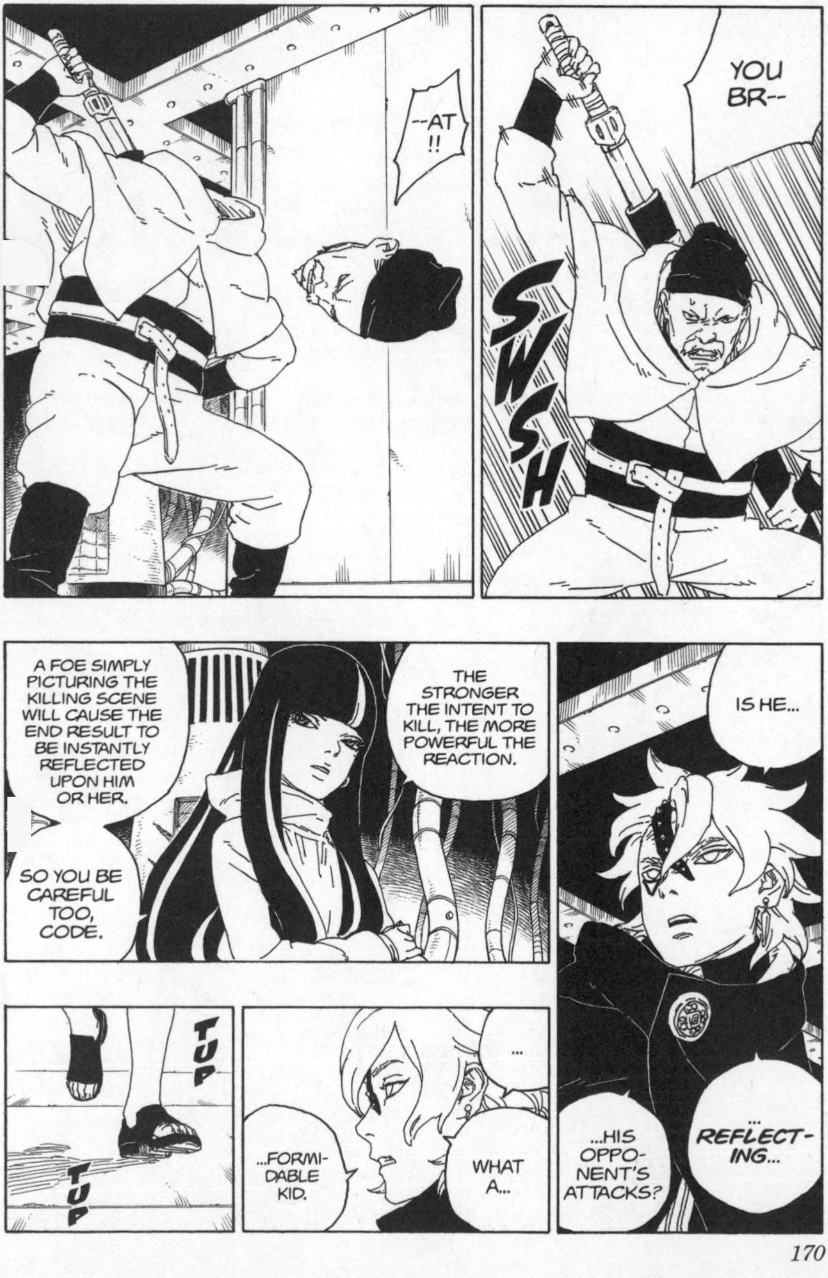
YOU BR--
SWSH
--AT !!
IS HE...
... REFLECT-ING...
...HIS OPPO-NENT'S ATTACKS?
THE STRONGER THE INTENT TO KILL, THE MORE POWERFUL THE REACTION.
A FOE SIMPLY PICTURING THE KILLING SCENE WILL CAUSE THE END RESULT TO BE INSTANTLY REFLECTED UPON HIM OR HER.
SO YOU BE CAREFUL TOO, CODE.
...
WHAT A...
...FORMI-DABLE KID.
TUP
TUP

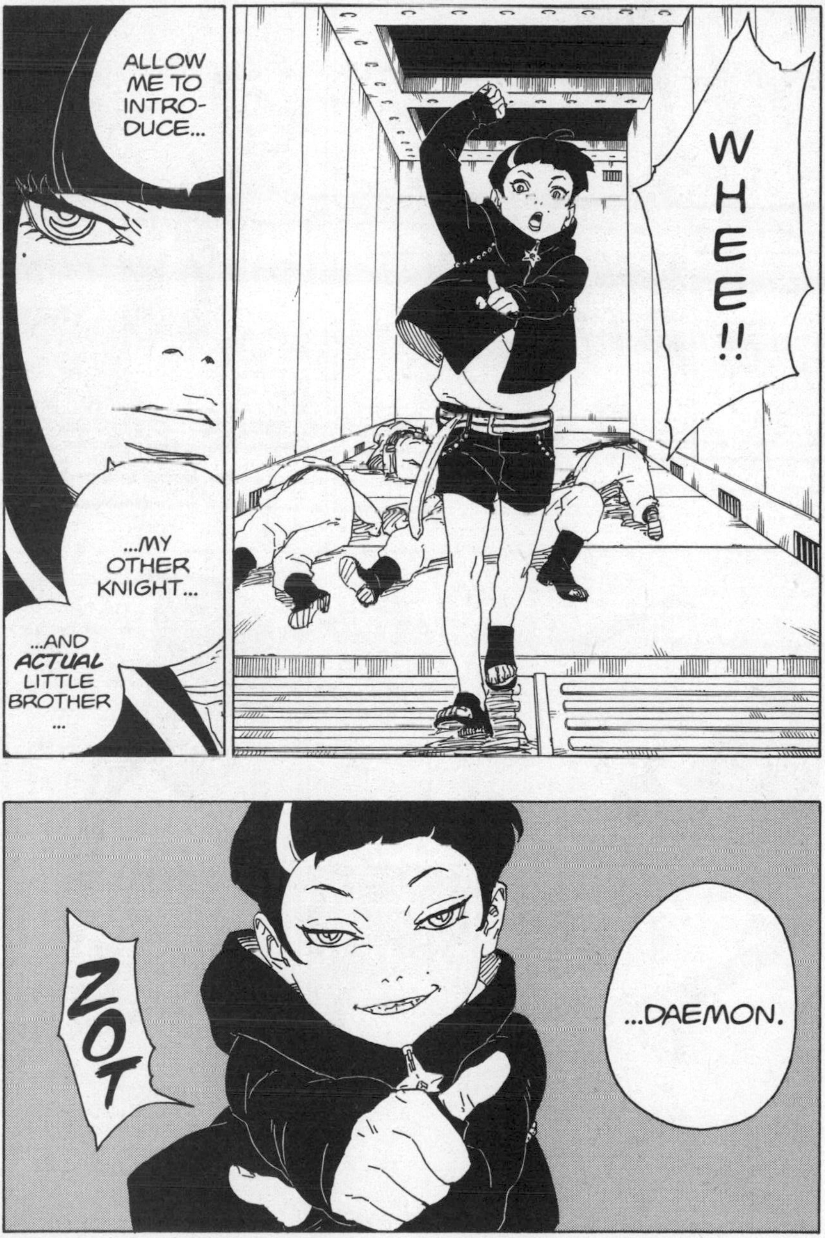
WHEE!!
ALLOW ME TO INTRODUCE...
...MY OTHER KNIGHT...
...AND ACTUAL LITTLE BROTHER...
...DAEMON.
ZOT

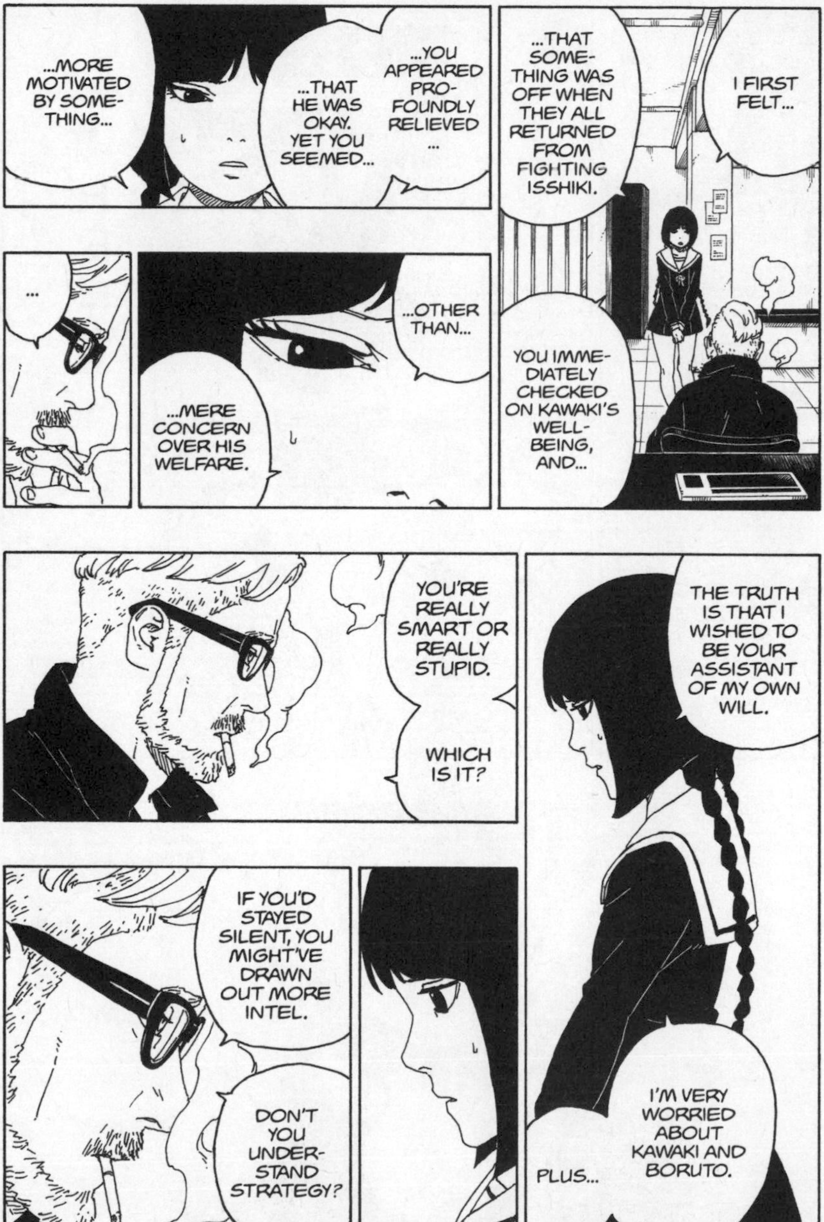
I FIRST FELT...
...THAT SOMETHING WAS OFF WHEN THEY ALL RETURNED FROM FIGHTING ISSHIKI.
YOU IMMEDIATELY CHECKED ON KAWAKI'S WELL-BEING, AND...
...YOU APPEARED PROFOUNDLY RELIEVED ...
...THAT HE WAS OKAY. YET YOU SEEMED...
...MORE MOTIVATED BY SOMETHING...
...OTHER THAN...
...MERE CONCERN OVER HIS WELFARE.
...
THE TRUTH IS THAT I WISHED TO BE YOUR ASSISTANT OF MY OWN WILL.
I'M VERY WORRIED ABOUT KAWAKI AND BORUTO.
PLUS...
YOU'RE REALLY SMART OR REALLY STUPID.
WHICH IS IT?
IF YOU'D STAYED SILENT, YOU MIGHT'VE DRAWN OUT MORE INTEL.
DON'T YOU UNDERSTAND STRATEGY?

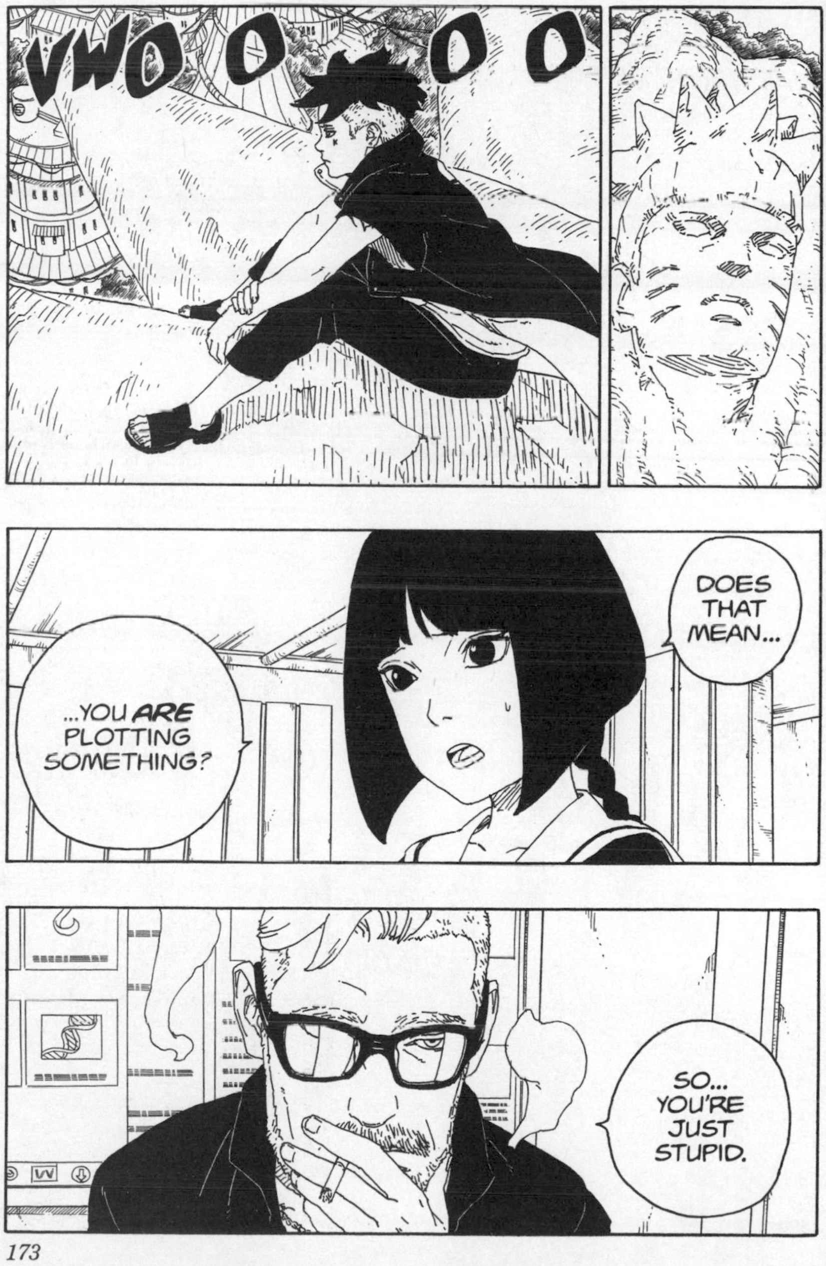
VWOOOO
DOES THAT MEAN...
...YOU *ARE* PLOTTING SOMETHING?
SO... YOU'RE JUST STUPID.

Black ✤ Clover

STORY & ART BY YŪKI TABATA

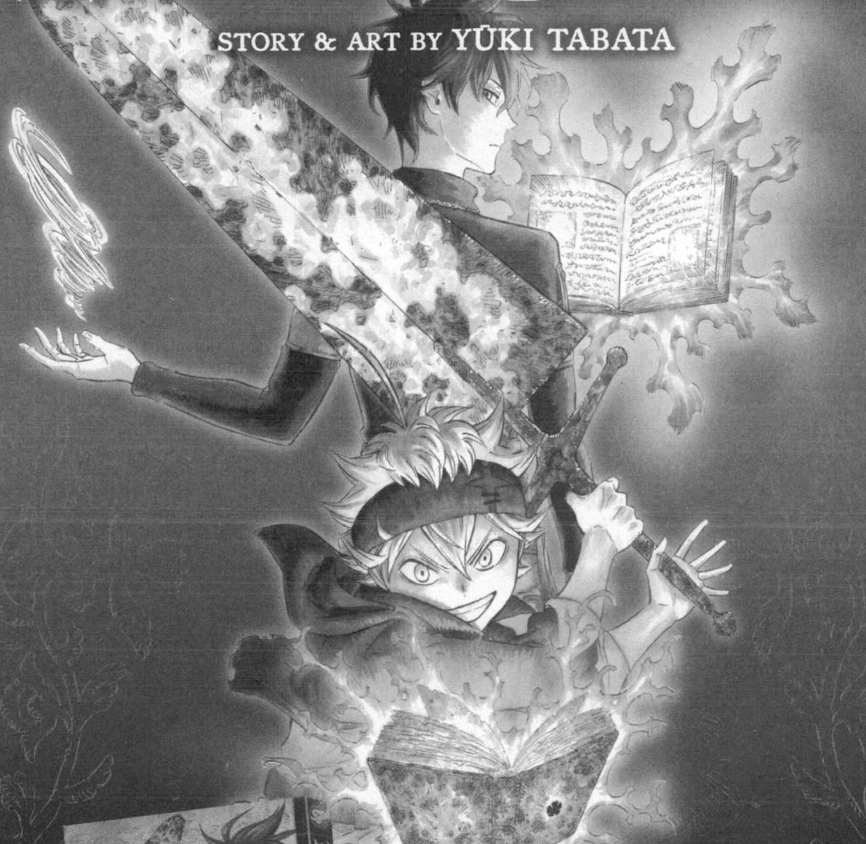

Asta is a young boy who dreams of becoming the greatest mage in the kingdom. Only one problem—he can't use any magic! Luckily for Asta, he receives the incredibly rare five-leaf clover grimoire that gives him the power of anti-magic. Can someone who can't use magic really become the Wizard King? One thing's for sure—Asta will never give up!

SHONEN JUMP

VIZ media

www.viz.com

YOU'RE READING
IN THE
WRONG DIRECTION!!

WHOOPS! Guess what? You're starting at the wrong end of the comic!

...It's true! In keeping with the original Japanese format, **Boruto** is meant to be read from right to left, starting in the upper-right corner.

Unlike English, which is read from left to right, Japanese is read from right to left, meaning that action, sound effects, and word-balloon order are completely reversed... something which can make readers unfamiliar with Japanese feel pretty backwards themselves. For this reason, manga or Japanese comics published in the U.S. in English have sometimes been published "flopped"—that is, printed in exact reverse order, as though seen from the other side of a mirror.

By flopping pages, U.S. publishers can avoid confusing readers, but the compromise is not without its downside. For one thing, a character in a flopped manga series who once wore in the original Japanese version a T-shirt emblazoned with "M A Y" (as in "the merry month of") now wears one which reads "Y A M"! Additionally, many manga creators in Japan are themselves unhappy with the process, as some feel the mirror-imaging of their art alters their original intentions.

We are proud to bring you **Boruto** in the original unflopped format. Turn to the other side of the book and let the ninjutsu begin...!

—Editor

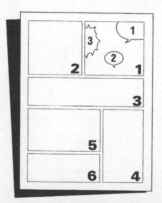